INDIA

IN

TRANSITION

INDIA
IN
TRANSITION

MANABENDRA NATH ROY

GYAN

Published by

Gyan Publishing House
5, Ansari Road
Daryaganj, New Delhi-110002
Phone: 011-47034999, 9811692060
E-mail: books@gyanbooks.com

Distribution Network
gyanbooks.com
India, USA, Canada, UK, Australia

ISBN: 978-93-6780-477-3 (HB)
First Published, 1822

2nd Impression 2024

Printed at: Gyan Press, Delhi.

INDIA IN TRANSITION
Author: MANABENDRA NATH ROY

MANABENDRA NATH ROY

INDIA IN TRANSITION

INDIA IN TRANSITION

By

MANABENDRA NATH ROY

With Collaboration
of Abani Mukherji

GENÈVE

Edition de la Librairie J. B. Target

1922

CONTENTS.

INTRODUCTION.

It is recognized by all that India is in a state of transsition. She finds herself in the period which links the past lived through and left behind, with the dawning future of new activities, new hopes and new aspirations. Indians of all shades of political opinion and social tendencies have written and are writing about this stage of transition. Everybody has defined it according to his understanding or his desire. Even writers belonging to the imperialist camp have dealt with the question. They have done it of course from the imperialist point of view. All hold that a "New India" — "Young India" is in the process of birth. Various theories about the character of this rising Indian nation are formulated. Multifarious plans and schemes regarding the education of this coming child are discussed. The British ruling class is anxious to be the god-father of this child and has appointed the clever midwife of imperial Liberalism to help its birth. And at the same time all precautions are being taken in order to prevent this belated child growing too fast and eventually revolting against the hegemony of paternal protection. The politically minded Indians-economically most advanced, therefore, the most conscious vanguard of the rising nation-find this transition leading up to their aggrandisement, which they identify with an imaginary prosperity of the inhabitants of a politically autonomous India. They propose that the people of India should be guided by them step by step along an orderly and constitutional channel, through this period of transition. There is a third school which also takes notice and talks about this transition. They are the extreme nationalists who have been dominating the stage the last several years. Their socio-political philosophy is the hardest to comprehend, being hopelessly confused. The reason of this confusion is that they hold an entirely wrong conception of this transition, in spite of being the most rudely tossed and toppled by this great wave of popular upheaval. To them it is not so much a transition, but a revivalist period, through which India is passing. Because they think that the Indian people are struggling to liberate themselves from the political and economic bondage which obstructed their progress for centuries, not to begin a new life with a new vision, but to revive the old. But the past is doomed by history, one of whose most important chapers is the present transition.

All these diverse definitions and interpretations, nevertheless, do not alter the fact that India is changing and changing fast. Her people are out, consciously or unconsciously, to change their life. This is the fundamental phenomenon in all that is happening in India today. Neither the anxiety of the British Imperialists, nor the desire of the constitutional patriots, nor the fanaticism of the orthodox nationalists will be able to lead the rising Indian nation astray from the path marked out by those historical forces which determine human progress. Jointly or severally they may retard, confuse the forward march of the Indian people; but they cannot stop it for ever. The real significance of the period of transition through which India is passing, is that after long and long years of forced stagnation, the progressive forces latent in the Indian society are asserting themselves. The future of the Indian nation is going to be shaped by the inexorable evolution of these forces.

The following chapters are written with a view to analyse the present situation and the prospective developments. In this analysis nothing has been taken for granted; realities, cold facts, have been examined in order to determine which way the wind is blowing. An attempt has been made to investigate the past, analyse the present and visualise the future, from the point of view of Historic Materialism. To re-write Indian history is a tremendous, although much-needed task. No such pretension entered into the writing of these pages. They are written with an eye to problems much more immediate. The object of this work is first to point out the material forces that are pushing the various classes of the Indian people in the present struggle; second to point out the deep-rooted social character of the present unrest; third to analyse the social tendencies embodied by the two principal schools of nationalism; and fourth to indicate the revolutionary trend of the growing mass movement and to impress upon those concerned the necessity of conforming their programme and tactics according to it.

The materials necessary for realising the above stated objects satisfactorily are not easily available. We are obliged to learn about the past of the Indian people from two sources viz. the imperialist historians, who write more about the civilizing mission of their illustrious countrymen than about the life and conditions of the conquered people, and 2. Indian authors, who are very apt to sacrifice historical facts on the altar of patriotism. At best we can have some idea of the glories and grandeur of the Hindu and Moslem courts. Thanks to the painstaking researches of some modern historians, one can learn how many sacks of kishmish the great Aurangzeb consumed in his life or how the noble Shirajadawlla has been painted in such a black colour by the English writers; but scrutinizing study of such impressive volumes provides one with but little information as to the economic condition of the toiling masses. Nevertheless, the searchlight of Historic Materialism reveals to us many things even in the dark dephts of such historical treatises. Thus we have succeeded in establishing a rational background of history upon which the picture of contemporary India can be drawn in none too blurred and irregular lines.

One has to be disappointed if he expects anything better from the records of the British government. After raking the brain over the mountains of Statistical Reports published by the government one wonders whether it is really true that the English are ruling India out of charity. Our object not being limited to the overdone task of pointing out the heavy Home Charges and other forms of drains from India, we had to read the same statistics in various ways in order to find out the fullest extent of exploitation to which the Indian masses are subjected not only by the foreign rulers, but by the native propertied class as well.

With the help of the materials available, the real character of the transition through which the Indian society is passing, has been shown in the first three chapters. Taking this analysis of the economic development of one section of the population and the corresponding exploitation of the rest, the future life and struggle of the rising Indian nation are to be judged. Neither a "New India" nor a "Young India" is going to be born from this transition, which will simply result in ushering the people of India into a more advanced stage of socio-economic development. India is not only struggling to free herself from the political domination of a foreign power, but she is moving ahead in the path of human progress and in doing so finds many cherished traditions of old prejudicial to this movement forward. Therefore her entire store of popular energy is in a state of revolt against everything which has so far kept her backward and still conspires to do so. This revolt, this great social upheaval, is the essence of the present transition, which marks the disappearance of the old, bankrupt socio-economic structure in order to be replaced by one which will afford the people greater facilities for progress.

These pages were written more than six months ago when Gandhism was at its highest. But the subsequent events have proved that no mistake was made in the analysis of the movement and the criticism of its leadership. The conflicting social tendencies, that were mixed up confusedly in the superficially united national struggle, are in a process of clarification. A readjustment of forces is taking place before the struggle can enter into a more advanced and intense phase. After having been for several years the organ of orthodox nationalism dominated by the dying forces of reaction, the National Congress has landed in political bankruptcy. Today it stands at the cross-roads. It must either adjust its socio-political convictions in accordance with the forces behind the great mass upheaval, or put itself straight on the tracks of constitutional democracy. The latter course will take it back under Moderate leadership, which is convinced that the British connection is beneficial to the economic interests of that class of the people whose political representative they are. To carry the discussion of this possibility farther does not come under the purview of this book, which does not go beyond pointing out the social tendencies latent in the contemporary political movement. The question of practical politics and the formulation of a programme commensurate with the nature recently revealed by the movement, will have to be dealt with in a subsequent work.

The most outstanding feature of the Indian national movement has been its lack of theoretical foundation. A modern political movement involving a sweeping mass-action, cannot go on forever with antiquated religious ideology. On the other hand, the impotent constitutionalism of the Moderates falls miserably short of the mark, although it serves the purpose of the bourgeoisie. The Indian people is engaged in a social struggle of historic and to a certain extent of unprecedented character. There must be a socio-political philosophy behind this great movement. This much-needed ideological background of our struggle is not to be invented from the imagination of great men; it will be evolved out of the material forces making the birth, growth and success of such a struggle possible. To study out social conditions, actual as well as of the past, and to watch the evolution of the economic forces, is indispensable for those who desire to understand that the people of India are progressing along a course common to the entire human race. We have our peculiar problems to solve; there are peculiar obstacles to be overcome on our way. But the fact remains that we are involved in a great struggle which calls for profound understanding of the socio-economic forces making for the progress of the Indian people.

The following pages are devoted to this study, which will help to direct the movement.

Manabendra Nath Roy.

March 1922.

INDIA IN TRANSITION

CHAPTER I.

The growth of the bourgeoisie.

Contrary to the general notion, India is not under the feudal system. In India, feudalism was destroyed or more correctly speaking, undermined not by a violent revolution, as in Europe, but by a comparatively peaceful and gradual process. Feudalism as the basis of social economics, received the first deathblow in the earlier years of the British possession in the middle of the 18th century, when the political power passed into the hands of the representatives of a foreign commercial bourgeoisie. In proportion as the British East India Company went on making the power of British commercial capital supreme in India, the foundation of the feudal system could not help being undermined. But it took the East India Company almost a hundred years to consolidate its supremacy all over the country. Therefore, though weakened, feudalism maintained its existence, at least in form, throughout this period. From the very beginnning of the British occupation, the final proprietorship in land was taken away from the Indian landowning class, either by force or by fraud, and was vested in the British Government. In other words, in place of the feudal lords, the representative of British commercial capital became the owner of the land. The last vestiges of feudal power were shattered by the failure of the revolution of 1857, which is known as the Sepoy Mutiny. The revolution of 1857 was nothing but the last effort of the dethroned feudal potentates to regain their power. It was a struggle between the worn-out feudal system and the newly-introduced commercial capitalism for political supremacy. At the same time, when feudalism was crumbling down in Europe before the rising bourgeoisie, a vibration of this great social struggle did not remain unfelt in India. But during the one hundred years preceding 1857, the normal economic development and the rise of the native bourgeoisie had been prevented in India by the following causes: First, the forcible export of more than 70 % of the accumulated wealth of India by the East India Company in order to help the industrial development of England. Second, the deliberate destruction of the craft industries and the consequent forcing of the artisan class back to the land, instead of into the modern machine industries, as in Europe. The craft industry was also in process of destruction in Europe, but the difference lay in the fact that, whereas in Europe, it succumbed before a higher form of production, namely the machine, which evolved as a new social force, — in India the process of destruction was premeditated and violent. Indian craft industries did not die in order to give place to a higher form of production within the country. They were the victims of the industrial growth in England. But historically speaking, the broad results were the same, namely, the political power passed on to the hands of a new social class, controlling superior means of production, thus bringing about the undermining of the feudal system as an economic force and the destruction of the craft industries. Practically the whole country was brought directly under capitalist exploitation after the failure of the revolt of 1857. The Government of India was removed from the hands of the East India Company and transferred to the crown.

Today, India is divided into four distinct classes, namely; 1. the landed aristocracy, including the native chiefs, 2. the bourgeoisie and the intellectuals, 3. the petty peasantry and 4. the working class, including the landless peasants.) Of the 17,328 big landowners, 700 are classed in the category of Native States. Their chiefs are called Feudatory or Protected Wards of the British Government. One-third of the area of the entire country or 709,555 square miles, is governed by these Chiefs, and is known as Native India. The biggest of these States is Hyderabad, or the Nizam's Dominions, which equals Italy in area, with 13,500,000 population. The smallest is limited to only 5 villages. The aggregate population of Native India is 72,000,000, a little less than one fourth of the entire population of the country. The existence of these native States is responsible for India's being called a feudal country.

Theoretically, the native Chiefs enjoy the sovereign power within their respective territories, but practically, they have no power whatever, much less do they constitute the backbone of the social-economic structure of the country. The internal administration of none of these States is feudal; except a few, none of these ruling chiefs is directly descended from the feudal nobility of pre-British India. To all intents and purposes, they are puppets in the hands of the British Government. Besides the local and municipal administration, all these States are governed politically and militarily by the British, commercially and industrially by the native bourgeoisie. In fact, the native bourgeoisie has more influence in the Government of the Native States than in the Government of India. All these States have Legislative Councils of their own, representing the local commercial and landowning class, and lately the industrial bourgeoisie is fast making itself supreme. But the autocrat in whom the absolute power is vested for all practical purposes, is the Resident, who is the representative of the British Government. Originally, these Residents were sent to the Courts of the Native Princes, as ambassadors of the British Government, but being the representative of the more advanced social class, namely, the bourgeoisie, these Residents have in course of time become the arbiters of the States. Therefore we see that even in these Native States where at least the shadow of feudalism still clings to a certain extent, it is the bourgeoisie which wields the political power.

In the internal administration of many of the larger Native States the progressive tendency of the bourgeoisie is more clearly manifested. In States like Mysore, Travancore, Baroda, Cochin &c. the percentage of illiteracy is much lower than in British India. Whereas in the latter primary education is not even free, in some of the Native States it is free and compulsory. In recent years, the industrialisation of the country has been more rapid in the Native States than in British territories. The condition of the peasantry in these States is the same as in British India. In short, the remnants of feudalism are not to be found in the Native States any more than in the British territories, except in the courts of the pampered puppets.

The Native Chiefs, oppressed as they are by the British, are nevertheless conscious of the fact that their continued existance is doomed to destruction, and it is only by grace of the British Government that they are maintained as a conservative factor in the society. British power in India has never been based upon these scions of an extinct feudalism; on the contrary, it is the Government of India, representative of the British bourgeoisie, that maintains them grafted upon the social order. Consequently, they know very well that they owe their existence to the British power, so they are heart and soul pro-British, and will help the latter in any exigency, as was shown in the last war.

The remaining 16,628 of the above mentioned 17,328 big estate-owners are also directly or indirectly connected with the feudal monarchs who ruled over India after the fall of the Moghul Empire. Thus they, together with the 700 native Chiefs, constitute the landed aristocracy of India. These aristocrats, together with their families and dependent relations, number 540,175 out of a total population of 320,000,000. The total number of persons who live on land rent is 8,500,000, according to the census of 1911. (Figures for 1920—1921 are not available.) Except for the 540,175 mentioned above, who belong to the aristocracy proper, the remaining eight million belong to the landholding class. The difference between the landowners and the landholders is that the former nominally own their estates under the protection of, or as feudatories of the British Government, and their properties are subject to the feudal laws of inheritance, being handed down from father to eldest son. The second class hold their land on permanent or temporary lease from the Government. The rent paid by them to the Government is sometimes permanently fixed, sometimes assessed periodically, according to the changed valuation of the land.

The landholding class can be counted as old as the British Government in India. It rose out of the chaos which followed the fall of the Mussulman Empire and preceded the consolitation of the British power. Its foreunners were the usurers and high officials of the latter years of the Mussulman administration. In the last part of the 18th century the country was ravaged by widespread famines caused by the deliberate destruction of the craft industries, the unrestricted export of food-grains, heavy fall in the total production of food-stuff owing to climatic conditions, the transfer of extensive areas of land to the cultivation of indigo and jute and the laying waste of large tracts due to the continued state of civil war. As a result of these things, the great bulk of the peasantry found itself heavily indebted, and their holdings fell into the hands of the usurers and former government officials who had accumulated a certain amount of capital. The East India Company, which in those days was unable to control alone the disturbed population because of its numerical weakness, encouraged the growth of this class of landholders, who were allowed to hold the land on behalf of the Government, in whom the title of final ownership was vested. Thus the elements that might have given rise to a native bourgeoisie were diverted from their natural development into a landholding class, for the convenience of a foreign bourgeoisie who conquered the political power and wanted to monopolize the right of exploiting the whole population. The modern Indian bourgeoisie is largely derived from this landholding class, which is investing its accumulated wealth more and more in commercial and industrial enterprises, now that the British Government has been forced to change its policy of holding back the industrial development of India. The smaller landholders find it more profitable to get rid of their land and to invest their money in trade and commerce, and the result is a growing concentration of land in the hands of big capitalist concerns. This tendency towards concentration will be shown later on in detail. (chap. II.)

The Indian intellectuals who, together with the progressive element in the landholding class, form the basis of the modern bourgeoisie, are the creation of the British Government. Already in the earlier years of its rule, the British Government found out that it was more profitable to employ natives in the clerical and administrative posts of lower ranks than to bring out men from England for these works. Besides, it was necessary to depend on the Indians for the purpose of local administration. It was impossible that the numerous personal required to maintain the cumbersome British bureaucracy in India could be recruited from the home country. On the other hand, the big British commercial firms in India needed the services of the cheaply paid clerks and other employees. For any one of these capacities, in the earlier days of the British occupation, no less than fifty Indians could be hired for the amount of money to be paid to an Englishman coming out of England. Therefore, modern education was introduced by the British Government in the second decade of the 19th century. Since then, the modern intelligentsia has been growing very rapidly, transcending the limits marked out for them by the foreign rulers, and capturing entirely the professions of medicine, law and teaching. Today, the English are practically ousted from these professions by the Indians. According to the census figures of 1911, the number of people employed in public administration and professions amounted to 7,973,662. This figure does not include the clerks and employees of the commercial firms. These professions proved to be lucrative, and money began to be accumulated in the hands of the upper strata of the intellectual class. In 1850 the total accumulated wealth of this class, as shown in the investments in Government securities, amounted to £ 69,000,000. Since there was no industrial or other profitable means of investment, this whole amount was invested in Government securities. The total capital invested in Native banks at that time amounted to £ 19,000,000. Land offered the only other form of profitable investment at this period, and the accumulated savings of this class were also invested in land-leases, which were in the process of transfer from the hands of the big holders on account of their failure to meet higher government assessments, as well as from the small holders, because of their heavy indebtedness. Thus a considerable portion of land has been passing out of the control of the old conservative holders and into the hands of the more progressive rich intellectuals. This class of progressive landholders, which simultaneously is engaged in many instances, in the lucrative liberal professions also, is rapidly marching itself in the ranks of the bourgeoisie proper, since in proportion as the capital accumulated in its hand grows, it extends its investments to industrial enterprises. Today in India are to be found numerous instances in which the rich landholder and industrialist are combined in the same person.

In the earlier years of British rule, there existed in India a great deal of inter-provincial activity in banking and commerce. This internal trade was completely destroyed by the introduction of the modern banking system and the establishment of British commercial houses in the first half of the 19th century. The result was that the prosperous Indian banking and merchant class was reduced to petty shopkeepers. After 1860, this inter-provincial commerce again revived, with the accumulation of wealth. The reason for this revival was the continued expansion of European capitalistic enterprise, which pushed its exploitation further and further into the country, in search of raw materials and a market for their manufactured goods, and created a class of Indian middlemen in the process. The growth in the volume of foreign trade led to the enrichment of this native mercantile class, which soon found itself in the possession of considerable capital for investment, but foreign trade and international banking being monopolized by the foreign ruling-class, the Indian merchants found this way blocked to them and an outlet for their energy and capital was found in industrial enterprises. The first power-driver cotton-mill was erected at Ahmedabad in 1851.

Modern industry owned by native capital remained insignificant in India till 1880. In that year there were 58 cotton-textile mills with a paid-up capital of £ 3,832,000 and 22 jute-textile mills with a capital of £ 2,246,000. The number of workers employed in these two industries was 68,000. Besides these, and other private industrial enterprises, including native inter-provincial commerce and banking houses, there was £ 90,000,000 invested in savings banks and joint stock companies. This capital was all in the hands of the Indian mercantile class except for. 02 % which was owned by English capitalists. Thus as far back as the '80's of the last century, Indian capitalism, as represented by the liberal professions and landholding class, and the Indian merchants and traders, was ready to enter into its industrial phase, but the foreign Government was opposed to it. The Imperial Capital of Britain wanted to hold India as a source of raw materials and as a market for finished goods. Consequently, the young native machine-industry was subjected to special taxations which seriously checked its growth, and in many cases, ruined it in the very beginning. But the cheapness of raw materials and labor kept the textile mills going, in spite of the fact that they were the main object of governmental attack.

The increasing wealth of the intellectuals and the absence of profitable means of investment made them discontented with the British Government. Finding it beneath their dignity to carry on trade, and industrial outlets being denied by the Government, land and Government securities were the only remaining sources of investment left to this class. The interest on securities was very low, being but 3 to 3½%. It was not at all attractive for an ambitious class. Neither was the income from land-investments very high. Besides, the area of productive land being comparatively limited, no very large scope was presented. The native capitalist class was excluded from building railways, tramways, exploiting mines and other industries whose development was not obstructed by the Government. All these industries were the monopoly of English capital. The liberal professions were overcrowded, so the rich intelligentsia found its further economic development blocked on all sides. The British Government was seen to be the cause of all this, and there arose the necessity of fighting against it. Economic necessity forced the intellectual bourgeoisie to begin its political struggle, which was initiated in the form of the Indian National Congress, whose first session was held in 1882 in Bombay, under the Presidency of W. C. Banerji, a rich lawyer who had his savings invested in commercial and industrial enterprises. The object of this political movement was manifest, — it was to replace or at least to curtail the power of the British Government, which was standing in the way of the economic development of the bourgeoisie. This movement was headed by rich lawyers, merchants, mill-owners, physicians, &c. or in other words, that progressive element of the society which possessed capital to be invested.

In the last years of the 19th century, the power of Indian capital went on growing, though rather slowly, because of the fact that it was denied the outlet of industrial development. Nevertheless, since there was a class with money to be invested, and great masses of people were looking for employment, having been deprived of their land and of their ancient handicraft occupations, industries kept growing despite all obstructions created by the Government.

* * *

The big landholders of the province of Bengal enjoy a privileged position under the permanent settlement introduced in 1793. According to this system, they pay a fixed scale of taxation, their holdings being exempt from new assessments. According to the Bengal Tenancy Act, the cultivators to whom the big landholders leased out their lands, enjoy the right of occupancy. As a result, the agricultural production of the province of Bengal has always been high, and the rental value of the land increased enormously. But the Permanent Settlement prevented the Government from participating directly in this increased land-value. A means to nullify the effects of the Permanent Settlement was found in the partition of Bengal in 1905. By this partition, the eastern half of the province, containing the rich rice-producing area, was placed under the administration of a newly-created provincial government, with the power to revise the old system of taxation. Thus arose a new conflict between the Government and the rich landholding class which, as stated before, contained a large number of intellectuals.

The unification of landed and capitalist interests as against British rule, was achieved. In 1905 the political movement of the Indian bourgeoisie as represented by the Indian National Congress, backed by the progressive landholding class, used the economic weapon of boycott against British capitalism. The 25th session of the Indian National Congress held in Calcutta in 1906, under the presidency of Daddabhai Naoroji, also a rich merchant lawyer, declared a boycott of English goods until the Partition of Bengal Act was repealed. The economic power of the Indian bourgeoisie, composed of the intellectuals, mercantile capitalists, liberal landholders, and the industrial capitalists, had acquired sufficient strength to enable it to declare an open struggle against the foreign capitalistic monopoly.

The number of factories in 1905 amounted to 2,688. Of these, only 718 were non-power, the rest being either steam or electricity-driven. The textile industry had grown to count upon 178 weaving mills, with a capital of £ 10,762,000 and 750 ginning mills owned by individual capitalists, (figures for capital invested not available). The jute industry counted 38 mills for weaving, with a capital of £ 5,393,358, and 100 pressing mills owned by private capital. According to the Government statistics, the capital of joint stock companies registered in India, engaged in industrial enterprise amounted to £ 57,000,000. The amount of capital invested in industries had increased almost tenfold since 1880, whereas investment in Government securities had increased by only £ 4,000,000 the total amount being £ 94,616,740, during the same period. With industrial development, Indian capital also began to create modern banking institutions. In 1905 there existed in India nine banks with Indian capital. These were in addition to the native banking firms based on usury. There were six woolen mills and seven paper factories.

The theory on which the Boycott Movement was based was that this growing native industry should be protected and stimulated in order to increase the national wealth, the only way of improving the economic condition of the people, according to the bourgeois reasoning of that epoch. Owing to the fact that Indian industry was too new and weak to hold its own in a competition with British capitalism, the object of the boycott movement was not attained. British goods could not be thrown off the market, simply because Indian industries were not able to produce the amount needed for consumption. But the Government found it necessary to recognise the strength of the bourgeoisie. In 1909, the Morley-Minto Reforms were introduced, conceding to this class some nominal share in the administration of the country. For the first time, an Indian was appointed in the Viceroy's ExecutiveCouncil, which corresponded to the board of advisors of an autocratic monarchy. The choice fell on one of the premier lawyer, who was at the same time a rich landholder. The number of elected members in the Legislative Councils, both Imperial and provincial, was increased. Special electorates were conceded to the landholding class as well as to the

Mussulman bourgeoisie. A royal Commission was appointed to investigate the possibility of increasing the percentage of the native element in the public services. In 1911 the first phase in the political struggle of the Indian bourgeoisie culminated in the repeal of the act of the Partition of Bengal. The Indian bourgeoisie was very much encouraged by its first political victory. It kept on the struggle until a year later, the Government of India had to declare through the mouth of the King-Emperor, who visited India expressly for this purpose, that self-government would be conceded to the Indian people at the earliest possible moment.

Nor was the victory of the bourgeoisie in the industrial field altogether negligible. In 1908, the number of cotton weaving mills had increased to 212, with a proportionate increase in the amount of capital invested therein. The number of jute mills (weaving) also increased to 56, with about 50% increase in the invested capital. In both these industries, a small percentage of English capital had always been invested, but after 1905 the proportion as well as the actual amount of English capital invested in these industries, showed a noticeable decrease. Besides the cotton and woolen textile, which benefitted most by the boycott movement, a general impetus was felt in the industrial field as a whole. New industries were started, and existing ones extended and modernised. The following industries felt the impetus most:

Coal-mining, glass-making matches, flour and rice-milling, oil-mills, tanning, leather manufacture, metal-works, pottery, soap, pencil, paper, dyeing, &c. &c.

The number of joint-stock companies increased from 1,530 in 1905 to 2,061 in 1910. The amount of capital invested in industrial enterprises was calculated at £ 72,800,000 in 1908 and £ 108,606,000 in 1910. The number of banks owned by Indian capital increased to 14 and 16 respectively. The industrial and commercial concerns run with private capital, about which no figures are available, also showed a great increase. The iron and steel industry received a great impetus when in 1907 the Tata Iron and Steel Co. was organised with a capital hitherto unprecedented in India.

Urged on by its initial political victories, the Indian bourgeoisie went on consolidating its position economically. Although it was not until the Great European War that Indian capital received the fullest opportunity to assert itself, a considerable amount of industrial and commercial activity was felt all over the country in the years preceding the war. The growth of modern industry is shown by the fact that the value of machinery imported in the year 1913 amounted to nearly £ 10,000.000. Besides, in the same year, 2½ million pounds sterling worth of parts of machinery were manufactured in India. In 1914, the capital invested in Government securities amounted to £ 121,500,000, drawing interest at 3½ to 4%, whereas there were 2,545 joint-stock companies with — an aggregate — capital of £ 113.396.000. The figures for the capital invested in privately-owned industrial enterprises are not available.

The war opened up a new era for the Indian bourgeoisie. The necessity for mobilising her entire industrial strength for the production of war materials, combined with the dislocation of marine transport, owing firstly to the transfer of merchant vessels to naval purposes and secondly to the submarine warfare, made it impossible for England to keep the Indian market supplied with manufactured goods. This placed the Indian manufacturers in an unexpectedly advantageous position. The overwhelming competition of the imperial capital was suddenly removed and Indian capital was presented with a free field of development. But this was not all. The British Government itself, which so far had persistently followed the policy of keeping India industrially backward, found it necessary to change its policy. Since the beginning of the century, there had been growing discontent in the country. In the years preceding the war, this discontent had become widespread and acute, because of the increasing poverty of the masses and the enormous growth in the number of unemployables among the intelligentsia. So at the outbreak of the war, things looked rather threatening in India. Attempts were made to overthrow British rule by organising armed uprisings. Signs of revolt appeared among the Indian troops. The political movement for national liberation, originally, started under the auspices of the wealthy intellectuals, and growing bourgeoisie, had been largely captured by the so-called Extremists, whose ranks were swelled by the lower strata of middle-class intellectuals. Terroristic societies had been active since 1904. The tendency towards complete separation of India from the British Empire by means of a violent revolution was no longer confined within the secret revolutionary organisations. It began to spread among the ranks of the Extremists, who constituted the Left Wing of the Indian National Congress.

There were two factors behind the political movement in India. First, the rise of a class which had accumulated a considerable amount of capital in its hands and which wanted to have the right of participating in, if not monopolising the exploitation of the natural riches and labour power of the country. Second, the growing poverty and the existence of a great number of unemployed and unemployables, due to the intensive and extensive exploitation of foreign capital which so far, had found it profitable to keep the country industrially undeveloped. Both these factors were working against British rule. But socially speaking, they were contradictory one to the other. The fact that they had a common enemy to fight made it possible for them to unite, and a united effort of these two factors would bring about the destruction of British rule. To prevent this union was naturally the desire and purpose of the British Government. Among the bourgeoisie was found the element which could be won over, or at least whose actions could be moderated by means of political concessions. But in India, the bourgeoisie of 1916 was not the same as in 1909. It was no longer possible to placate it with hollow political and administrative privileges. It wanted economic concessions, a share in the exploitation of the country.

In the first years of the war, Japan began to capture a considerable part of the Indian market, formerly supplied by English manufacturers. It was practically impossible for the British capitalists to keep the Japanese goods out of the Indian market. All these internal and external reasons taken together, made the British Government take the Indian bourgeoisie into confidence. In the very beginning of the war, the promise of giving India self-government was repeated, provided India would help England in the prosecution of the war. As self-government means the transfer, wholly or partially, of the administration of the country to the Indian bourgeoisie, this promise won the active support of the propertied class to the cause of the war. Hoping to gain at least a considerable control over the government of the country, this class suspended its political struggle and helped the British Government in the recruitment of Indian troops and in discouraging the nationalist movement, now led by the lower middle class. These valuable services were paid by the granting of a 3½% import duty on cotton imports in 1916. This was a protection granted to the principal industry of India, and it meant such a great economic concession to the bourgeoisie that the latter readily helped the Government of India to raise a war-fund of £ 100,000,000 as a gift to England. The immediate effect of this was that the amount of capital invested in the textile factories owned by registered joint-stock companies, rose to £ 24,500,000 in 1917, the number of mills being 276. Besides, there were 1800 cotton-ginning factories and a considerable number of weaving factories owned by individual capitalists or private companies. Since 1880 up to 1917, the cotton-textile industry had increased 375% in the amount of capital invested, 792% in looms, and 411% in spindles employed, the all-round increase being 427%. By the year 1917, India could produce the entire quantity of yarn needed for her textile industries and half the amount of textile-woven goods, or in other words, the native production was 94.6% of the imports as compared with 42% in the years preceding the war. In 1917, India produced 1,614,216,458 yards of woven cotton-goods valued at £ 18,100,000, besides a considerable quantity of yarn of great value.

The average total capital of companies registered every year from 1910 to 1914 was approximately £ 12,000,000. The figure rose to £ 18,000,000 in 1917—18; and in the two years following the conclusion of the war, it reached the enormous heighth of £ 183,000,000, and £ 100,000,000 respectively. Of course these figures, especially the latter ones, do not represent the actual amount paid up on registering the companies; but they signify nevertheless the large industrial and commercial prospect the promoters had in view. Besides, this capital inflation was intended to give a tolerable appearance to the extraordinary rates of dividends paid to the shareholders.

The profit made in the Indian industries in the last few years is veritably fabulous. Cheap, ignorant and unorganized labor, together with an abundance of easily available raw materials enables the owner to make such excessive profits.The average dividend paid by the important cotton-mills in 1920 was 120%, the highest figure being as much as 365%. The number of mills coming under this category is quite large. The actual profit made in some of these mills came up to 500% if the habit of capital inflation so frequently indulged in by the Indian companies, is taken into consideration. The average rate of dividends paid by the jute mills in the same years was still higher, being not less than 140%. One concern, the Hoogly Mills of Calcutta, paid as much as 400%. In many other industries, for example, tea-plantation and manufacture, coal and gold-mining, leather works &c., the rate of profit, if not so high, is also very considerable. The average in the collieries is 90%. From this it is very easy to imagine the rapidity with which the Indian capitalist class is enriching itself. The inevitable result of this enormous profiteering is the accentuated growth of industries, because the profit is constantly increasing the capital ready for new investment.

The economic and industrial condition of the country in 1917 may be well appreciated from the following facts. There were more than 36.135 miles of railways, light railways not included, owned almost exclusively by English capital, a considerable portion of the light railways being Indian-owned. The number of workers employed on the railways including the industries directly allied with them, was 1,500,000. There were altogether about 9000 industrial establishments, employing more than 2,000,000 workers. Over four thousand of these were driven by steam or electric power. There were 1800 tea and coffee plantations, employing 900,000 workers. Great activity was shown in coal, petroleum, manganese, mica, iron and gold mining. The amount of business transacted through the principal ports and dockyards can be estimated from the fact that no less than 1,000,000 workers were employed. In 1919 the total profit made in the cotton, jute, woolen, paper, mining and leather industries was £ 45,000,000. The gross income of the railways was £ 77,600,000. It should be remembered that the amount of capital invested in the English-owned industries like railways &c. is not taken into account here.

Great impetus was felt in the jute industry also. In 1917, the number of mills rose to 78 and the capital invested to 13,215,000 pounds. The amount of Indian capital invested in this industry has increased by 311% since 1914. The entire industry has grown by 362% in volume, and 528% in capital since 1880. Manufactured jute exported in 1917—18, was valued at £ 30,000,000, 34 times more than the export of 1880. The wollen mills produced £ 1,405,000 in 1917 as against £ 400,000 in 1913. The production of paper-mills increased to £ 1,253,000 from £ 545,000 during the same peroid.

In 1917, India produced 18,200,000 tons of coal whereas the total consumption for that year amounted to 17,849,000 tons. The increase in the coal output was 2,000,000 tons more than the 1913 output. In the same year, the coal exported from India amounted to 408,117 tons worth £ 253,000. The consumption of coal in Indian industries for that year was 9,000,000 tons, as against 10,326,000 tons in the Japanese industries, exclusive of her merchant marine. The petroleum output of India in 1917—18 was 288,759,523 gallons valued at £ 1,093,000. Of this, only 139,000,000 gallons were consumed in the country, leaving the rest for export.

Indian commerce grew in proportion to. Of late Indian merchants are taking an increasing part in overseas commerce. She has become a competitor in the markets of the Dutch Indies, Malay Peninsula, East Africa, Afghanistan, and to a certain extent, China. She supplies these markets with manufactured or partially manufactured cotton goods. Her export of finished goods is increasing, whereas the export of raw material, especially jute and cotton, is decreasing.

That the Indian bourgeoisie has not been slow to seize the opportunity presented to it by the war conditions and the changed economic policy of the British Government is proved in the following table, which shows the percentage of decrease in the investment of Indian capital in Government

Securities as against increase in the various industrial pursuits.

	1914	1917	1918	1919	1920
Govt. Secur.	100	70	67	74	62
Banks	100	106	112	116	137
Munic. Deb.	100	89	84	84	81
Jute Mills	100	311	467	383	563
Cotton Mills	100	132	162	167	386
Woolen Mills	100	106	125	125	187
Coal Mines	100	136	134	157	149
Tea	100	137	125	123	136
Flour Mills	100	137	206	238	406
Iron and Steel	100	332	295	284	207

The change in the economic policy of the British Government was marked by the appointment in 1916 of the Indian Industrial Commission, with the object of finding the best means of fomenting the industrial developmentof the country. The Commission constituted ten members, out of which four were Indians, one being a leader of the Right Wing of the Indian National Congress, which is the political organ of the bourgeoisie, and the other three were the premier industrialists of the country. The Commission was instructed to examine and report upon the possibilities of further industrial development in India and to submit its recommendation with special reference to the following questions:

A. Whether new openings for the profitable employment of Indian capital in commerce and industry can be indicated.

B. Whether, and if so, in what manner, Government can usefully give direct encouragement to industrial development, 1) by rendering technical advice more freely available, 2) by the demonstration of the practical possibility on a commercial scale of particular industries, 3) by affording, directly or indirectly, financial assistance to industrial enterprises, or 4) by any other means which are not incompatible with the existing fiscal policy of the Government of India".

The Commission completed its work and submitted a lengthy report in 1918. The following are the features of the recommendations contained in the report: 1) That in future Government must play an active part in the industrial development of the country. 2) That India produces all the raw materials necessary for the requirements of a modern community, but is unable to manufacture many of the articles and materials essential alike in times of peace and war. Therefore it is vital for the Government to ensure the establishment in India of those industries whose absence exposes us to grave danger in the event of war. 3) That modern methods should be introduced in agriculture so that labour now wastefully employed would be set free for industries. 4) That universal primary education should be introduced, but that it would be unfair and unjust to impose upon employers this duty which devolves rather upon the State. 5) That institutions for technical and mechanical training should be introduced widely. 6) That the policy of laisser faire in industrial affairs to which the Government clung so long, should be abandoned. 7) That the establishment of Industrial Banks should be encouraged by means of Government financing if necessary. 8) That the necessity of securing the economic safety of the country and the inability of the people to secure it without the cooperation of the Government, are apparent. Therefore the Government must adopt a policy of energetic intervention in industrial affairs."

The political expression of the British Government's reconciliation with the Indian bourgeoisie is in the Montague-Chelmsford Reform Scheme. Taking advantage of the unexpected opportunity presented to it by the war conditions, of 1917—18, the Indian capitalist class acquired such a secure economic position that it was no longer possible for the Government to ignore it. To revive after the war, the old policy of obstructing the industrial growth of the country would surely force the Indian bourgeoisie, which had developed its political consciousness and organisation sufficiently, to place itself actively at the head of the revolutionary movement which was spreading wider and wider throughout India. The only way of preventing such a catastrophe was to devise means for divorcing the political ambition of the bourgeoisie from the spontaneous revolutionary upheaval among the masses. Already in 1911, the Indian bourgeoisie had been promised self-government, a promise which was repeated in the beginning of the European war in order to win its support.

The war was over. The Indian bourgeoisie had stood faithfully by the British Government. The time had come when some considerable concessions had to be made to it. These concessions were made by the introduction of the Montague-Chelmsford Reforms, whose principal features were as follows: 1) The control of the British Parliament over the Government of India exercised through the Secretary of State for India was modified. 2) The number of Indian members of the Viceroy's Executive Council was increased. 3) The system of dual-chamber was introduced in the Legislature and the number as well as proportion of elected Indian members was increased. 4) The franchise was so extended as to embrace all owning property, exceeding a certain minimum. 5) The actual power of law-making which had so far been vested in the Executive, was partially conceded to the Legislature. 6) Indian ministers were appointed to assist the provincial governors; these members being recruited from the leaders of the moderate nationalists. 7) The size as well as power of the provincial Legislatures was also extended. 8) The number of Indian elements in the superior posts of the Civil Services was increased to 33 per cent. 9) New facilities were provided for entering the Civil Services by holding the examinations in India as well as in England. 10) The difference between the scale of salaries of the Indian and English officials was reduced. 11) Municipal administration was given over to the local bourgeoisie to a great extent.

But the remarkable feature of this Reform, which is said to have brought a new political era to India, is the economic concessions made to Indian capital. The following passages quoted from the Reform Scheme speak for themselves.

"As the desirability of industrial expansion became clearer, the government of India fully shared the desire of the Indian leaders to secure the economic advantages that would follow the local manufacture of raw products. English theories as to the appropriate limits of the State's activity are inapplicable to India. We believe that this is true in case of industries, and that if the resources of the country are to be developed the government must take action. We feel no surprise that there remained a feeling of bitterness among the advanced parties. The people have recognised their inability to carry out their programme (of industrial development) without the help and guidance of the government. The war has created a new position. The prohibition of imports from enemy countries was welcomed as giving India an opportunity of replacing foreign articles by home products. After the war, the need for industrial development will be all the greater, unless India is to become a mere dumping ground for the manufactures of foreign nations, which will then be competing all the more keenly for the markets on which their political strength so perceptibly depends. India will certainly consider herself entitled lo claim all the help that the government can give her to enable her to take her place as a manufacturing country. On all grounds, a forward policy in industrial development is urgently called for, not merely to give India economic stability, but in order to satisfy the aspirations of her people, who desire to see her stand before the world as a well-poised, up-to-date country; in order to provide an outlet for the energies of her youths, who are otherwise drawn exclusively to government services or to a few overstocked professions; and in order that money now lying unproductive may be applied to the benefit of the whole community. Imperial interests also demand that the natural resources of India should henceforth be better utilised. We cannot measure the access of strength which an industrialised India will bring to the power of the Empire. Mere traders may be disposed to regard each new source of manufacture as a possible curtailment of their sources of profit. But each new acquisition of wealth increases the purchasing power of the whole. The war has thrown a strong light on the military importance of economic development. Now-a-days the products of an industrially developed community coincide so nearly with the catalogue of munitions of war that the development of India's natural resources becomes a matter of almost military necessity. We believe that this consideration is not a matter of indifference to India's political leaders; and that they are anxious to see India self-supporting in respect of military requirements. The government must admit and shoulder its responsibility for furthering the industrial development of the country.

"We have been assured that Indian capital will be forthcoming once it is realised that it can be invested with security and profit in India; a purpose that will be furthered by the provision of increased facilities for banking and credit. The real enthusiasm for industries, which is not confined to the ambitions of a few individuals but rests on the general desire to see Indian capital and labour applied jointly to the good of the country, seems to us of the happiest augury — — — — —."

This rather long quotation is made because (herein are indicated the reasons which forced the British capitalist class not only to recognise the Indian bourgeoisie as a factor to be taken into consideration, but to help it develop by conceding it the position of junior partnership in the exploitation of India. The object behind this remarkable change of policy on the part of British Imperialism was to split the revolutionary movement by making clear to the bourgeoisie that it was no longer impossible for it to realise its ambitions under British rule. The opportunity to develop as an economically powerful class was what the Indian bourgeoisie was striving after; their political movement was a struggle to conquer this right. The economic and industrial advancement secured during the war was strengthened by the declaration of change in the governmental policy, and the Indian capitalist class entered a period of spectacular development from 1918. The growth of industries was very rapid and commerce extended enormously.)

In 1918—19 the capital invested in joint-stock companies was £ 255,000,000 as against £ 135,000,000 in 1913—14, besides there were 3600 factories owned by private capital whereas in 1913—14 the number of factories owned by private capital was 1300. The amount of wealth accumulated in the hand of the bourgeoisie as shown by the investment in Government securities, — to find a profitable investment of which wealth was the principal burden of the commissions appointed and reforms introduced by the government, — rose to £ 359,000,000 in the same year*. As a result a considerable development took place in the industries of jute and cotton textile,

* One hundred year ago i. e. in 1820 the same class had only £ 20,000,000 invested in Government Securities.

engineering, iron and steel, coal mining etc. Another factor helped the transfer of a large capital from trade and commerce to industries during the war. This was the closing down of German and Austrian firms, which used to carry on a large export and import trade in raw and manufactured products through the Indian middleman.

With the growth of the native industries, a considerable change took place in the sea-borne trade. In the imports, an increase was shown in machineries, while there was a decrease in cotton-textiles. The amount of raw materials exported decreased. According to the report of the Director of Commercial Intelligence, the volume of Foreign Trade of India was valued at £ 600,000,000 in 1920 as against one-sixth this amount twenty years ago; the greatest increase in imports was in machinery and kerosine. In presenting his report, the Director General said: "India's purchasing power must be developed by developing her industries. Manufactured and partly-manufactured goods are of greater value than raw materials. This tendency has been marked in the last years. Jute is exported manufactured. A great portion of the oil-seeds are crushed and the oil exported. Thus, India has been capable of buying more machinery and other foreign goods for her industrial development."

The amount of manufactured cotton imported in 1920 showed a decrease of 60 % in the quantity of yarn and 36.5 % in the quantity of woven goods as compared with 1914. In 1920, cotton-goods constituted 28 % of the total import of India, whereas in 1914, it was over 50 %. On the other hand, the export of raw materials has decreased by 19 %. In the pre-war period, India used to import a considerable amount of railway materials but in the last years, an increasing part of her demand is being met by native industry. The contract to supply steel rails to one state railway and to two other systems owned by English companies has been given to the Tata Iron and Steel Co., an Indian firm.

Jute, raw and manufactured, used to form a great part of India's export trade, being 24 % of the total. A great change has taken place in this. The export of raw jute in 1919—20 was only 77 % of that of 1913—14. At the present time, nearly 75% of the raw produce is consumed in the local mills as against 50 % in the pre-war years.

The export of raw cotton decreased by 22 % in 1920 as against 1914, whereas the increase in the export of cotton-woven goods was 120 %. The total production of the cotton-textile industry rose by 41 %. The latest figures as to the growth of the Indian manufacturing industry are not available, but it is generally held that the industrial capital of India today is 2000 % greater than in the pre-war days.

This vast increase of wealth of the Indian bourgeoisie has not been achieved by depriving British capital of the full benefit of Imperial exploitation. We will see in the next chapter that with the increase in the wealth of the bourgeoisie, the poverty of the masses has also increased. Today, the bourgeoisie in India is not a negligible factor. If the British Government is trying to win it over to its own side, this is because it can no longer suppress it or ignore it as a socio-economic factor. But on the other hand, in comparison with the vastness of the country and its population, as well as in competition with the Imperial capital, the Indian bourgeoisie cannot help being conscious of its weakness. Therefore, its political tactics are determined by the desire to acquire concessions and support from the British Government, in order to further its own development. It does not as yet feel itself strong enough to challenge the right of the British Government to be in India, but by virtue of its increasing wealth and rapidly concentrating capital in industrial enterprises, it has grown into a political power, so much so that the Government has to recognise it as such. The Government has made political as well as economic concessions, not because it finds in the new Indian bourgeoisie a mortal enemy, but because the growing revolutionary movement among the masses is forcing upon the authorities the necessity of compromising with that section of the people which is closer to themselves by class-interest. The Government is willing to admit the Indian bourgeoisie to a junior partnership in the exploitation of the country, but the Indian capitalist class, which already controls 75 % of the industry (excepting railways, mining and plantation) as well as a big share in the commerce, is not satisfied with this.

The more the British Government makes concession to the Indian bourgeoisie, the more ambitious the latter becomes. It knows quite well that it is necessary to make compromises with the Imperial capital, till the time comes when it will be in a position to openly contend for the right of monopoly of exploitation with the foreigner. But it also knows that British Imperialism cannot be overthrown without the help of the masses. So to deceive the workers, whose revolutionary consciousness is steadily growing, owing to their increased poverty, which is accentuated by the concentration of wealth in the hands of the bourgeosie, the latter has thrown open the doors of the Indian National Congress to the masses. But at the same time, by declaring the boycott of British goods for the second time, the Indian bourgeoisie shows its tendency to aggrandize itself at the cost of the people. In the Indian bourgeoisie as well as in the masses, are to be found the objective forces making for a revolution. But these two factors are divided by class interest and this class differentiation is growing and is bound to grow wider in proportion to the further development of the Indian bourgeoisie. Both the forces are solidifying themselves in their own way; the masses in the growing number of trade-unions and peasant movement; the bourgeoisie in the political movement expressed by the National Congress. The fact that the Indian National Congress, under the leadership of Ghandi, succeeded in raising more than 10,000,000 rupees in three months for a National Fund demonstrates the growing solidarity of the Indian bourgeoisie. The All-India Muslim League, founded in 1905 under the auspices of the Government, to marshal the Mussulman capitalists and landed aristocracy in a political opposition to the Indian National Congress, (originally composed of the Hindu elements of the population with a sprinkling of liberal Mussulman intellectuals) has abandoned its original rôle and merged itself into the national movement of the Indian bourgeoisie as a class. In short, to-day the latter constitutes a social class enonomically and politically well-knit, conscious of its historic mission. Undoubtedly, it is going to be at the vanguard of that national upheaval which will overthrow foreign rule, but the more class-conscious it becomes, the more it will lose the power to deceive the masses. The more the country develops, economically and industrially, under the leadership of the native capitalist class, the wider will grow the class-cleavage. Therefore, to rely on the national solidarity under purely bourgeois leadership for the purpose of destroying British rule in India, may not be always safe. The overthrow of the British rule will be achieved by the joint action of the bourgeoisie and the masses, but how this joint action can be consummated, still remains a question. It will be easier to solve this problem when the condition of the masses is analyzed, in order to understand what a great gulf divides these two revolutionary factors.

CHAPTER II.

The Condition of the Rural Population.

In 1911 the total population of India was 315,000,000. This showed an increase of 21,000,000 over the figure of 1901, when the population amounted to 294,000,000. But a study of the census statistics shows that the actual increase by births was but 10,000,000, the remainder being due to more efficient methods of taking census, and to the inclusion of new territories within the census area. Thus the actual increase of the population of the country could not be called high, nor even normal in comparison with that of the European countries. The cause of this low birth-rate is to be looked for in the chronic poverty of the rural population. Many statisticians, both official and non-official, have testified to the fact that the great bulk of the agricultural population lives in a state of perpetual starvation. According to Sir William Digby, who held various high posts in the Indian Civil Service for twenty-five years, more than fifty percent of the entire agricultural population never have their hunger satisfied once in their lives. Sir Charles Eliot, former provincial governor of Bengal, declared that 40,000,000 of the inhabitants of India never get one full meal a day. Such testimony can be added to ad infinitum, while the history of Indian famines is known to all the world. Instances are not rare in which millions of people are swept away by famine and the resulting pestilences. According to Government estimate, 6,000,000 people died in 1918 of Spanish Influenza (non-official estimates place the total mortality for that year from famine and disease at 32,000,000).

Although detailed statistics of 1920—21 census are not yet available, the present population is estimated at nearly 320,000,000. This figure shows an increase of less than five million in the last ten years, despite the fact that the methods of census taking have become more accurate, and the limits of census area have been extended to include outlying border districts.

Indian nationalists of all shades of opinion unite in declaring British imperialism responsible for all these evils, and the precarious condition of the people is laid solely at the door of the present governmental abuses. Their idea of a panacea for all these ills lies in the termination of foreign rule and the establishment of an autonomous or independent government. Their attitude can be summed up in the words of Sir Surendranath Bannerji, one of the veteran leaders of the Indian National Congress in its session held in Lucknow in 1916: "I have demonstrated that we are the natural leaders of the masses, the protectors of their interests, and those interests will be safe, far more safe in our hands, than in those of the foreign bureaucracy."

Nobody can minimize the disastrous offects of British Imperialism upon the Indian people, but in their political agitation, based consciously or unconsciously upon class-interest, the Indian Nationalists neglect to investigate other causes which are also responsible for the present condition of the agricultural population and which will continue after the termination of foreign rule, unless and until far-reaching changes in the present mode of production are brought about.

In 1911, 280,000,000 of the entire Indian population lived in villages and small towns of less than 5000 inhabitants. But there existed a general tendency towards decrease in the rural population and an increase in that of the towns, especially of the great industrial cities. For example, in the ten years ending in 1911, the population of the city of Calcutta showed an increase of 14 %, that of Bombay 25 %, and of Ahmedabad 16 %, whereas the population of religious centers, in which there is always a great number of people engaged in non-productive professions, decreased, Benares by 5 %, Muttra by 4 % etc. The urban population in 1911 was 35,000,000. There were thirty cities of more than 100,000 inhabitants, but in the last decade, this distribution has greatly changed. An increase is to be noted in the population of the newly-grown industrial centers. The growth of several of the principal urban industrial districts has been almost spectacular, as for instance, the population of the city of Calcutta, which rose from 1,300,000 in 1911 to 1,800,000 at the beginning of the war, and at present it is estimated at over 2,000,000. The growth of Bombay has been still more rapid, proportionately, if not in actual numbers.

Taking into consideration the vastness of the country and its population, India still remains predominantly agricultural, despite the rapid development of industry in recent years. Since the production is mainly agricultural, the the economic condition of that part of the population engaged in an industry so important, is necessarily a determining factor in the national life, therefore, the forces and agencies which affect this class must be carefully investigated and analyzed, in order to determine the potential relation to the political movement of the country as a whole.

The entire rural population of India can be divided into two great classes, namely, those engaged in the exploitation of the earth's surface, and those engaged in handicrafts, transport and trade. The census of 1911 puts the number of the first class at 224,000,000. Of these, only eight and a half million lived on agricultural rent, i. e. belonged to the landholding class who took no part in actual production. All the rest were cultivators of the soil. Thus we find two-thirds of the entire Indian population engaged in agricultural pursuits. Before proceeding to an analysis of the present economic condition of this great class, we will briefly consider the condition of that other section of the rural population, consisting of handicraftsmen, transport workers and traders.

When the British first came to India, a prosperous artisan class existed. Not being able to compete with the imported machine-made commodities, this artisan class was forced to abandon its occupation and go back to the land. but the destruction of Indian handicrafts was achieved more by violence than by peaceful competition, in order to secure a monopoly for the imported goods on the market. As a result of this violent destruction of the means of livelihood of a large section of the people, a greater part of the population was forced to live by agriculture than the land-area justified, and so it is that ever since the British occupation, more people lived by agriculture than could, under normal circumstances, be provided for. The results of this crowding-out and destruction of handicrafts was first felt in the large towns and districts adjacent to big trading marts, leaving the handicraftsmen of the remote village partially unaffected. Thus we find even as late as the last decades of the 19 th century, the modest necessities of the rural population manufactured or produced either by the cultivator himself or by the village artisan. But of late, the increasing importation of foreign manufactured goods, as well as the production of new native machine-industries have been driving a great portion of the village artisan class out of their occupations. The population thus displaced has been partially absorbed, either among the land-workers or the city proletariat. The extension of railways and river-navigation has brought about very great changes in the local trades and primitive transport system of the rural area. In the earlier days, as in all the industrially backward countries, the Indian village used to be a self-contained economic unit. Its cloth and often the raw material for it, its food-stuff, its fuel and its scanty need of agricultural and industrial implements, together with the rest of the household necessities, used to be produced in the village itself. But in spite of the fact that large-scale machine industry remained almost unknown in India until hardly twenty years ago, the influence of imported machine-made commodities did not leave the Indian village untouched. It is long since cheap, machine-made commodities began to penetrate farther and farther into the country, ousting the artisan from his means of livelihood. Modern means of communication have brought the Indian villages closer to the cities, where the machine-made articles are imported from foreign countries. The village trader, to whom the peasant sells the surplus product of his land, brings within the reach of the peasant's slender purse comparatively larger quantities as well as varieties of domestic and ornamental articles made by machinery in some far-off land. The village trader who deals in these imported machine-products, gives the peasant more of such articles as cloth, metal pots and utensils, cutleries, etc. than can the village artisan. Busy trade centres have sprung up along the railways and the river steamship routes, where the peasant can dispose of his product for ready money and can buy cheaply those necessities of life for which he formerly used to depend on the village artisan. He sells his cotton, for example, to the exporters or the native mill-owners' agents and buys machine-made cloth cheaply from the local dealer.

Thus the village weaver is being gradually eliminated as an economic factor of the community. And when we take into consideration the fact that the craft of weaving became so widespread and well developed in India for centuries that it could survive the onslaught of machine production, the ultimate undermining of the weaver may be looked upon as the death of the rural artisan class. The same process of elimination is going on in all other craft industries; as the transportation by bullock cart has been greatly replaced by railways, the once prosperous industries of wheel-wright and cartwright have been ruined. Such has also been the fate of boat-making industries, owing to the fact that an increasing bulk of the water-traffic is carried in river steamers or steam-launches owned by big river navigation companies. The village leather worker is disappearing under the competition of organised industries.

In short, the economic position of that portion of the rural population which has been for centuries engaged in non-agricultural pursuits, has changed. The village artisan finds it more and more impossible to earn a living by his craft. This being the case, a great bulk of the artisan class is thrown out of occupation. And since the population which earned a living by handicrafts was to be counted by tens of millions in India and also on account of the fact that the large-scale machine industry of the country has been and still is too small to absorb an appreciable portion of these displaced artisans, the latter had to turn either toward the land, which was already over-crowded, or to stick to their bankrupt professions in order to eke out a miserable living. There is still to be found a large population in the rural districts engaged in handicrafts, but its economic condition is absolutely hopeless. If these unfortunate people are still sticking to the occupations which cannot prevent death from starvation, it is not because they are too fond of these ancestral pursuits to abandon them, but because all other ways of earning their livelihood are blocked. According to the census report of 1911 no less than 25,000,000 of the rural population were engaged in handicrafts, a third of which number belonged to the weaving industry. The increasing influx of machine-made cotton-cloth, not only foreign but Indian manufactured as well, has thrown a considerable part of these people out of their calling. The actual number thus displaced is hard to be ascertained, as the census figures of 1920—21 are not available. But in the words of the Industrial Commission (1916—18) "the extended use of cotton cloth of native and foreign manufacture by the poorer classes has very prejudicially affected the communities of weavers scattered over the country".

While the economic position of the rural artisan has become desperate, that of the trader on the contrary, is improving. The same agency, that is the imported manufactured articles, which has undermined the social foundation of the handicraft industry, has at the same time been a cause of prosperity for the trading class. The most powerful man in the rural districts of India to-day is the trader, who is at the same time the usurer and in many cases happens to be the person, who, by virtue of the liquid capital he is in possession of, speculates in the small-holdings of the cultivator. The Indian peasant is entirely under the thumb of the country trader, who not only lends him money at an exorbitant rate of interest, but who controls practically the entire economic life of the country-side. He loans, sells and purchases seeds and grains, besides dealing in cloth, salt, oil, utensils, drugs and other household articles no longer produced in the village but imported from outside. The position of a village farmer with grains, oil-seeds or cotton to sell, but at the same time heavily indebted to the village trader, his only customer, makes the former a helpless victum of the latter. Thus this rural trading-class is looked upon by both the peasant as well as the ruined artisan as the cause of their misery. The peasant thinks so because the grip of the trade-usurer is becoming tighter on his throat every day, while the artisan is deprived of his living by the import of cheap machine-made commodities. The country dealer, possessing trades' and usurers' capital, sucks the blood of the peasantry on the one hand, and as representative of industrial capital on the other, has ruined the artisan class.

As in most parts of the country the production in on a small scale, it is practically impossible for the farmer to take his product to the larger markets where he can get a better price. But there is another factor which deprives the peasant of the right of selling his crops in the open market. It is again the trader engaged in usury. He loans the cultivator money either in cash or in seed grains in exchange for a mortgage on the prospective harvest. Naturally he imposes his own terms. Thus bound down, the farmer loses the right of even removing his crops from the field before the claims of the usurer as well as that of the big holder or the government (as the case may be) are satisfied. The disastrous effects of this system will be dealt with extensively in its proper place, but it is evident from what is said that the trading class is the master of the situation in the rural districts.

In 1911 the number of people living on trade was 17,800,000. Of this a considerable part belonged to the urban population, but no less than 70 % could be classed among the rural traders. It is through the agency of this comparatively small section of the people that the most outlying parts of the country were brought within the orbit of capitalist exploitation. The rural trading class of India, obstructed in its normal growth as the pioneer of the future native bourgeoisie, has proved itself a very efficient instrument for extensive and intensive exploitation in the hand of foreign capital. It is through the medium of this class that the peasantry, in spite of being largely engaged in very backward methods of land culture, has been reduced to capitalist exploitation. In the person of the village trader, the agent of the big export firms is to be found in almost every corner of the country. These agents have elaborated a system of taking away by far the greater volume of the produce of the soil in exchange for cheap machine-made commodities, a considerable portion of which consists of domestic necessities and worthless ornaments, thus leaving the peasant starving and submerged in debt for the rest of his life. The crops on the fields are sold to the large capitalist concerns before they are harvested or often before they are sown.

On account of the influence of capitalist commerce exercised over agriculture, which still remains the basic industry of India, its social significance has undergone a radical change thanks to the mediation of the rural trader. The value of the agricultural production of the country is no longer determined alone by its capacity to feed the population, but also, and to an ever-increasing degree, by its usefulness to serve as raw materials for modern industries. Or in other words, the rural population of India, though apparently untouched by modern means of production, is no longer left to produce what it needs for its own maintainance; the land tilled by the Indian peasant has to produce what is needed for the machines somewhere else. The productive power of the land and of those who toil on it has been drawn into the orbit of the capitalist system. In short, the rural population of India has been to all intents and purposes, reduced to capitalist exploitation, without having in appreciable degree its standard of living raised and mode of production revolutionised, as would have been the case under normal circumstances.

The cultivation of the soil in India, although to a great extent still backward, is being adapted more and more to the exigencies of trade and industry than to the primal necessity of feeding the cultivator and his family. In form, agriculture still remains almost the same as a century ago, but its social character has been modernised. In this peculiar phenomenon lies the cause which is going to determine the economic and political movement among the rural population of India. Thus we find an increasing degree of local specialisation of particular crops, especially in those grown for export or for supplying the necessities of the modern industrial centres of the country. For example, cotton is no longer grown in small patches in almost every village, but it is concentrated in areas specially adapted for it. In the irrigated dry planes of the Punjab, United Provinces and Sindh, the growing of edibles like wheat, sugar canes, etc. is declining gradually, owing to the inability of the peasantry to meet the excessive rate of taxation and various kinds of rents imposed on these lands in return for the improvement made by artificial irrigation.

In place of food-crops, the cultivation of long-staple cotton has been introduced, because on account of its superior commercial value, cotton enables the peasant to meet his increased liabilities. On the irrigated lowlands of Madras cotton, ground-nuts and other oil-seeds which are in great demand in the export market, are replacing the staple food crops. In Central Provinces, sugar-cane is being ousted by cotton, which is readily exchanged for cash, with which the cultivator can buy the cheap imported sugar without taking the trouble of manufacturing it by his crude methods. The great fertile delta of the Ganges, which produces nearly one-fourth of the entire rice of the world, is rapidly coming under the cultivation of jute at the expense of the grain which is the staple of the province as well as of a great portion of the country. The reason is that the poor and indebted peasantry can realise cash immediately after the harvest from jute, and as a rule receive advances in money in order to meet the cost of sowing by mortgaging the coming harvest to the agents of the exporter or manufacturer, who are to be found even in the remotest villages. Instances are not rare in which the cultivator is found to be so hopelessly at the mercy of the local dealer or exporter's agent, that he has to part with his rice crop from the very field and to go hungry all the year round, or to buy what is left after the choice grains have been exported, at a price often several times more than he has received for his crop. And this bad purchase he can make only by mortgaging his landholding or by selling his cattle and plough.

Thus we find not only the peasant ground down to abject poverty, but the economic life of the Indian village in rapid process of transformation. Owing to the demand for raw materials in the industrial centres outside as well as inside the country, the kind of crops raised is undergoing a change and the method of marketing is altogether different from what it used to be before. The peasant can by no means be called the owner of the product of his soil and toil. His labour-power has been socialised in the sense that he is no longer allowed to enjoy the product of it, as well as that it is employed, not in order to satisfy the hunger of himself and his family, but for supplying the commercial and industrial needs of somebody else. The entire agricultural industry of India, in spite of its backward state, has also been socialised, in so far as its scope is no longer limited to producing food for the toiler, and the value of its products is determined more by their exchangeability for other commodities than by their intrinsic character as articles of consumption.

Now we turn to examine the deplorable economic condition of the agricultural population of India as well as the causes which underly it. Above has been given a general picture of the rural population with special reference to the ruined state of the non-agricultural class, that is, the artisans and craftsmen. The new tendencies and the deep changes in the economic life of the rural population, agricultural as well as industrial, have also been surveyed. But all the changes, cross-currents and upheavals in the rural population can be estimated according to their proper magnitude and character, only by a thorough knowledge of the economic condition of that bulk of humanity engaged in agriculture, the basic industry of the country.

In 1911 the number of people living on the cultivation of the surface of earth and pasture was 224,000,000, that is more than 70 % of the entire population. Of these 8,500,000 lived on agricultural rent, taking no part in actual production; they belonged to the landholding class. Therefore the number of people engaged in agricultural production and living on it along with that of the allied industries was 215,500,000. This bulk of population can be divided into three sections according to their relative economic status. Owing to the absence of any reliable material, it is very hard to make this classification accurate, but in broad lines it is as follows:

1. Peasant proprietors, not in the sense of owning the land they cultivate, but that their holdings are large enough to leave to them a certain surplus to sell after having satisfied their needs.
2. Small farmers, living partly on the produce of land held on rent and partly on wages.
3. Land workers living exclusively on wages.

Besides these three main classes, a population of about 7,000,000 live on cattle and other stock raising.

In 1920 the total population of India rose to 320.000.000 and the area under cultivation of both food as well as non-food crops amounted to 291,000,000 in the same year. Thus the average cultivated area per head of the population was a little above $^9/_{10}$ of an acre. But the actual distribution of the cultivated land was as follows: Deducting the 8,500,000 living on agricultural rent, and 7,000,000 dependent on stock raising, fishing and hunting, the agregate number of people subsisting exclusively on agriculture amounts to 208,000,000 of which 41,000,000 are land workers living exclusively on their wages without owning or holding any land. Thus we have in round numbers 167,000,000 people belonging to the first two classes of the agricultural population, viz. peasant proprietors and small farmers. Large scale farming is practically unknown in India. In spite of the fact that there is a rapid process of concentration in landholdings, the capitalists, rich intellectuals, traders and land-speculators, in whose hands the holdings are being concentrated, are not given to agriculture. Except in certain cases, for example, tea, indigo, coffee, partly ground nuts and other oil seeds, the tendency of the Indian bourgeoisie is to invest its capital not in agriculture, but in land. Of late this tendency has been showing signs of decline, and capitalistic production is being introduced into agriculture, especially in the cultivation of cotton, sugar, oil-seeds, and such other non-food crops which are in growing demand as raw materials in the new industries of the country. But on the whole, practically the entire cultivated area of the country is held on rent, under various systems of land tenures, by the first two classes of the agricultural population. The number of this two classes is 167,000,000, including women, children and dependents. This number is divided among 28,000,000 families, averaging 6 members. About 5,000,000 of these families can be put in the first class (peasant proprietor), and the other 23,000,000 in the second (small farmers). The average holding of the first category amounts to about 20 acres and that of the second to about 8-acres per family. Informations available about the average holding per family of cultivators and the difference between the holdings of the two classes are very scanty and unreliable. The size of the holding varies from one province to the other.

The tenant's holding per family goes as low as 2.8 acres in the Punjab while that of the big farmer goes as high as 59 acres in Bengal.

Of the 42,000,000 people living on agricultural wages 25,800,000 are actual workers, men and women included, the former being 13,100,000 and the latter 12,700,000. The rest are evidently children and infirm dependents. A considerable portion of the land workers are employed by the peasant proprietors and big landowners cultivating a part of their field directly, that is, not renting out to the tenants. A small number of the field workers is also employed by the petty farmers in the sowing and harvest seasons. These land workers can be called agricultural proletariat, in every sense of the word. Their economic position is much worse than that of the pauperized peasantry, being that of wage-earners pure and simple. The classified figures of the 1920 census are not yet available, but according to semi-official reports and other sources of information, the number of field workers living exclusively on wages has increased by 60 % in the last ten years, causing a decrease of about 40 % in the petty peasantry and small landholders. This increase in the number of land-workers is due on one hand to the tremendous rise in the cost of living, forcing women and young people into manual labour, and on the other, to the rapid process of land concentration caused by the growing indebtedness of the petty peasantry.

This huge mass of agricultural workers is a dead-weight on the rural population of India. It came into existence not by the process of the economic evolution of society as in the European countries; it was created by the destruction of the native craft industries, which till the earlier decades of the 19th century employed 25 % of the entire population of the country. Craft industries, which supplied the means of livelihood to such a considerable portion of the people, was ruined as stated before, not by the growth in the country of a higher form of production, viz. machine industry, but partly by violent methods and partly by the introduction of machine-products imported from a foreign country. Thus by the '30's of the last century, nearly half a million families of artisans were thrown out of work completely. As the normal industrial development of the country was obstructed artificially in order to preserve the monopoly of a foreign capitalist class on the Indian market, this huge mass of rural population dislodged from its occupation by machine production, could not be turned into a city proletariat in the same manner as in European lands. A great part of it was driven back to the land which had already been supporting too many people, and consequently crowded others out. Thus came into existence the large rural population living on agricultural wages. The number of these field workers has constantly been augmented from the small farmers overwhelmed by indebtedness on one side and on the other, from the village artisans ruined by the steady penetration of cheap-imported machine-made articles into the farthest interior of the country.

The condition of these field-workers is very bad. At least six months in the year they are without work or are employed very irregularly. Since nearly two-thirds of the entire cropped area of the country is cultivated by small farmers holding on an average 8 acres per family of 6 (at the minimum) and since the distribution of the greater part of the remaining one-third (about 100,000,000 acres out of 106,000,000) is also so sub-divided as to preclude the employment of any considerable number of hired labourers, the possibility of this large mass of field workers being absorbed into the agricultural industry is very limited. The peasant proprietors (that is, the farmers holding on an average 20 acres per family) cannot employ a very large portion of the agricultural workers, and these only in the season of seeding and harvesting. The area covered by large scale forms is hardly 6,000.000 acres, and this is the only place where a steady employment is provided for the field workers; but no more than a couple of millions can be provided for there, under the best circumstances.

This being the case, the field workers of India constitute what is called the floating population. Not having a place where they can be steadily employed, these toilers wander over the country in large masses in search of employment. According to the climatic conditions and those of the soil, different crops are sown and harvested in different parts of the country in different parts of the year. Crops like rice, which need speedy seeding, transplanting as well as harvesting in short spaces of time, supply work to a great bulk of these land-workers; but the total duration of this employment does not last more than two months a year. The average wages of the field-worker is hardly 8 pence during the working period; thus if the whole year, including the unemployed months, are taken into consideration, the amount dwindles down to 3 or 4 pence a day. The agricultural wages have gone up during the last two years by 20 % while the rise in the cost of living has been over 400 %.

Along with the change in its industrial policy, the Government of India has recently been adopting measures to improve the agriculture as well. The object is the same, viz. to increase the agricultural productivity of the country. The only way of achieving this end is the introduction of modern methods of cultivation by using machinery. But the smallness of the average holding of the farmer is a great obstacle to the use of machinery. A free transfer of the agricultural industry from the present system of small scale individual production to large scale capitalistic production, entails the necessity of driving an increasing percentage of the rural population to wage slavery, because large farms can only come into existence by depriving the small peasants of the petty holdings to which they cling, although starving perpetually. Thus the scheme of increasing the productivity of the land by introducing improved methods would swell the wealth produced by the agricultural industry, but the economic condition of the population living on small holdings or field labour would grow worse in proportion, since the introduction of improved methods will drive the small farmers off the land and increase the number of rural wage earners. But the growing use of labor-saving machineries in agriculture will deprive the field workers of employment, thus accentuating their present precarious plight. This problem seems to be taken into consideration by the government in its new economic policy, even if the political movement of the bourgeois intellectuals still remains oblivious to such vital questions of social-economics. The British rulers appear to appreciate the grave danger of the existence of an ever-growing mass of unemployed and unemployables in the country. In recommending that the

Government should encourage and help the introduction of machinery in agriculture, the Industrial Commission (1916—18) remarks: „It is clear that, if the basis of employment also be widened, crop failures will lose much of the severity of their effects, and the extension of industries, in as great a variety as circumstances will permit, will do more than anything to secure the economic stability of the labouring-classes."

Of course this view of „securing the economic stability of the labouring classes" is taken from the exploiter's angle of vision and adapted to their interests. While the occasional crop failures have their effects on the economic condition of the people, it is only the theory of capitalist imperialism which ascribes to crop-failures the entire responsibility for the havocs wrought by the famines in India. The same Industrial Commission admits in another part of its report: "Famine now connotes not so much a scarcity or entire absence of food, as high prices and a lack of employment in the affected areas". It also testifies to the fact that "the development of irrigation and the improvement of agriculture enable the country to grow a much larger quantity of foodstuffs than before".

The secret of the misery of the rural population lies in the fact that the agricultural production of India has been brought completely within the sphere of capitalist exploitation, foreign and native combined. The unrestricted export of food grains, together with the merciless speculation carried on by the native traders, raises the price continually on the one hand, while on the other, the lack of employment among an ever-growing section of the rural population creates great scarcity of money. So, even when there is food the people die of hunger because they have no money to buy it with.

In the province of Madras, the use of machinery in agriculture has been more than in any other part. As a result the productivity has been increased, especially of the land under oil-seeds; but the other side of the picture shows a great decrease in the number of unemployed field workers.

Finding it impossible to absorb this mass of unemployables within the country, a large number of these had to be sent out to earn a living somewhere else. The rubber plantations of the Malay States provided a field. The emigrant workers have been helpless victims of the same class of native traders who found it profitable to speculate in human labour. In the last years, the slump in the rubber market has thrown hundreds of thousands of these plantation workers out of their employment.

So it is evident that the problem of finding employment for the growing mass of field workers can be solved neither by the capitalist method of increasing production by the use of labour-saving machineries; nor by the bourgeois nationalist programme of conferring on the big landholding capitalist class the right of ownership, thus exempting it from the liability of paying augmented taxes to the government; nor by the petty-bourgeois liberal reformism which prescribes the abolition of large holdings and leaves the basic industry of the country in the hand of the small farmers. We will be better able to formulate our solution after having analyzed the system of land tenures as well as the economic condition of the first two sections of the rural population, viz. peasant proprietors and small farmers.

In India the ownership of the soil, both cultivated and uncultivated, is vested in the State. The land tenure is divided into two classes, viz. Zemindari system and Ryotwari system. The former again is divided into two categories, permanent and temporary. The system of land settlement that prevails in India is based on the imported idea of English feudal aristocracy mixed with the native tradition of peasants owning the land and paying the State tribute through the medium of a class of tax-collectors. Of course none of these old basic ideas can be found in toto in the present systems of land tenure; but the latter is the development of the two old systems adapted to the modern necessities of capitalist exploitation.

Under the first system of tenure, that is the Zemindari system, the land revenue is assessed by the State permanently or temporarily as the case may be, on individual families holding large estates and occupying a position analogous to that of a landlord. These holders in their turn lease out small parcels of their estates to tenants who cultivate the land. When the revenue is assessed directly by the State on small holdings occupied and cultivated by the peasant, the tenure is called Ryotwari. The second class of tenure is always temporary.

In order to understand clearly the agrarian problem of India and the economic condition of the population engaged exclusively and living on cultivation of the earth, it is necessary to go into the history of the development of tenure, distribution and taxation of land. When in the middle of the 18th. century the British East India Company assumed the political control over the province of Bengal, the ryot or cultivator had been in the habit of paying a fixed share of produce either in kind or cash, to the large land-holders called the Zemindars. Under the Moghul Empire, these Zemindars paid to the central government nine-tenths of what they received from the cultivator, retaining one-tenth for themselves. Besides they had the right to assess additional local cesses which entirely fell to their share. At the time of the Emperor Akbar was introduced the custom of renewing assessment on the holding of the landlords every ten years. Nominally the landlords held their estates under mandates from the Emperor, in return for meritorious services rendered. The right of collecting revenue passed on to the heir after the death of the Zemindar, on the former's paying the Emperor a gift or fine. With the decline of the Moghul power the well-regulated feudal land-laws introduced by Akbar ceased to function, and chaos and anarchy in land taxation as well as administration was the order of the day, when the British became the supreme political ruler of the country. In its first attempt at revenue administration, the Company adopted the prevailing custom of annual assessment; according to this system, the right of collecting rent was sold annually to the highest bidder, that is to the person who could guarantee the government the greatest amount of revenue from the land. The result of this method of collecting the largest amount of revenue was disastrous. The Company's government was satisfied with receiving from the landholders the guaranteed amount, without minding the methods employed in collecting it as well as the share that the collector chose to take for his own. Between the government and the people there came into existence a class of tax-farmers, who by their very economic position were not at all interested in the actual agriculture, but only in getting as much as possible from the cultivator. Knowing that the holding might pass away from his hand the next year, the tax-farmer's philosophy was to make hay while the sun was shining. Consequently, the peasantry was ruined, agriculture was largely abandoned, and the amount extracted from the cultivator even by the most merciless procedure, diminished. It was not long before the Company came to understand the wrong economics of the system.

The British East India Company, in its character as the representative of trading capital, naturally desired to exterminate the Indian feudal land-tenure, in order to bring the producing forces within territories occupied by it, under its own direct exploitation. The procedure of leasing out gradually the right of collecting land revenue ruined the heridatary landowner families. In a short space of time, the former hereditary right of collecting land revenue passed away from the ancient feudal families into the hands of a new class of leaseholders and tax-farmers, who were at the same time officials, traders and usurers. But this fundamental change in social economics alarmed the British Parliament, which in those days (1777—80) still greatly reflected the political views of the English landed aristocracy. True to its feudal traditions, which were not dead as yet, the British Parliament could not watch idly the peaceful passing off of its peers in India. Accordingly it was enacted in 1784 that "whereas divers Rajas, Zemindars, Polygars, Talookdars, and other native landholders within the British territories in India, have been unjustly deprived of, or compelled to abandon or relinquish, their respective Indian Jurisdictions, Rights and Privileges, the Court of Directors should take measures for establishing, upon principles of Moderation, and Justice, the Permanent Rules by which their respective Tributes, Rents, and Services shall be in future rendered and paid to said United Company by the said Rajas, Zemindars, &c." Thus we find the struggle of the two philosophies of the social economics of the England of those times, viz. the reactionary tendency of the landed aristocracy to cling to the undermined feudalism, and the bourgeois mission of freeing the peasantry for unfettered exploitation by capital, reflected in the administration of India in the earlier days of British domination. The disastrous effects on revenue as a result of the system of annual assessment, together with the opposition raised by the British Parliament against the destruction of the Indian feudal families, thrust upon the Company's government the necessity of reforming its land policy. The political power wielded by the British rulers in those days was not sufficient to enable them to assume the task of bringing the entire population under the exploitation of trades capital, without some native intermediary. Nor were the English invaders numerically strong enough to undertake the task of collecting the land tax directly from the cultivators. Therefore, it was resolved to create out of the new revenue collecting class, 'a class of landholders. Being originally a class of usurers, traders and land speculators, this new landholding element could be counted upon as the social basis of the foreign rule.

The reformed land tenure was introduced as an experiment in 1789 in the form of a Ten Years' Settlement. It was a reversal to the old system of Akbar. This policy of reviving the dead landlordism, although in a modernised form, was inaugurated under the auspices of Cornwallis — that champion of the British landed aristocracy, who had but a few years before met his defeat at the hands of the rebellious colonial bourgeoisie at Yorktown. The experiment was found to be satisfactory to all concerned; the income of the government was stabilised, a loyal supporter was found in the contented class of newly-created landholders, and the agricultural production was increased, the peasantry having been saved somewhat from the ravenous exploitation of the irresponsible tax-farmers. On the expiration of the experimental period, Cornwallis reported that the new system had worked very satisfactorily and recommended that the next assessment should be made in perpetuity. Consequently the entire cultivated area of the provinces of Bengal, Behar, and Orisa was assessed permanently, the Government's share in the revenue being fixed at 90% of the whole economic rent. This is known as the Permanent Settlement of 1793. The effect of this settlement was that a permanent landholding class living on agricultural rent was created out of the tax farmers, or in other words, those who had been collectors of revenue became practically the owners of their leaseholds, while the cultivators, who had been the owners of the soil they tilled, became tenants at the mercy of the Zemindars, who soon began to burden them with rack-rent.'

The Permanent Settlement of 1793, which is looked upon even by the Indian Nationalist as one bright spot in the history of British rule, and for the general extension of which all over the country the political leaders have been stoutly fighting during more than half a century, has been the most sinister event in the annals of modern India. It checked the growth of the Indian bourgeoisie in its infancy and diverted it into a wrong way. In the latter part of the eighteenth century, there came into existence in India a prosperous trading class with a considerable capital accumulated in its hand. This trading class was largely responsible for undermining the foundation of feudalism in the days of decay of the Moghul Empire. All the big landowners as well as the rulers of the various independent states that sprang up on the ruins of the Moghul Empire, were heavily indebted to this class of usurious traders. The land was rapidly passing out of the hands of the hereditary feudal owners into the control of usury and trades capital. The latter was interested in seeing more people engaged in industries than in agriculture. In the middle of the eighteenth century in the province of Bengal alone, there were several million people employed in one industry — that of cotton-spinning and weaving. There were textile factories employing more than 100 workers. Woven cotton cloth formed a considerable part of the commodities exported from India by the East India Company, even towards the end of the eighteenth century. So this class of traders was the advance guard of the coming Indian bourgeoisie and would have developed into the modern capitalist class had not its normal growth been obstructed. The representative of the British bourgeoisie recognised in the Indian traders and land speculators their rival, historically destined to compete for the right of monopoly of exploiting the country. In the pious request of the English landed aristocracy assembled in Parliament, not to wipe off landlordism in India, was found a way to side-track the energies of Indian capital. Feudalism as a hereditary element in social economics had already been irretrievably undermined; the land had been freed from feudal fetters. By the Permanent Settlement, the land liberated from feudal ownership was given over to the trading class still in its infancy. Thus the capital and energy of the trading class, which under normal circumstances would have proved to be the forefather of the Indian bourgeoisie, was diverted to the investment on landwhich offered a promising prospect. In the struggle between two trading classes the less developed one succumbed before the more developed. The Indian trader and usurer were not only prevented from constituting themselves eventually into rivals of British capital, but were converted into a loyal support of British rule. But the hand of history cannot be kept back for ever. As has been shown in the first part, this very landholding class, created by the British government for its own benefit, has contributed largely to the rise of the modern intellectual, commercial and industrial bourgeoisie of India. The social forces assert themselves unfailingly.

Of course by the Permanent Settlement, the absolute ownership of the land was not forfeited by the government. The land was leased out to a number of middlemen at a rate of assessment fixed in perpetuity, who were given the right to collect the revenue in behalf of the State. Thus under the Zemindari system, which is in many respects analogous to landlordism, the land rent in India is not, as in other countries, a tribute paid to the State out of the income of the landowner, but on the contrary, it represents the relinquishment of a portion of the land revenue in favour of the handholders. Or in other words, under the Permanent Settlement the British Government, instead of exacting tribute from the landlords, concedes to them a part of the net rental of land. besides the privilege of sucking the blood of the poor tenants by a thousand and one ways, which will be dealt with presently. The British rulers adopted this method of subsidising a parasitic class for its own purposes as demonstrated above. But the reactionary character of that wing of the Indian political movement, which demands the extension of this system of tenure over the entire country, is betrayed when we find that under it, it is the small class of landholders that thrives at the cost of the cultivators. Even to the government this system has ceased to be useful, since it has played out its role to divert India's trades capital from industry to land; whereas on the other hand, in the provinces where this system is in force, the government is deprived by this privileged class of a great part of the land-rent. For example, in the three provinces of Bengal, Behar and Orissa, where the Permanent Settlement was first introduced, the total revenue paid to the government by all the Zemindars taken together is £ 3,500,000 the sum fixed as the 90% of the entire economic rent a century and quarter ago, while the actual rental has gone up to more than £ 14,000,000.

The Permanent Zemindari system holds good in five-sixth of the provinces of Bengal, Behar and Orissa, one tenth of the United Provinces and a quarter of the province of Madras, — representing in all about one-fifth of the area of British India. Another 32% of the area of British India is under temporary Zemindari system which allows a new assessment every 20 to 30 years. In the rest of the area, that is 48 %, the Ryotwari system is in force. In the Native States the temporary Zemindari system prevails, although a considerable portion of land is under Ryotwari tenure. Accurate figures about the land tenure in the Native States are not available. Though for reasons stated above, in the earlier days of their domination, the British rulers were forced to bring into existence a new class of landholders, after the old feudal landlordism had been destroyed by the development of new social forces, — in course of time, those reasons gradually lost their potentiality. The procedure of collecting land rent through the medium of a privileged class soon proved to be uneconomical. The Permanent Settlement precluded the government from participating in the actual profits of land rent, which kept on increasing owing to the more settled condition of the country. To its discomforture, the foreign capitalist government found that it had signed away its right of exploiting the agricultural population, in so far as the proceeds from the land rent were concerned, to the new landholding class, which was growing wealthy under the protection of the government. But the British rulers did not think it was yet possible to maintain their power over the vast population and extent of the country without the help of a solid and contented native element. So they did not dare to do away with the Zemindars; but they decided not to concede so much privilege to them in the newly acquired territories. Thus we find the Permanent Settlement in force in those provinces which fell into the hands of the English first, viz. Bengal, Behar, Orissa, Madras and the United Provinces. Even in those provinces. The Permanent Settlement was not introduced into those portions which came under British domination subsequently. The new system was Temporary Zemindari tenure. Under this system, the class of intermediary landholders was still retained in order to collect the rent for the government, but the latter reserved the right of enhancing its share in the total economic rent of the land from time to time. The government still needed such a class of landholders in order to avoid the troubles and worry of collecting the revenue. This system prevails in those parts of the country, which came under British administration while the British power was not yet well consolidated; that is, in some part of Bengal and Behar-Orissa, nine-tenths of the United Provinces, the whole area of the Punjab, four-fifths of the Central Provinces, the entire North-Western Frontier provinces and small tracts of Bombay. As stated above, 32% of British India and by far the greater part of the Native states come under temporary Zemindari system. In British India alone, 195,000,000 acres are held by Zemindars (temporary) 122,000,000 acres (permanent) of the entire area of 614,000,000 acres.

Under the Temporary Zemindari system, the right of collecting rent in return for a share in it, is conferred, in addition to individuals, upon joint villages. The revenue system which treats the village as a unit, and makes a Collective assessment is only applied to the „joint villages" of the north, that is, in those parts of the country where the old village communities existed at the time of British occupation. For the convenience of collecting revenue, the British Government thought it wise to utilise these communities as economic or proprietory units; the services of the P a t w a r i (the village headman) were found particularly valuable. Theoretically these so-called "joint villages" are held jointly and severally liable for the revenue charge, local rates &c., the burden of which they distribute among the co-sharers according to the rule and principle of their constitution. But in practice, the Patwari is the supreme power, being the representative of the Government and abusing his authority to much an extent that instances are not rare when he is killed by the villagers.

Now we will proceed to analyse the effects of the Zemindari system, both permanent as well as temporary, on the cultivators. It is held by a great majority of the Nationalists that the Zemindari system, and especially the Permanent Settlement of the Bengal type, is most beneficial to the cultivator, because it protects him from the exploitation of the Government. But the facts disprove this opinion, which manifestly is based upon class interest. Under the Zemindari tenure, the tenant suffers more than anybody else. He has absolutely no protection against being rack-rented.

The excesses committed by the Bengal landholders became so flagrant that the Government found it imperative to curtail their power by granting Occupancy Right to the cultivator. By the Bengal Land Act of 1859, the government recognised the right of the tenant holding land since 1793 or for twenty years, to remain in possession of the holding without the Zemindar's having the authority to eject him or to enhance his rental without a civil suit. But these guarantees count for very little in the practical life of the cultivator. By the privilege of appropriating a large portion of the entire economic rent, the Zemindars have accumulated considerable wealth; thus they can afford to buy off all the petty judicial, revenue and executive officials on whom rests the task of enforcing the law. And on the other side, the object of the government in enacting such laws was not to safeguard the interests of the toiling class against the landed rich, but to weaken the position of the landholders by posing as the protector of the poor cultivator against the oppressions of the latter. Thus, while in recent years there has always existed growing acrimony between the government and the landholding class over their respective share in the proceeds of exploitation, the position of the peasantry has been getting worse and worse, because both are desirous to extract as much as possible from the cultivator. The fact that the public exchequer receives less revenue from the area under Zemindari system than from the Ryotwari area, that is, the area under direct government assessment, does not by any means substantiate the contention that the cultivator under the former is any better off economically than under the latter. Under the Zemindari tenure, the actual payment, including that made in kind, is much more than the legal rate of rent payable to the landholder. The cultivator pays a fixed rent, assessed at an average of 35% of his net income, plus contributions for the upkeep of the Zemindar's household and rent-collecting staff, the latter being a permanent demand and is considered a part of the tenant's liabilities. The salary of the Zemindar's collectors is £ 1 per month on the average. This terribly insufficient wage naturally makes the Zemindar's officials extremely corrupt; they exact all kinds of contributions from the tenants under one pretext or another. Most of the rich landholders are absentees, living most of the year in the cities, where their luxurious life is supported by the rent exacted from the peasantry. Thus the cultivator is left entirely at the mercy of the unscrupulous rent-collectors, who at the same time indulge in petty usury. Over and above all these liabilities, which are more or less constant, the peasant has to pay contributions, mostly in kind, for the various religious and other festivals celebrated in the household of the Zemindar. All these taken together constitute no less than 75% of the net income of his land and labour, which the cultivator has to part with for the benefit of the idle Zemindar. Should the poor peasant refuse to meet all these legal and illegal liabilities, the landlord, who is usually also the usurer and is on friendly terms with the local native officials, finds means of getting him into various complications, which result in his ejection from the holding and ultimate ruin.

The entire cultivated area (56,803,000 acres) of the province of the Punjab is under temporary Zemindari system, the term of every assessment being fixed at twenty years. This province, being one of those parts of the country where modern irrigation has greatly increased the productivity of the soil, is considered as heaven for the cultivator. But when one turns to the actual condition of the people, quite another picture is found. The entire benefit accrued from the improvement of land and the consequent rise in its value goes to the government and to the native tax farmers. In 1894 it was found by an enquiry that more than 20% of the total cultivated area had been either sold or was heavily encumbered with debt; between 1892 and 1896 more than 50,000 acres had passed from the hand of the small farmers to that of the money lenders and other non-agricultural holders. In the year 1899—1900 120,000 acres were sold, and the area under mortgage was 300,000 acres. In 15 years (1902—1917) the net increase in the mortgage debt of the province exceeded £ 10,000,000. Of this nearly 90% falls on the peasant farmers. The real cause of this ruined economic condition of the peasantry is to be looked for neither in the government's contention that the cultivator is improvident, nor in the nationalist theory of the excessive rate of land revenue exacted by the state. It lies in the fact that the comparatively backward agricultural production of India has been reduced to the modern form of capitalist exploitation. It is not the rent with which the present government of India is principally concerned, as was the case with its predecessors; today the source of government income from the land lies in the commercial value of its produce. Thus the peasant's relation with the state or the landlord is not liquidated, as before, by paying a certain portion of the crops; the entire quantity of the product of his land and labour is under the control of capitalist commerce. That land revenue does not constitute the principal factor in the field of economic exploitation of the present Indian state is proved by the following figures which show a gradual diminution in the percentage of it:

Proportion borne by the land rev. to	1870	1880	1900	1910	1920
The gross income of the State . . .	39%	29.5%	23%	19%	—
The taxation proper .	43%	41.8%	40.8%	38.6%	35%

In order to disprove the nationalist contention that the peasantry is becoming impoverished on account of the heavy burden of taxation imposed on the land by the government, the latter points out the fact that in all the provinces where the assessment is subject to periodical revision, it has been the policy of the government to reduce gradually the proportion borne by the assessment to the net assets. For example in the province of Agra the standard of assessment was reduced from 90% in 1812 to 50% in 1885, the percentage having been lowered considerably since then; in the province of Orissa the reduction was from 83.3% in 1882 to 54% in 1900 and the present rate is below 50%. But this decrease does not actually affect the total revenue; on the contrary, the amount of income to the public exchequer from land revenue has increased.

The development of the land revenue of British India since the revolution of 1857 is shown by the following figures:

	Rupees
1856—57	173,000,000
1870—71	199,000,000
1880—81	219,000,000
1890—91	240,000,000
1900—01	262,000,000
1910—11	317,000,000
1920—21	351,000,000

Territorial expansion of any fiscal importance during this period was the aquisition of Upper Burmah in 1886. Thus the extension of cultivation, resulting in larger production and rise of prices may be held responsible for this substantial increase in the total land revenue. Today, in actual land rent, the Indian peasant pays less in proportion to the gross produce of his land than before, but the amount he pays is more than he used to pay formerly. Because the part left to him has ceased to be his property in the sense it used to be. The commercial value of the entire agricultural production is of much more importance to the present capitalist government than the rent on the land. This is equally the case with the landholders, the majority of whom look upon land not in the same spirit as their feudal predecessors used to, but rather as a profitable means of investing their capital. The difference between the economic outlook of the government and that of the landholding class is this; while the former, being the political apparatus of a foreign bourgeoisie, completely conscious of its interest, is desirous of increasing the productivity of the land, the latter, having its capital invested in the land, tries to recover the greatest amount possible in rent and interest. Thus it is but natural, looked at from the point of view that the two exploiting factors represent two categories of capital, one more advanced and more conscious than the other — that the common victim, that is, the cultivator, should be exploited in different ways. That is why we find the peasants in those parts of the country directly assessed by the government superficially more prosperous than their fellows living under Zemindari tenures.

The government's policy is to let the peasant toil on his land with the least encumbrance possible in order that at the end of each year there may be an increase in the total production, since the greater the productivity of the land and labour of the country, the more profit accrues to the capitalist class, whose representative is the government. But agriculture in India being still very backward, there is a limit to the increase in its production. Therefore the insufficient agricultural production of the country has been brought under intensive capitalistic exploitation, thus throwing the peasantry into a state of hopeless and perpetual poverty. The grip of the money-lender is becoming tighter and tighter every day. In order to bring the product of the cultivator's labour freely in to the open market of capitalist commerce, the government would like to do away with the intermediary of the native trader and money-lender; but it cannot be done, — the latter have become an integral part of the structure of the exploiting apparatus.

Twenty years ago the province of the Punjab found itself in an agrarian crisis. The money-lender was the master of the situation, being in alliance with the Zemindar. The cultivator was losing his hold upon the land. The cultivated area redeemed was always less than the area newly mortgaged. At last in 1901 the government found it necessary to turn its back on the tax-farming barons and take up the cause of the peasantry. The Zemindars were a convenient class to have in order to save the government the troubles and worries of collecting the rent, and to be relied upon in case of emergency; but as soon as they constituted a fetter on production, bourgeois economic theories of the freedom of the peasantry and the security of its tenancy were turned against the once useful class. Thus was passed, to the great discomforture of the Zemindars and in the face of strong opposition from the camp of the nationalists, the Land Alienation Act. By this legislation, the cultivator was given the right of occupancy on the land, that is, the land-holder could no longer enhance the rate of rent arbitrarily. Formerly it had been well nigh impossible for the cultivator to hold on to the same piece of land for any length of time. Unless the peasant was secure on his holding, he could not be expected to work hard on it and increase its productivity. The cultivator was freed from the vagaries of the Zemindar in order to be more intensively exploited by the capitalist government and the native trading class. Under the old system of tenure, the Punjab peasantry was inextricably in the grip of the usurer, who used to lend him money to pay the exactions of the Zemindar. The land was rapidly being transferred from the hand of the agricultural to that of the non-agricultural class. It was ceasing to be a souree of production and becoming a medium of speculation. The result of this process was a fall in production, therefore the government, controlled by a foreign bourgeoisie, found it imperative to "protect" the cultivator. But so long as the accumulated wealth of a certain class of the native population finds its way to higher forms of investment blocked, it must follow speculative and usurious pursuits. If it is prevented from speculating on land rent, it speculates on agricultural product; and the government being interested in complete commercialisation of the product of the land, needs the services of the native trading class. Thus we find the peasant still in the grip of the usurer, even after he has been secured on his land, somewhat immune from the exactions of the Zamindar.

The secret of the incurable misery of the Indian peasantry lies in the fact that it is being ground between two mill-stones viz. foreign capital in a higher atage of development and the native capital in a lower stage. In the field of exploitation the two depend upon each other, while at the same time, owing to the very historic inevitability of the evolution of capitalism, they cannot help clashing with each other. When they depend on each other, the native trader brings the farmer directly under the commercial exploitation of the foreign bourgeoisie; when they conflict with each other, it is again the peasantry which perishes in the clash.

As stated before, the average holding of the Indian cultivator is so small that it is very hard for him to subsist on its produce. When, under the Zemindari system, a greater part of the produce is taken away from him in the form of rent, interest and contribution, he has to starve because what is left to him is too insufficient. On the other hand when, under the benign protection of the capitalist government, the relative amount of the various kinds of direct taxation to be borne by him is reduced, the portion of his produce spared him may be somewhat more, but the prices of other necessities have already gone up and he finds himself in the clutches of the trader. Such being the case, a great majority of the rural population live on the verge of starvation all their life. Not being able to sustain himself and his family on the produce of his small holding, the petty peasant sinks into indebtedness, which goes on increasing till he is thrown off of his land, no matter what sort of tenure he theoretically enjoys. The existence of a considerable amount of capital invested in land is forcing its rapid concentration in the hands of the non-agricultural class. The registration of Land Records shows a growth in the cases of land transfers. In the year 1918—19 no less than 994,000 holdings changed hands, involving 4,676,000 acres. The figures available about the cases of land transfer are very incomplete. The Statistical Reports of the government on this subject do not embrace three entire provinces viz. Bengal, Madras and Behar and Orissa; no informations are available about the number of transfers executed through the Civil Courts; and it is stated in the official statistics that the figures contained in the official reports are also incomplete. Thus we can put the number of transfers at three or four times above that indicated. Or in other words, an average of about

20,000,000 acres of cultivated land is passing on to the control of non-agriculturists annually. Therefore to that extent, agriculture in India is ceasing to be determined by the village economy of the petty peasantry.

This transfer of land from the cultivators to the land speculators is gravely affecting the production of the country. We call this class, in whose hand the land is being concentrated, "speculators", because they invest their capital not in agriculture, but in land. The method of cultivating the land thus concentrated is not modernised; capitalist large scale production is not being introduced in the place of small scale individual production. Thus we find an increase of 50% in the land lying fallow in British India in 1917—18 and the proportion increased to 62% in the year following. The cause is the growing pauperisation of the small farmers, who are abandoning their land because they find it impossible to eke out a living on it. The government is naturally alarmed at the fall of production resulting from this diminution in the area cultivated. Therefore it is adopting a "forward policy" in agriculture as well as in industry. It does not find any other solution of this grave problem than to hand over the agricultural industry to the capitalists, who have so far been speculating in land and the limited product of primitive agriculture. "To encourage the introduction of modern machinery in agriculture" is the new policy of the government. Considering the fact that machinery cannot be used economically while agriculture continues on the prevailing small-holding system, the inevitable corollary of this new policy inevitably must be the wholesale expropriation of the small farmers. The consequence of this will be the enrichment of the landholding and money-lending class which has a surplus capital to avail itself of this new policy, and a tremendous increase in the mass of rural population living on agricultural wages. And since there already exists a great scarcity of employment for the field workers, the misery of the land proletariat can be easily imagined when their number will be greatly augmented by the introduction of labour saving machineries in agriculture on one hand, and by depriving small farmers of their land holding on the other, — the two inevitable results of large scale farming.

Though the cultivator living under the Zemindari system is so much exploited by the idle class of modern land-barons in some provinces and by capitalist tax-farmers in others, the economic condition of the Ryotwari tenents cannot be called in any way better. Under the Zemindari system, specially the permanent type of Bengal, the rate of rent legally paid by the cultivator is often less than that borne by his fellow living on Ryotwari tenures. But this advantage is more than out-balanced by innumerable other contributions having their origin in the tradition of feudalism, long dead and gone as an economic force. The Zemindari tenents are "protected" by the government with land laws which render the former secure against the excessive exploitation of the landholder. Of course the real object of this protection is to cut into the enviable large income of the rich landholding class, whose continued existence is becoming more and more undesirable, and even prejudicial to free capitalist exploitation of agriculture. Nevertheless, while the Zemindari tenents are "protected", the cultivators living on Ryotwari land are exploited directly by the government. And, since the capitalist background and consciousness of the British Indian government is much more scientific and developed than that of the native land speculators, landed bourgeoisie and usurers, the exploitation exercised by the former is naturally more efficient and cuts in deeper. The Ryotwari system prevails over 48% of the entire area of British India and a greater portion of the 32% under temporary Zemindari system, to all practical purpose, falls under the former. The land under these two kinds of tenure can be said to have been "nationalised" if the ownership by a state in the hands of a foreign power, can be called nationalisation. This system of government dealing directly with the cultivator is claimed to have been adopted according to the tradition of the country. It is true that in India, historically, land revenue is an economic factor prior to private rent on land. In the pre-British period, the monarchs, both Hindu and Mussalman, used to take directly a share of the produce of the land; this claim was not based on the right to participate in the contributions gathered by the landowning nobility, but directly on the produce of the soil. Thus the revenue idea evolved before that of rent, which all through the pre-British period was theoretically non-existent. The rent enjoyed by the feudal holders was identical with that portion of revenue relinquished by the Crown in favour of its nobles. The real rent and rent-yielding property in land was introduced into Indian economics by the British. It has been indicated already how the English idea of landed aristocracy was reflected in the Permanent Settlement of Bengal.

The British Government in India being a political apparatus of the bourgeoisie, could not for ever stick to the policy of creating a rent-getting landed aristocracy for India. For various reasons pointed out before, especially in those earlier days of the Indian Empire when the British rulers were still closely connected with and were under the political control of the English landowning class, the creation of a class intermediary between the State owning the land and the peasant cultivating the soil, was found necessary. But the economic policy of the Indian government changed in proportion as the social character of the English bourgeoisie went on changing.

Thus came the time when the Indian government decided to keep to itself (that is to the British bourgeoisie), both the revenue as well as rent from land. The intermediary landholding class appropriating the land-rent was no longer necessary. In order to justify this combined state-landlordism and state-capitalism (in agriculture), the British official revenue experts resort to the history of ancient and medieval India to establish that "the right of the state to the rent is superior to that of the private holder".

For all practical economic purposes, the area under Ryotwari tenure and a considerable portion of that temporary Zemindari tenure granted to small holders cultivating the land by themselves with the aid of hired labour, could be called a huge farm. The government, in its character of landowner receives the rent and in that of capitalist proprietor, is interested in the increase of production, which as social production, belongs to it. Thus the peasants are nominally independent small farmers, but in fact laborers on a huge capitalist farm. The productivity of those tracts directly under government control, has been greatly increased by the introduction of artificial irrigation. But this advantage has been more than out-balanced by new taxations. The average rate of rent on the land actually under cultivation is 2.8 rupees per acre; considering the backwardness of agriculture and the consequent low output as well as the smallness of the average holding of the cultivator, this is a very high incidence. But the actual amount paid by the cultivator in the irrigated tracts is much more than this, taking into account other indirect taxes on land such as cess, contributions for the expenses of guarding the canal zones &c. The actual amount paid goes up to 35 % of the net produce. All these liabilities have to be liquidated in cash; consequently the cultivator finds it necessary to sell his crop immediately after the harvest. This forced sale makes it impossible for him to get a fair price. Thus, while on the one hand the productivity and therefore the value of land is increased, the wealth in possession of the peasantry, on the other hand, is decreased. He toils on his land to sell out his produce at a low price, and has to incur debts in order to obtain the seeds and capital for sowing and cultivating his land the next year. This bankrupt position of the peasantry is greatly helping the commercialisation of agriculture. The cultivation of non-food crops is increasing, while that of food-crops is decreasing proportionately. Finding himself under all kinds of liabilities to the government as well as to the money-lender, the peasant is forced to grow the crops in demand for industrial use in preference to food grain, because the former are sold more readily and at a higher price.

The following table containing the percentage of increase in the area as well as yield of the principal food and non-food crops, shows the change in the agrarian economy of India:

Crops	Unit in 1900	Increase in yield 1919	Increase in area 1919
Rice	100	50%	50%
Wheat	100	50%	30%
Cotton	100	100%	90%
Jute	100	70%	60%
Oil Seeds	100	105%	60%
Tea	100	200%	55%

The output of rice, the staple of the larger part of the population, has never been in excess of the needs during the last 6 years; but in 1919—20 there was a striking expansion in the shipment of non-food articles like cotton (both raw and manufactured), jute (raw and manufactured), oil seeds, tea &c. The value of food grains exported in 1919—20 was £ 7,200,000 in excess of that of 1913—14, whereas the value of non-food agricultural product exported was £ 60,610,000 more. In 1909—10 jute and cotton exports had constituted 13 % and 10 %, while in 1919—20 they were respectively 24 % and 19 % of the total export.

Taking into consideration the fact that a great bulk of raw materials like jute and cotton is of late consumed in the large scale industries developing in the country, it is evident that the production of non-food crops must have increased much more than is shown by the rise in export figures. And this increase must have been at the cost of food grains, since the increase in the total area under cultication has not been considerable. In the last two years the movement has been decidedly to the contrary: The total cropped area decreased by 12% and the extent of cultivated land lying fallow increased by 50%. Besides, there is another factor to be taken into consideration, viz., there is a tendency towards decrease in the area under more than one crop a year. Only in one year (1918 to 1919) the decrease was from 37,000,000 acres to 27,000,000 acres. Neither have modern methods of cultivation been introduced in the area under non-food crops, to any appreciable extent. Therefore, obviously, the proportion of land under non-food crops needed for industrial purposes in India as well as in foreign countries, is increasing and that under food crops conversely, is decreasing.

From this movement of crops it is evident that the agricultural industry, on which by far the greater part of the rural population of India depends, is ceasing to be determined by the needs of the cultivators themselves; it is becoming commercialised, and has become so to a great extent already. Capitalist industry and commerce, British as well as native, have in their hands the control of Indian agriculture. Or in other, words, the Indian peasant is the victim of capitalist exploitation, and is becoming more so every day. The big landholder, small tax-farmer, money-lender, country-trader, land-speculator, liberal intellectual with his capital invested in land, as well as the government, under whose collective and several economic pressure the Indian peasant is reduced to a state of abject and chronic poverty, are consciously or unconsciously all parts of one and the same structure of capitalist exploitation which holds the country in its hand.

A study of the production and export of agricultural commodities in India will give a further insight into the economic condition of the rural population. It will also show that the exchange value of the produce of the comparatively backward and seemingly individualistic agriculture of the country, has become predominant over its use value. Let us begin by giving a summary of the total agricultural production in amount as well as in price, of the last year (1919—20):

Articles		Amount	Price
Rice	Tons	33,956,000	£ 684,552,960
Wheat	„	10,297,000	209,244,280
Sugar	„	3,000,000	80,096,800
Tea	Lbs.	337,055,600	18,527,780
Cotton in bales of 400	Lbs.	480,000	342,063,000
Jute „ „ „ 400	„	8,482,000	101,790,360
Linseed	Tons	430,000	13,826,680
Rape and Mustard seed	„	1,200,000	37,296,000
Sesamum	„	614,000	24,558,000
Ground Nuts	„	800,000	10,200,000
Indigo	cwts.	446,000	2,200,000
Barley	Munds.	58,540,000	29,270,000
Jawar	„	153,660,000	96,005,000
Baj	„	80,500,000	56,350,000
Maize	„	58,540,000	31,026,000
Gram	„	900,000	72,000,000
Minor Products including fruits		—	181,005,480
Total in round numbers			£ 2,000,000,000

(The Indian unit of measure, Mund, is equivalent to about 70 pounds.)

In comparison with the pre-war standard, the price of food stuffs has gone up 76 % wholesale and 400 % retail.

If the cultivator had been the owner of his produce after having liquidated all his legal liabilities in revenue, rents, and taxes, he would be in a rather prosperous position today, since 90 % of the food consumed in India is produced in the country. The following figures about the rise in the price of a few staples will give an idea as to the general increase in the wealth produced by agriculture:

Articles	Selling prices calculated in seers per rupee 1913	1920
Wheat	14 seers	6 seers
Rice	10 seers	4 seers
Grains	20 seers	7 seers
Pulses	12 seers	4,5 seers
Meat	4 seers	1,8 seers

Now, when the price of food-stuffs has gone up so tremendously, what has been the effect on the cultivators who produce these articles and who are supposed to be proprietors of the produce of their toil, if not of their land? We can just as well have the peasant's life described in the words of Sir O'Moore Creagh, who was the Commander-in-Chief of the Indian Army in the last years.

"The peasant digs, sows and reaps, the rain falls and the crops prosper and are reaped, but no sooner is the harvest over than the crop is divided. The landlord, be he government or a great landlord, takes the lion's share. The village shop-keepers and the village servants are paid from what remains, when the producer has nothing left. The money-lender, town Vakil (lawyer) and medical men cannot squeeze him drier then they do. He again gets credit for his food and seed for the next crop from the village shop-keeper, which cost him dear, and he goes home to plough, sow and live in the hopes of a better time which never comes."

So, this is the condition of the great bulk of the population engaged in the principal industry of the country, — an industry whose production in increasing as far as possible within the bounds of its backwardness, and the value of whose produce has gone up almost fabulously. Then, who is benefited by the increase of production as well as rise in price? Into whose hand falls the wealth produced by the peasantry? To the government, Zemindar, and the land speculator goes a part in the form of revenue, rent and tax; and the rest, which is the more considerable part, goes to swell capital, both foreign and native, — commercial as well as industrial. So the agricultural population of India is the victim of a system of exploitation which works through various agencies in various ways.

It is held by nationalist economists that the enormous rise in prices and the resulting misery of the peasantry is due to the export of food grains. On the face of it, it looks reasonable, but facts don't corroborate the contention. Of the £ 180,000,000, which constituted the approximate value of the total agricultural produce exported from India in the year of 1919—20, only a little more than £ 42,000,000 was covered by food-stuffs. This cannot be called a very considerable amount. It is an increase of 16.5 % over the value of the food grains exported in 1913—14. But the prices have gone up by 75 % wholesale, not taking into account the tremendous rise in retail price. How is the difference of 50 % to be explained? Evidently there is great speculation in food-stuff going on inside the country. The produce of the land is controlled by trades capital, which by various neans expropriates the peasant of the fruit of his toil, in order to sell it back to him for a price several times higher.

Large scale capitalist farms do not exist in India, agricultural production is mostly in the hands of small farmers producing on their own account. The only exception to this is the tea plantations and other minor cases. This being the case, ordinarily the total net income of the agricultural classes of India in 1919-20 should have been £ 1,611,000,000. This figure is obtained by subtracting from the total value produced, £ 327,000,000 exported, £ 52,000,000 paid in land rent and £ 10,000,000 paid in other taxes and contributions indirectly connected with the land. If this amount is divided among the 209,000,000 people, including land workers, living on land there results a per capita of £ 8; but according to official statistics, the per capita income of the entire Indian population is calculated at less than £ 2. This is the average; that is, when the income of the rich which is included in the average, is taken into consideration, that of the poor is reduced to very little. So there must be some social element which absorbs by far the greater part of this £ 8 that would belong to the peasant otherwise. The rise in the price of food-stuff as well as other agricultural produce means the prosperity of this social class on the one hand, and poverty and starvation for the cultivator on the other. This class is the Indian bourgeoisie, the tale of ,whose rather spectacular development has been told in the preceding part. The wealth wrung from the peasantry is being accumulated in the hand of the Indian bourgeoisie and invested by it in a more profitable field, — modern industry. Of course it is to be understood that British capital stills holds the monopoly of exploiting India; but a certain class has always tried to break the absoluteness of this monopoly, and of late has grown to the status of a powerful competitor will who no longer be ignored and is thus being invited into the corporation as a junior partner.

As in the industrial field, so in the agricultural, India has for a long time been reduced to capitalist exploitation, without receiving the benefits of capitalist development. In the industrial field, as shown before, handicrafts were destroyed in competition with higher means of production, the artisan class was pauperised, but the city proletariat in the strictest sense of the term, did not come into existence till very late. Likewise, while it is long since the land as well as the agricultural produce came under capitalist economy, the cultivation of the soil was left largely in the hands of small farmers given to backward processes of production. Since agriculture remained undeveloped, the population engaged in this industry could not even derive the little benefits that accrue as side-issues of capitalist exploitation. Although it is true that in case he would not be by one way or other expropriated of the scanty produce of his land and labor, the Indian cultivator could save himself and his family from starvation, still it is a known fact that the actual agricultural production of the country is very low, and the methods and implements used for tilling the soil are almost primitive. Since agriculture had for a long, long, time been the main national industry of India, the land and its produce have always been the means of speculation conducted by trades as well usury capital. A helpless victim of the money-lender, the Indian has always been in great lack of working capital. This conspicuous lack of wealth accumulated in the hand of the caltivator prevented the development of a class of rich farmer-proprietors who could avail themselves of the modern means of production in order to augment their income. The greater part of the burden of supporting the society falls on the back of the Indian cultivator, who has always been ground down to the earth. The wealth in the hand of the peassantry at the present time can be judged from the following figures:

In 1919 the total number of livestock amounted to 150,000,000 bovines (bulls, oxen, buffaloes and cows), 56,000,000 ovines (sheep goats &c.) and 5,000,000 pack animals. The number of ploughs and carts in the same year was 19,500,000 and 5,000,000 respectively. These figures are only for British India, those for the Native States not being available. The method of cultivation is very backward; the old-fashioned hand-made plough-share is still in vogue; and the ploughing is practically all done by cattle, the use of mechanical implements being very limited.

Small-scale farming and backward methods of cultivation are the causes of low production. Density of population and lack of fertile waste land, to a great extent have prevented the growth of large scale farming in India. Although low in production to the area, the total amount of agricultural production of the country has always been considerable and it has greatly increased in the last half a céntury. This production was found to be sufficient for the industrial and commercial needs of the British bourgeoisie. So instead of investing its capital in agriculture as has been done in other colonies, the British bourgeoisie found it more profitable to develop first the means of communication and transport, in order to bring the entire agricultural produce of the country under capitalist exploitation. The Indian bourgeoisie was encouraged to invest its accumulated wealth in trade, tax-farming and land speculation. For a long time the Indian bourgeoisie occupied the place of a speculating middleman dependent on the capitalist structure of the foreign bourgeoisie. Therefore large scale farming was not developed by native capital either. The production increased very little in proportion to the degree of exploitation of the producing class. The result has been the impoverishment of the latter. The incurable economic bankruptcy of the agrarian population of India is due to the fact that a backward and antiquated method of production has been reduced to the most modern and highly developed form of exploitation.

The British rulers have always followed the policy of exploiting the peasantry through the medium of a native agency, — at first the permanent Zemindars, then the temporary tax-farmers, the village headman and always the native trading and money-lending class. These privileged classes sucked and still suck the blood of the cultivator under the auspices of the government, in return for the meritorious services they render to the latter. These parasitic elements participate in the traffic in production without in any way helping to increase production. They have been grafted on to the body of social production and distribution by the policy of imperialist capital, by which for a considerable time the normal growth of the native bourgeoisie has been prevented. The principal factor in the ruin of the Indian peasantry is usury. The pent-up energy of the capital debarred from a freer field of investment expresses itself through usury, which takes its most virulant form in advancing seeds to the peasant. As stated before, the usurer, trader and often the land-holder, are as a rule united in the same person. In olden days the cultivator used to be at the mercy of the money-lender as a result of his futile efforts to liquidate the-never-to-be satisfied demands of the landlord; of late the rise in price puts the peasant more under his control. In order to pay rent, the cultivator borrows seeds or money at 'an excessive rate of interest, which often goes up as high as 600 % and is never lower than 100 %. The loan sometimes takes the form of "conditional sale" by which, in case of default in payment of interest within a specified time, the mortgaged leasehold passes to the creditor automatically. The harvest is often sold to the trader even before sowing. Thus it is not the peasant nor the big landholder, but the trader and usurer, who are the practical owners of the agricultural produce of the country.

Formerly, and still to a great extent, the landholder and the trader were the usurer. But in 1914, the government decided to include usury in the general scheme of capitalist exploitation. This was done by passing the Co-operative Credit Societies Act., ostensibly designed to benefit and protect the cultivator. But the real object was to centralise usury-capital under the supervision of the State, in order that the former might not prejudice agricultural production by its irresponsible methods. On account of the fabulous exactions of usury capital, in the beginning of the century, the land was passing into the hands of speculating non-agriculturalists at an alarming rate. This naturally affected production. The British bourgeoisie, with its advanced means of production and more developed consciousness, again came to the rescue; it had already "freed" a considerable portion of the peasantry from feudal serfdom; now came to the time to "protect" it against a backward form of exploitation. Another motive behind this move was to find an outlet for the capital accumulated in the hand of the petty bourgeoisie. The Co-operative Credit Societies have grown fairly well. In 1918 there existed 32,439 of them with a capital of £ 17,554,000 of which only 1.9 % constituted state aid. In 1900 the number of Co-operative Credit Societies was 3498. The Co-operative Credit Societies flourish more in those provinces where big landholders do not exist. By reducing the rate of interest the cultivator has to pay, on the loan he must contract under any circumstances in order to be able to sow and harvest his land, the Credit institution has stabilised him on his land, thus safeguarding agricultural production. On the other hand, supported by the petty bourgeoisie, which has its capital invested in them, the government through these credit societies can exercise the minutest control over the agrarian economy of the village. When the land does pass out of the hand of the cultivator, it is no longer to be a mere object of speculation; but the present tendency is to have it concentrated in the shape of large — scale capitalist farms.

The poverty of the peasantry has become so chronic and the chances of any radical change so non-existent that a complete agrarian revolution remains as the only solution. Neither the reformed land policy of the government, nor the frankly conservative, if not reactionary program of the nationalist movement, offers any prospect for betterment. The growth of large-scale farms worked by machinery would deprive millions and millions of people today living on land, of the means of livlihood; and a step back to landlordism would make the progress retrograde. The population is so vast that it would be impossible for the modern industries, even if they increase to a hundred — fold their present magnitude. to absorb the mass of unemployed which would come into existence as a result of an extensive introduction of labor-saving machinery in agriculture. Besides, the growth of industry would throw into unemployment another large section of the population — the artisans. Thus nothing short of a radical readjustment of the national economy can improve the situation. There must be a revolution in order to change not only the superstructure, but the very basis of social-economics.

Significant signs of this coming revolution are to be found in various parts of the country. The peasantry is revolting. Although there have been isolated instances of peasant revolts from time to time during the last century and a half, it is only in recent years that the agrarian trouble has assumed an acute and wide-spread aspect in the national life of the country. The first agrarian revolt during the British period, occured in 1835—38 when the English indigo planters, together with the newly created Bengal Zemindars, endeavored to reduce the small farmers to a state of serfdom. The uprisings were of quite a serious nature and were headed by the liberal intelligencia. The revolt was ultimately crushed, but the government passed legislation restricting the rights of the English Squires transplanted into India, and of native landlords, to revive a dead and uncivilised form of exploitation under a full-fledged bourgeois regime. In 1877, the peasants in the centre of Bombay Presidency revolted against the excessive rate of taxation imposed by the Zemindars as well as by the government. In 1907 there took place in the northern part of the province of Punjab, serious agrarian disturbances which had to be quelled by the declaration of material law. This movement was due to the exorbitant increase of canal taxation; as a result of the riots the canal administration was somewhat reformed.

During years and decades the forces have been accumulating; the economic position of the peasantry was becoming absolutely hopeless. At last came the period of the enormous rise in prices during the war. This brought the situation to a climax. The condition of the peasantry became so bad that riots began to break out in different parts. In 1917 a series of uprisings ocurred in the province of Behar; this movement was directed against the big landholders, who had increased the rent by 25 % in spite of the failure of crops and the rise in prices. Since then the peasant movement has been spreading in other provinces; at the present moment the entire north of the country is affected and of late the movement has broken out in the south in the form of the Mophla rising. The agrarian troubles are assuming such tremendous proportions that they are causing growing disquietude among the Indian bourgeoisie, which never took the agrarian problem seriously in its political reckoning. A member of the Legislative Assembly from Madras writes:

"If the government believes that the present taxes can be continued or that fresh taxes can be levied or that the unfortunate owner of small holdings can be ground down any further, they would be living in a fool's paradise. They would be instrumental in this country in giving impetus to the agrarian unrest which is slowly developing itself all over the peninsula."

Making due concession to the typical bourgeois nationalist psychology of throwing all the blame on the foreign ruler, one can find in these words the recognition of the seriousness of the agrarian unrest. Now let us have the estimtion of the peasant movement from another source. A member of the Punjab Provincial Legislative Council, in his speech moving a resolution to amend the land laws, expressed the following sentiment:

"In coming to a just decision on this point we must bear in mind that a vast majority of land proprietors in the Punjab possess small holdings from 3 to 10 acres. If it is true, and it is true, that these wretched proprietors are living from hand to mouth; if it is true, and it is true, that they are buried in debt up to the eyes; if it is true, and it is true, that they are generally ill-fed, ill-clothed and without any education, then I say, with all diffidence to the official point of view, that the Land Revenue Administration in India generally, and in the Punjab particularly, has not succeeded. The condition of the agriculturist, labourers and cultivators, is even worse, and the agrarian movement in the neighbouring provinces is not without causes. The origin of such movements as communism, nihilism, and agrarian movements lies in the stomach."

So we find that the rebellous mood of the peasantry is becoming so manifest that it is causing alarm to the government and the landed aristocracy alike. Both are very much concerned in checking it. Before the Imperial as well as the Provincial Legislative Councils are being brought various measures and suggestions for the readjustment of land settlement. But since none of the parties, by virtue of their belonging to the exploiting class, is capable of striking at the root of the trouble, the situation is getting more serious and complicated.

Since 1918, the peasant movement in the north of the country has become a standing affair. Local risings and riots are very frequent and of such a serious nature that the military is often called in to cope with the situation. Appreciating the potentiality of the agrarian movement, the Indian National Congress admitted in its session of 1916 a great number of peasant delegates. But the bourgeois political movement has demonstrated its utter inability to understand as well as to lead the agrarian movement.

In the winter of 1920, the agrarian movement broke out in the most violent form; it almost assumed the proportions of an insurrection. This happened in the province of Oudh, where the Zeminardi system prevails and the power of the land-holders is very extensive. The peasants' actions were well organised; they were directed only against the rich landholders, until the government sent troops to protect their lives and properties. Houses were burned, estates looted and crops destroyed by the rioters. The immediate cause of this serious outbreak had been the highhanded methods with which the Talookdars (big landholders) extracted from the cultivators the large sums of money which the former had contributed to the war fund in the previous years. This made the already heavy economic burden, caused by excessive taxation and rise of prices, unbearable for the poor peasants. Of course, the government rushed to the aid of the propertied class, and crushed the revolt with military force. But the movement has not died; on the contary it is steadily spreading to other parts. These agrarian disturbances have, during the course of the last year, crystallised into a political movement, the character and activities of which will be dealt with in a subsequent chapter.

The latest phase of the agrarian trouble is the Mophla risings, on the coast of Malabar. Subsequent informations show that the movement has been advancing to the east coast as well. The Mophlas are the descendents of the Arab traders who came to India centuries ago. Their number does not exceed a million. They are very poor, agriculture being their means of livelihood, and have always been under the thumb of the money-lenders, who are Hindus. The majority of the big landholders in that part of the country also happen to be Hindu. The recent revolt is caused by purely economic causes. It was started by looting the houses of the landholders and money-lenders, with a demand for remission of rent and for getting back the land that had been concentrating in the hands of the speculator and capitalist agents. But in every instance of peasant disturbance the government promptly demonstrates its class affiliation by rendering military aid to the landholders; thus the class differenciation of Indian society is brought into evidence for those who care to see it. The Zemindars and landholders may struggle with the government to maintain their privileged position, unchanged by the new economic policy of the latter; and the government may "protect" the cultivator from the abuses committed by the Zemindar; but as soon as the peasant revolts against the system that starves him to death, he finds the ranks closed in the enemy camp. Such is the social and economic position of the agricultural population of India.

It stands between two classes of exploiter viz, 1. the foreign capitalists and 2. native landholder, usurer and trader. The two may disagree and struggle about the share each should have in the exploitation, but both of them are indentical in their fundamental social significance — they live and thrive on the labor of the toiler, be he a worker in the factory or cultivator of the soil.

CHAPTER III.

The Proletariat.

1. Historical and Social Background.

The class of industrial workers living exclusively on wages earned in cities, is a comparatively recent phenomenon in Indian society. Of course, since in 1820 the first coal mine was worked by mechanical process, the beginning of the steam railways dates as far back as 1853 and the first factory moved by steam power was built in 1851, workers were employed in these industries; and the number of industrial workers went on increasing in proportion to the growth of these modern industries. But, as has been shown in the previous parts, in a wide sense, India did not enter an industrial age till 1880, and the real industrialisation of the country began still later. Therefore, though existing in small numbers and confined to a few localities, the proletarian class did not become a factor in the social organism till rather late.

This belated growth of the city proletariat is naturally due to the retarded industrial development of the country. Until very recently, India remainded an agricultural land, and even to-day she is predominantly so, 72% of her entire population being engaged in and living on the cultivation of the soil. But when we take into consideration the fact that in 1911 no less than 87% of the entire population was dependant on agriculture and auxiliary industries, the rapidity with which the country is being industrialised becomes evident. It is needless to say that India did not choose to remain in a backward state of national economy so late as in the earlier years of the twentieth century; nor was it that the conservatism of her people and the shyness of native capital were the factors responsible for her industrial backwardness, as is held by the imperialist historian and is commonly believed. If the Indian people remained victims of conservatism till so late, it was not due to some peculiar characteristic of theirs, but because the great revolutionary agency, modern machinery, did not come into the country to shake the society to its very roots and make national conservatism an impossibility. And it was not that modern machinery was kept out of the country because the Indian people had a special dislike for it, but because it happened that, by one of those ironies of history, the capitalist class, which has used machine power to enslave the workers in other parts of the world, found it more profitable to do without it in India. If the wealthy class of Indian society came to the industrial field so late, it was not from any instinctive aversion to the pursuit on its part, but because the abnormal political condition of the country prevented it from developing along the same lines as did its peers in other lands. The economic development of India through the introduction of modern-driven means of production, was not allowed for a considerable time by the foreign bourgeoisie which usurped the political power. Not being able to utilise the political State power, the Indian middle class could not enlist the aid of mechanical inventions in order to exploit the natural riches and labour power of the country. Large scale machine-production, which in the countries of Western Europe made the trading class grow into a liberal bourgeoisie, and snatched the artisan from his tool and the peasant from his soil in order to herd them into crowded cities, affected Indian society in an entirely different way. In order to reap the full benefit of machine-production in one country, the foreign rulers found it profitable to keep machinery out of India.

Just at the same time that the spinning-jennies and fly-shuttles were contributing to the rapid growth of the Lancashire towns in which masses of ruined craftsmen were forced into factories, the product of the same mechanical agencies was creating a contrary effect in India. The imported cotton manufactures, forced upon the Indian market by the foreign conqueror, wrought havoc among the native weavers, but instead of driving them to factories, made them change their tools for the plough-share. The introduction of higher means of production in cotton manufacture marked an era of social and economic progress in England, but it had a retrograde effect upon India. The forces that helped to build so many industrial centres in the former, were used for the destruction of prosperous towns and urban industrial centres in the latter. The reason of this diametrically opposite effect of the same cause was that Indian as well as English society came under a more developed method of exploitation, but the improved means of production which made this new method of exploitation possible, remained the property of the bourgeoisie of one country, which became the political ruler of the other. Every force, physical or social, has two attributes — destructive and constructive, — negative and positive. Whereas England felt both the effects of the social force expressed through the mechanical inventions of the eighteenth century, in India, which became an economic and political dependency of England in consequence of the expansion of the system created by this force, only the negative, the destructive effect was felt. The self-same force of exploitation, which distinguished itself by bringing into existence the infamous century of slave-labour and child-torture in England, contributed to the breaking up of the artisan class of Bengal, but without bringing in its train great industrial cities with swarms of slum-dwellers, the progenitors of the mighty modern proletariat.

In the first part of the eighteenth century the economic structure of Indian society corresponded to that stage which precedes the industrial epoch. Handicraft was very highly developed; and a thriving trading class had grown, based on the productions of the prosperous and industrious artisan. Trade and industry had led to the rise of towns rich and populous. When Clive entered Murshidabad, the then capital of the Kingdom of Bengal, he found the city "as extensive, populous, and rich as the city of London, with this difference, that there are individuals in the first possessing infinitely greater property than in the last". Clive saw Murshidabad in 1757. When in the 80's of the eighteenth century the city of Dacca, the capital of East Bengal, came under the domination of the East India Company, it had a population of 200,000 and its export of manufactured articles was so large that the value of only one commodity, viz. muslin, amounted to £ 300,000 a year. Nor were these exceptional cases; all over the country, and especially in the province of Bengal, trade and industry flourished, and these had been concentrated in urban centres. Indian society was no longer confined within the narrow limits of agrarian economy. Industry had ceased to be a mere part of the village organism; it had grown too big for the necessities of the village communities and thus had long ago transgressed the boundaries of the village and diverged to the large urban centres, there to be commercialised by a wealthy trading class. It is very often forgotten that the economic relations of the Western nations with the East, and particularly India, is not the same today as it was in the beginning of the eighteenth century. European traders were first attracted to the Indies not by raw materials, but by manufactured wares. By the end of the eighteenth century, the textile industry of Bengal was so well controlled by native trades capital and capitalist exploitation had obtained such a high degree of efficiency "that cotton and silk goods of India up to 1813 could be sold for a profit in the British market from 50 to 60% lower than those fabricated in England". (H. H. Wilson, "History of India".)

Such was the economic condition of India when industrialisation took place in England and subsequently in other European countries. While the most highly developed imperialism of to-day is marked by the export of capital to the colonies, the movement was the reverse in the early days of imperialism. Then wealth was imported from the colonies; and this imported wealth helped greatly the growth of modern industry. But curious as it may seem, the product of these capitalist industries not only prevented but destroyed the growth of industrial capitalism in the colonies. India is the most remarkable example of how capitalism, being by its very nature a force of social progress, has nevertheless led to social stagnation, if not retrogression. The capitalist industries built in England with slum-labour as their social basis aided greatly by the wealth imported from the colonies, were solidified and extended endlessly by selling their products in countries like India, to the serious economic detriment of the latter. Although India, in respect of craft and trade, stood on the eve of capitalist industrialism in the eighteenth century, the general economic tendency since then has been more towards agriculture and less and less towards manufacture. This state of economic affairs held good till the closing years of the nineteenth century, when the social forces of history broke the bonds of artificial restriction and asserted themselves. Thus it was not less than a century and a half that India was held in an abnormal state of economic progress. The expression "abnormal state of economic progress" sounds strange; but it expresses exactly what took place in India during the period from the middle of the eighteenth century till the end of the nineteenth. The political control of the country passed to the bourgeoisie, which, however, happened to be foreign. Under the political rule of the bourgeoisie the economic exploitation of the society could not remain in the fetters of antiquitated methods. Gradually the entire production of the land was brought under capitalist exploitation on the one hand, and manufacturers of capitalist industries destroyed to a great extent the backward form of craft production, on the other. So the national economy could not be said to have stayed stationary, since under the capitalist system and modern political regime of the bourgeoisie, the total production of the country increased; but the power of productivity and the kind of produce were determined by the needs and convenience of foreign capital, which reigned supreme. The economic basis of social production underwent a radical change in consequence of the fact that a capitalist government ruled the country, but no great transformation took place in the form and method of production. The productivity and labour power of India were included in the general scheme of capitalist exploitation, but she had to remain on the outskirts, occupying the place of a reserve force, so to say.

The industries of England needed a market as well as raw materials. India promised to supply both. But an India with her own modern industrial production would cease to do so. Therefore, the same British capitalist class, which found the machine an invaluable instrument of exploitation in the home country, prevented its introduction into India.

While at home machinery aided the English capitalist, in India the absence of it was found to be more conducive to the interest of the foreign bourgeosie. If Great Britain is what it is to-day as the result of capitalist production, India is what she is to-day due to capitalist exploitation. If capitalism has concentrated 67% of the population of the British Isles in the cities, it is also capitalism which has driven 75% of the population of India to the soil. While the proportion of the total population of India engaged in arts and crafts was 25 % in the latter part of the eighteenth century, it dropped to 15 % a hundred years later. At the time of the British conquest, in the province of Bengal alone, several million people were occupied in the weaving and spinning industry; the numerical strength of this class of artisans is reduced to less than half a million at present. This is, of course, the consequence of higher forms of production introduced into the textile industry. But how negative has been the effect of mechanical inventions in India may be judged from the fact that in the beginning of the present century the number of operatives in the power-driven cotton textile factories of the country was less than 200,000. It shows that machine production eliminated from the field of social economics an older form of production without replacing it, as in other modern countries, by large-scale capitalist industries. This method of imperialist exploitation dislocated the social organism. Millions and millions of people were deprived of the means of livelihood by the destruction of craft industries brought about by the import of machine-made commodities, but modern industries were not allowed to grow in the country; thus the artisans ousted from their craft by the machine could not be tied to the same machine as wage slaves. The Indian artisans, after having lost their independant means of production, were not absorbed into large industrial centres, but were driven to the land. In India, the social expression of machine production did not take the form of a city proletariat, but that of a vast mass of land-workers and pauperised peasantry.

In order that the class — day differentiation of the present Indian society be properly understood, it is necessary to make a brief review of the process by which the country was reduced to capitalist exploitation without having felt the social re-adjustment that comes in the train of capitalist development. The economic transformation of Indian society has gone through such confusing up-and-down, backward-and-forward stages during the last two hundred years, that not a little difficulty is encountered, even by the modern-minded Indians themselves, in determining its present character and the immediate outcome, social and political. There is a tendency to think that Indian society is not divided into classes but castes. This tendency assumes active expression in the social theories of the liberal reformers of the nationalist movement. This tribe of social reformers can be divided into two categories; the radical religionists with strong national jingoism and the class-conscious modern bourgeoisie with liberal tendencies. The first take upon themselves the great task of proving that Indian culture has been a unique thing, that it developed in its own way and that the structure of Indian society has not been subject to the action and reaction of material laws. And, following this course of reasoning, these apostles of Indian culture come to the conclusion that the class-struggle never soiled the sanctity of Indian society, and that it is never going to be the principal factor in the process of social readjustment. They preach that class-struggle is the peculiar outcome of the materialist civilization of the West and is not possible in Indian society, which is based on the knowledge of the spiritual essence of man. "Gandhism" is the political expression of this social movement. The second class of social reformers is the modern bourgeoisie. They are the disciples of the 18 th century school of ecomonics, and their philosophy is that of the nineteenth century freethinkers and utilitarians. No national egoism can make them blind to the class cleavage in Indian society; but class egoism, the idea that by the dint of their education and privileged positions they are the custodians of national interests, — makes them diffuse the social character of the present struggle. They encourage the development of a modernised version of religion, whose futile fuss about caste seeks to drown the din of class struggle. These bourgeois reformers, who are the most conscious leaders of nationalism, are very much interested in the uplift of the "depressed" classes; and while holding thousands of wage-slaves in perpetual starvation, don't hesitate in the least to have them shot when these slaves show signs of revolt, in order to uplift themselves.

It has been shown in the preceding chapter how the Indian peasantry, in spite of their belonging to various castes and to the two great antagonistic religions viz., Hinduism and Islam, — have been always weighed down in misery by the landlords, usurers, and traders; and how, at the present moment, the agrarian revolts are the result of accentuated class differentiation, the political movement for national liberation notwithstanding. We don't want to go into an analysis of the caste — system. But it is necessary to throw a look back on history to ascertain what was the economic basis of caste. In the Hindu scriptures and classics the caste system is glorified in various ingenious ways. But coming down to the origin of it, one discovers slavery. The caste-line was drawn first between the Aryan conquerors and the conquered aborigines. The distinction was made by colour, the conqueror being fair and the conquered dark. The Sankrit word for caste is Varna which means colour. The divisions and sub-divisions in the caste-system were subsequently evolved in accordance with the inter-mixture between the conquered and conquering races, and the development of tools. The social growth followed almost the same process of evolution as in the savage and barbaric periods in the human society everywhere, only with certain modifications in the super-structure, caused by local circumstances. The physical and climatic conditions told heavily upon the structure of Indian society. Slavery, Feudalism, Serfdom, — all took somewhat different forms. The country being mostly flat, and the fertility of the soil almost uniform, the distribution of population was rather even. For a considerable time and up to very recent date, the village formed the social unit; and the village community was based upon the hereditary division of labour stereotyped into the caste-system, which in the commercial and manufacturing epoch, developed into trade and craft-guilds resembling greatly their prototype in contemporary Europe. Caste as the basis of social-economics organised production, but did not prevent exploitation. The class-line ran through the caste-system. So when in recent years, by virtue of the increasing introduction of machine-made commodities and the growth of modern industry inside the country, caste has ceased to be a living social factor, its economic essence, — the class division, — stands naked. Neither the hollow shell of the decayed caste-system, nor the lingering traces of religion and priest-craft, nor the great movement for national freedom, can hide the class-line which divides the whole social organism horizontally into two distinct parts.

It is held that the great bulk of the Indian people still live in such an economically backward stage, that it will be long before the class-differentiation will be clear in the society. The caste-system is also looked upon as a factor which diffuses the class cleavage between exploiter and exploited. It is said that even the exploited class is divided into castes which prevent them from understanding their unity of interest. There are some who go as far as to say that a worker feels himself more akin to his employer if he be of the same caste, than to his fellow worker of another caste. It will be shown later that the facts disprove all these pre-conceived ideas. The main argument is however, that capitalism has not come to India, therefore the things that accompany the capitalist mode of production cannot be found there. This is a wrong theory and all confusions arise from it. Firstly, capitalist exchange and, to a certain extent, production of commodities prevailed in India at the time of, and even before, the British Conquest. Secondly, the British government is the political apparatus of the capitalist class, India, therefore could not have been left untouched by capitalist exploitation under its rule. During the hundred and seventy years of British rule, the social production of India has been reduced completely under capitalist economy. But, since the capitalist exploitation was carried on by a foreign imperialist bourgeoisie, the outward effects of the capitalist mode of production were not clearly felt on the Indian society. Nevertheless, the fundamental social transformations that result from the capitalist control of national economy have taken place, and the present as well as the future of the country is bound to be determined by these transformations. It is necessary to investigate how these social transformations occurred without causing serious disequilibrium on the surface.

In the middle of the eighteenth century, when the English merchant invaders were establishing their political domination in some parts of the country, India economically stood at a stage which under a normal course of development would have led up to modern capitalist industrialism. Although industrial production was still based on the hereditary craftsmanship according to the caste-system, another class had developed which controlled the distribution of the commodities produced by the guilds. The hereditary artisan had ceased in many instances, to be an independant member of the autonomous village community. His production was no longer the property of the community to be exchanged by himself into other necessities produced by other equally independant members of the community. Arts and crafts, which centuries ago had arisen as a part of village economy within the bonds of caste, had long ceased to be the exclusive concern of the isolated villages, but were taken from one province to another in order to be sold and resold by a prosperous trading class with considerable capital accumulated in its hand. The principal industries had been commercialised and their base had been removed from the village confines to the towns, hundreds of which flourished all over the country. Still confined to the caste-guilds in so far as labour was concerned, the social and economic control of the industrial products had gone out of the hands of the artisan. Instead of completely controlling production and distribution as before, the craftsman was supplied with raw materials by the trading middle-man, who took the finished product out of the former's hands, not to distribute according to the needs of the community, but to sell it for profit. By this class of traders, the artisans were spared the worries of securing raw materials, of exchanging their fabricated wares and looking about for other necessities of life. All these troubles had been taken over by the benevolent trader. Production was largely separated from the family and concentrated in towns under the control of Trades Capital. In the towns, manufacturies had grown, employing often more than a hundred hands, who worked for the trading capitalist, and thus had ceased to be independant artisans of the olden days. Individual or domestic production was to a great extent displaced by collective production, but the ownership had been shifted from the producer to the mercantile class. The secondary, exchange value of industrial products had acquired predominance over the primal use value. Busy commerce had developed, bringing in its train a prosperous class of capitalists who controlled the economic life of the society, in spite of the fact that the old caste divisions still persisted in the field of production. The magnitude of commercial capitalism that prevailed in India about the middle of the eighteenth century can be judged from the testimony among many others, of Verelst, one of the first English Governors of Bengal. He writes: "The Bengal silks, cloths, &c. were dispersed to a vast amout to the West and North, inland as far as Guzrat, Lahore and even Ispahan". The stage of India's social economics and the rise and power of a capitalist class in the first part of the eighteenth century are borne out by the following words of Burke:

"There are to be found a multitude of cities not exceeded in population and trade by those of the first class in Europe; merchants and bankers who have once vied in capital with the Bank of England, whose credit has often supported a tottering state and preserved their governments in the midst of war and desolation; millions of indigenous manufacturers and mechanics".

Thus we find that at the time of the British invasion, India stood at the stage of social economics which would have been the period of transition of her industry from manufacture to mechanofacture. But it did not happen; the machine did not come to India. She could not pass from mercantile capitalism to industrial capitalism. The social progress was obstructed. But the secret of the abnormal economic condition of India during a century and a half lies in the fact that with the machine, the effects of machine production were not kept out of the country. The destructive effects of machine production were fully felt on the national economy.

With the growth of machine indusfry in England, her economic relation with India changed. The trade was reversed. Instead of importing manufactured goods from India, the British East India Company began to export to India articles fabricated by machinery in England. The cost of production in India was so low that even the English machine industry had to be protected in its early days against Indian imports by the enormous duty of 80% ad valorem. Owing to this protective tariff, but principally on account of the introduction of a higher form of production, Indian manufactured goods were thrown out of the English market. But this was not all; the tables were turned before long. Cotton fabrics began to be exported from Lancashire to India. The cost of production in India was low, but that in England in those days was also low; besides the English manufacturers had the advantage of superior machinery. Thus, foreign mechanofacture was pitted against Indian manufacture. The result could not be anything but the collapse of the latter. Machine production destroyed craft-industry and trades capital in England as well as in India; but its effects on the economic distribution of the population were not the same. In both countries the artisans were dispossessed of their means of livelihood; but while in England they were herded into the factories, in India they were driven back to the soil. But there, the land was over-crowded; so the influx of the mass of ruined artisans from the town created a serious dislocation in the agrarian population. The newcomers could not be accomodated without displacing others. This pressure on land provided a chance of speculation to the trading class, undermined in the towns by the ruin of industry. Thus while in England, machine production attracted the people from the village to the city, and pushed the capitalist class from a lower to a higher form of exploitation, — from trade to industry, — in India, the effects of the same machine-production happened to be the contrary. It drove the town artisans back to the village, thus reducing their standard of living and dragging the structure of national economy backward. It induced capital to take to petty-trading and land-speculation instead of entering upon an era of industrial development. In short, India was reduced from the state of a manufacturing country, to that of an agricultural country. But on account of the scarcity of land, the ruined artisans could not become peasants; there was no land to get, at least for a large number of people. Thus, machine production did bring into existence in India also a vast number of people divested of all ownership. But the difference was, that instead of a city proletariat, there was born in India as a result of the evolution of higher means of production, a class of wage-earners tied to the land. Factories were not allowed to grow, thus these masses of dispossessed could not do anything but become superflous auxiliaries to agriculture. Since this vast number of agricultural workers came into being, unemployment has been a standing problem in India. On account of the small individual farms prevailing there, a large number of agricultural labourers could not be employed on the land with any steadiness. In consequence of this dislocation in the economic distribution of the Indian people, brought about by the one-sided influence of foreign machine production, a large section of the population could not be absorbed into the economic organism of the society. The permanent presence of this mass of unemgloyed and unemployables in the country constituted a serious obstacle to the economic struggle of the city proletariat when the latter came into existence subsequently, as a result of the rather laborious and stunted growth of modern industry in India.

India was prevented from developing machine-industry by two causes: First, in the early days of the rule of the British traders a tremendous amount of wealth was expoliated and exported from the country without having brought anything in return. Second, in order to preserve the monopoly on the Indian market, the export of machinery from England to India was prohibited by imposing heavy custom-duties. The heavy drain of wealth exhausted the economic vitality of India for a considerable time, thus disabling her capitalist-class and preventing it from showing any active signs of struggle. The effects of the export duty on machineries were such that till the 60's of the last century, the cost of building a factory in India was four times as much as that required to build the same in England. And it was so, notwithstanding the cheapness of Indian labour. The British bourgeoisie, which by virtue of possessing higher means of production, imposed its political power upon India, found it very important to deprive the Indian capitalist-class of the access to modern machine production. This policy was vital for the continuance of the exploitation of India by British capital. Looked at from the point of view of world economics, the social progress of India during the period from the middle of the eighteenth century to the end of the nineteenth has not been retrograde. Indian society, which was at the period of mercantile capitalism at the time of the British Conquest, has been brought under the exploitation of industrial, finance and imperial capital. Political power went into the hands of the bourgeoisie which, for the convenience of unhampered exploitation, broke down, either violently or peacefully, all obstacles that stood in the way. The social production and economic life of India to-day are inseparably interwoven with the structure of world-capitalism. The agricultural industry of India is an adjunct of the British industrial system, and for this reason, 72 % of her population engaged in the cultivation of the earth, to all intents and purposes, occupy the social position of proletariat in the wide scheme of capitalist exploitation. Capitalist exploitation under the political rule of a liberal bourgeoisie, has helped to clarify the class differenciation as well. Though the Indian capitalist-class was not allowed a free development, or to enlist in its service the modern mechanical inventions, it was not excluded altogether from the scheme of exploitation. As soon as its social aspirations were broken down in competition with a higher mode of production, its good offices were enlisted by the foreign ruler, who soon made out of it an admirable means of exploitation and the social basis upon which the extraneous political domination could rest.

So till the closing decades of the last century, the Indian capitalist remained a ridiculous adjunct to the imperial capital. It was not until the 80's that he demanded a more dignified position. This renaissance of Indian capitalism was marked by a strong tendency towards industrialism, and brought into being a city proletariat, separated from the ranks of a proletarian nation.

In the centuries preceding the British invasion, the development of industry and the consequent expansion of trade led to the growth of towns. The proportion of the population living in urban centres in the early part of the eighteenth century was greater than in the end of the nineteenth. A large section of the urban population was engaged in trades and industries. In proportion as industries were brought under control, the number of independant craftsmen were replaced by wage earners, complete or partial. So, in the first half of the eighteenth century, there was a proletarian element in the urban population of India. But industrial capital affected India in a different way; instead of being a revolutionary social force, it pushed the country to a state of national economy which it had already passed beyond. In the early years of British rule, Indian towns were destroyed by the products of English machine-industry. The population of Dacca, one of the principal textile centres, diminshed from 200,000 in 1770 to 90,000 in 1840. In the middle of the eighteenth century, the people living in urban centres was estimated to be 25% of the entire population; at the end of the nineteenth the proportion had fallen to 15%. The decadence of formerly flourishing towns occurred in all parts of the country, till new and modern cities began to be built; these did not grow up around industrial centres as happened in Europe, but on the seaboard, as a result of busy export and import trade, and inland, as administrative centres and as stations both for collecting raw materials to be exported and for bringing the imported manufactured goods within the reach of the people. Naturally, the great majority of the inhabitants of these new cities were wage-earners, but the absence of an industrial proletariat was conspicuous. The only national industry of any importance that was allowed to exist, or that could resist the attack of machine-made commodities, had to take shelter in the confines of far-away villages. The native trading class found it more profitable to sell cheap imported articles, than to handle the scanty produce of the bankrupt village artisans. Thus, even handicraft industry, which had been developed to the first stages of social production as far back as the end of the seventeenth century, was again pushed back on an individual basis. The new cities of India were not the outcome of the native social progress, but were the outposts of the foreign ruler and trade-counter of the foreign bourgeoisie. But this original artificial character of theirs soon changed; their petty bourgeoisie and pigmy intellectual wage-earning population gradually grew into the most progressive class of Indian society. Out of these elements, together with the progressive land-holder and country trader, arose the modern bourgeoisie. But the majority of them remained in an economic condition corresponding to that of the proletariat.

The economic and social position of the intellectual proletariat who form a great majority of the population of most of the modern cities, should not be passed unnoticed. In recent years, the enormous rise in the cost of living and the acute scarcity of accomodation, have driven most of these intellectual workers out of the city proper to the adjacent suburbs or villages, whence they come to work in the town every day. In social standard they belong to the intelligencia; by profession they are clerks, ministerial employees in the government offices, assistants in the large trading firms, teachers, &c. The system of modern education introduced by the British government, opened the schools for all, irrespective of caste divisions. Anyone who could afford to meet the expenses, sent their children to the schools. A product of these schools, the intellectual workers are recruited from all castes. To-day they all belong to the same class of wage-earners, though the artificial social traditions of caste-division still persist among them insofar as inter-marriage is not permitted. More than three-fourths of the intelligencia, which constitutes 5 % of the total population, belong to the rank of intellectual workers. The economic condition of these people is absolutely miserable, and it is more so, considering the fact that psychologically they belong to the bourgeoisie and not to the working-class. Their mode of living is that of the former; but the standard falls very short. The average income of this class of workers is 20 rupees (£ 2 at the present inflated rate of exchange) per month; and when the fact that each wage earner has several dependants to support is taken into consideration, the actual rate of income goes down by many times. Their standard of living, in so far as clothes and dwelling are concerned, has to be higher than that of the manual worker; consequently in actual nutrition they are worse off than the latter. Although many of them have come up from the lower castes, thanks to the modern semi-education, the environment in which they work has developed a petty-bourgeois psychology 'in them. Depending on the bourgeois institutions for their means of livelihood, they are supporters of the present system of society, in spite of the fact that in the latter they can never be anything more than wage-slaves.

Till a quarter of a century ago, all that had been felt on the surface of Indian society of the effects of modern capitalism, was commerce organised on a large scale, and the bureaucratic administrative institutions which mark a capitalist state. These were the reflex of the industrial system of England. They were the integral parts of the scheme of exploitation of British industrial capital, which held India in subjugation. So the class proletarianised in India by imperialist capital was not so much the ruined and expropriated artisans; the latter, though reduced to the level of pauperised proletariat for all practical purposes, were pushed back to the land, to sink into an economic condition worse than that of the wage-earners. Capitalism, exploiting India through the media of commerce and bureaucracy, created a different kind of proletariat; this was the petty intellectual workers. The labour power of this proletarian class was less mental than muscular, since all it could sell for a starvation wage was not so much intellectual assets, as the capacity to read, write, and count. The writing too, was not original; what was needed was a copying machine. But this class of petty intellectual workers, though economically belonging to the category of propertyless wage-earners, socially and psychologically clung to the bourgeois customs and tradition. Their economic condition was objectively destined to make them revolutionary, but their social prejudices not only prevented the growth of revolutionary class-consciousness, but actually dragged them deeper and deeper in the depths of decay and demoralisation. Still, it was from the ranks of this class of social slaves as well as from among the students that the revolutionary element in Indian nationalism arose. And when we consider the fact that 90% of the students in the primary and secondary educational institutions are doomed to enter the ranks of the petty intellectual proletariat, the class contradiction in the folds of the Indian nationalist movement becomes clear. Since the class of petty intellectual workers has always been directly exploited either by the government or English employers, it is but natural that the class-oppression should appear to it as foreign oppression. But this equilibrium is bound to be disturbed in proportion as the native capitalist class comes on the field to employ more and more petty semi-manual workers. Inevitably the development of native industrialism will bring the factory-labourers to the front lines of the revolutionary ranks, in contradistinction to the petty intellectuals, despite the latter's completely proletarianised economic condition. During the recent years, this process of re-shuffling of the revolutionary forces has been going on in the Indian movement, and at the present moment it looks quite probable that class-consciousness will ere long transoend the limits of nationalist pre-occupations.

The economic cleavage between the propertied and wage-earning classes of the bourgeois society is becoming wider. The poor proprietor among the intelligencia is being expelled from the blessed realm of ownership by the process of the concentration of wealth in the hands of those who know the art of converting wealth into capital. The following extracts from the report (1919—1922) of the Educational Commissioner of India, are indicative of the economic condition of the lower strata of the middle class:

"In the Central Provinces there has been a further fall of nearly 15 % in the number of pupils in the High School Department. This was due to the high cost of living . . . . There is a drop in the number of pupils in the high stage of the United Provinces, due also to hard times. In the province of Bihar, there is a fall in the number of students, due to the same cause. But the colleges in all provinces are overcrowded. The decline in Bengal of middle English schools can be attributed to economic distress."

This shows that facilities for higher college (Universisty) education available to the rich are not sufficient.

the colleges being overcrowded, but the very scanty provision for secondary education cannot be fully availed of, because the petty intellectuals are finding themselves economically unable to send their children to the schools. And the diminution of secondary education in the ranks of the wage-earning semi-intellectuals signifies a corresponding fall in their prospect of finding employment.

In order to have a reserve force, the British government brought into existence more of these ministerial workers than could be absorbed in the present organism of the capitalist structure. Since the closing years of the past century, unemployment has prevailed in the lower strata, or the wage-earning section of the intelligencia. This unemployed element grew till it became unemployable. And an element which finds no chance of getting fitted into the social organism, converts itself into a force of destruction. Even after the political independance of the country has been achieved, this army of petty and semi-intellectual workers will still remain considerably unemployable, because a bourgeois national government would not be able to absorb it completely, nor change radically its economic position in the social organism. The fundamental thing is, that in every sense of social economics, this class has been proletarianised, and the substition of one capitalist government by another cannot and will not change their position. Their social prejudices must succumb before pressing econmic necessities. It will not be long before they realise that their salvation lies in the frank recognition of their social position, and consciously take their stand where they really belong.

CHAPTER IV.

The Proletariat-cont.

2. Process of Development.

As the result of the devious working of the same force of capitalist exploitation, the modern urban centres of India, which grew as the outposts of capitalist civilisation, where until rather recently conspicuous by the absence of the inevitable counterpart of capitalism, viz, the proletariat. The proletarianisation of the Indian masses was not intensive, but extensive. The modern industries first introduced into India having been mining and transport, the workers employed in them were not concentrated in cities. The modern urban centres continued to be purely commercial marts till the earlier 80's of the last century, and predominantly so, as late as the beginning of the current one. The great majority of the working class, belonging to the category of wage-earners partially or totally, lived in the rural district. The cities offered very little attraction to the purely manual workers, except to those employed in domestic services and other non-industrial occupations of comparatively little importance. What little remains of the handicrafts that survived the attack of imported machine-made goods, had to do so by retiring within the confines of remote villages. In 1899 the industrial workers, in their partially or totally wage-earning capacity, were distributed as follows: The total number of people living on industrial wages was estimated at a little over 15,000,000, making a population of 33,000,000, with their families and dependants. This included about 6,000,000 women-workers. That is, about 8,5 % of the then population of the country was dependant upon industrial wages. Accurate information as to what portion of this class of industrial workers belonged to the city proletariat, is not available. But considering the magnitude of modern machine-industry that existed in those days, the portion cannot be placed higher than 15 %. That is, the number of workers employed in modern large-scale industries on the eve of the twentieth century could not be more than 1,500,000 which, together with their families numbered 3,300,000. At that period, the principal industries of the country were transport (including railways, tramways and river steam-navigation), mining (coal, gold, iron, manganese, mica etc.), textile (cotton, wool, silk, and jute), electric and gas works, and tea-plantations. The number of cities with a population of 50,000 or over was 45. But very few of them could be called modern industrial centres. Only Calcutta with its ship-building yards, railway workshops, gas works, and jute mills; Bombay with its harbour and dock-yards, railway work-shops and cotton mills; Ahmedabad with its cotton mills; Cawnpur with its woolen mills and leather factories; Jabbulpur with its railway workshops and goverment arms factory; Jamalpur with its locomotive workshops; Ranigunj with the surrounding coal fields; Cossipur, Ichapur, Dum-Dum and Kirkee with their government arms and powder factories; Rangoon with its rice mills and harbour; Karachi, Madras and Chittagong with their harbours and dock-yards; and the tea-plantation of Assam and Darjeeling could be called modern industrial centres with a proletarian population accumulated there.

The remaining 13,500,000 (that is 29,700,000 including families and dependants) of the population living entirely or partially on industrial wages in 1899—1900 were domiciled in the rural district. These people were occupied in the following trades: weaving and spinning, ceramics, tanning and leather works, carpentry, metal works, sugar manufacture, other food industries, manufacture of chemicals, building industry, manufacture of boats, carts and other means of transport, dress-making and manufacture of toilet articles, etc. etc. The precarious state of these handicraft industries and the uncertain economic condition of the workers engaged in them have been dealt with in the previous part. These artisans, once engaged in prosperous trade in the towns, were ruined and dislodged from their hereditary economic position by the introduction of machine made products imported from abroad. The busy towns, once centres of manufacture as well as trade, were divested of their character of centres of production and became exclusively those of distribution and administration. Thus, the urban population engaged in productive work was driven to the villages; but even in the remotest corners of the country the artisan class did not free itself from the competition of the cheap imported goods. Consequently, what remains of the rural industrial worker to-day is partially engaged in and dependant upon agriculture, and mostly upon agricultural wages at that.

This dislocation of the social equilibrium has destroyed the economic basis of caste-division. Industrial, professional, and cultural callings of the Indian society were confined within the limits of hereditary caste-divisions. In the eighteenth century caste, in so far as the industrial population was concerned, had taken the character of trade guilds, which were shattered by the higher method of production of industrial England. Nevertheless, till to-day the innumerable caste-divisions are found existing in the Indian society, and the superficial barriers, separating these castes have not been broken down as yet. But a little enquiry under the surface discloses the fact that the very foundation of the caste-system has been undermined. The craft divisions on which the castes were built to all practical purposes have ceased to exist with the ruin of the craft industry. It only remained for the large-scale machine-industry to gather the demobilised human forces and build up a new social structure; but this unifying force was very late in coming. Therefore, in spite of their destruction as factors of social-economics, the caste-divisions continued to exist; but they were but the memory of something dead and gone, — a social prejudice that cannot be forgotten easily unless a violent storm of new institutions based upon higher means of production, knocks the undermined structure to the dust and throws it to the four winds. The Indian worker, released from caste bonds, has not been enslaved to the machine; on the contrary, he has been tied to the soil which his forefather had left long ago. Unlike large-scale industry, agriculture does not kill individualism.

Therefore three-fourths of the Indian people, in spite of being engaged in the same industry, agriculture, can keep themselves hedged within various caste-divisions whose economic basis has ceased to exist long ago. The following figures taken from the Census Report of 1911 are interesting: They show that caste, which existed in so far as intermarriage and eating together were concerned, did not have any economic importance. Altogether 89 castes were found to be in existence including a large section of the Mussulman population as well. But the actual professional (industrial) divisions functioning were but 21. In most of these professional divisions were engaged members of various castes. Let us take some of the most important castes for instance. The number of Brahmans, whose profession according to the caste system is study, teaching and worship, was 14,598,708. Now in the same year, the number of people occupied in professions and callings allowed only to the Brahmins according to caste law was at the most, 5,695,049. Therfore about nine million Brahmins must have been engaged in non-caste or extra-caste callings.

On the other side, of the 5,695,049 engaged in Brahminic professions, more than 70 % belonged to other castes which are debarred from these noble and holy professions by caste regulations. Kshatryas or Chattris or Rajputs, all taken together, were numbered at 9,430,095. These are military castes. They are to occupy themselves only with national defence. The number of people engaged in works allowed to the military castes was 2,398,586 in the same years. Besides more than 50 % of the public forces of India is recruited from the Mussalman and other classes outside the Kshatryas. From this it follows that almost 90 % of the military caste were occupied in callings, below or above their caste-limits. The numerical strength of the Baniyas or trading 'and money lending caste, was put at 1,125,517. But the actual number of people dependant upon these professions was not less than 17,839,102. And among these could be found Brahmins of venerable parentage and direct descendants of valorous Kshatryas. There were 11,493,733. Chamars, that is leather and hide workers, one of the lowest and most despised castes. Now the same years found only

698,741 people engaged in this industry. Therefore the rest of these hated, untouchable Chamars must have been accomodated somewhere else in the social organism. Telis or the oil-crushing caste was 4,233,250. But the number of workers employed in this trade was hardly half a million (exact figure unavailable). By the year 1911 most of the oil consumed in the country was crushed in power-driven mills situated in urban centres employing workers from all castes, — not excluding even the Brahmin. All the different sub-castes belonging to the guild of the weaving and spinning industry was calculated at 15,306,041. But the workers employed in the textile factories were not recruited exclusively from the given caste and the actual number of people engaged in handicraft textile industry was less than 8 millions.

This same process of disintegration and economic chaos may be marked in all the castes. A Brahmin can be found sweeping the street or engaged in the kitchen, whereas the son of a washerwoman will be occupying a high administrative post, or the son of the weaver teaching philosophy in the University. In short, capitalism had done its work and done it well, but one-sidedly. The destruction was very nearly complete, but the process of re-construction was barred from setting in immediately. The working-class of the Indian nation had been expropriated of its means of production. It had ceased to be the owner of its tools, thus losing the power to wield them according to dictates of its own necessity; its productivity had been crushed under the mass-production of machine-industry. The productive elements of the community had been practically reduced to the state of wage-slavery. But it was only the distribution of capitalism that had so far been introduced into India. With the absence of mass-productive industrial centres, the masses of Indian workers, in spite of having been expropriated and pauperised, remained scattered in the rural districts. Their productive capacity was subjugated to capitalist exploitation quantitatively. So long as the economic exploitation of the country could be kept a monopoly of imperialist capital, the concentration of the propertyless workers in modern industrial centres did not take place. But at last the native capital began to make itself felt. It refused to remain forever in the fetters of usury, petty trading, landholding and speculation. It wanted industrial expansion and all the efforts of imperialist capital could not prevent it any longer.

With the advent of native capital in the field of modern machinery, began the period of social re-distribution of the people. British capital wanted the Indian worker to forsake his independant craft and dedicate himself exclusively to the production of raw-material for the British industries. To do this work, it was necessary for him to be held in the village, labouring on the soil. But this method of exploitation was not suitable to the interests of the native capitalist class. The latter did not enjoy the advantage of holding the British workers in his factories to produce surplus values for him. The toilers of India engaged in the production of raw material, supplied the British capitalist with labour power which supplemented that of the British proletariat, tied to the machine that manufactured commodities from these raw products. But to the Indian capitalist, the labour power of the Indian worker only in its supplementary capacity, was not enough, because he did not possess big industry to be supplemented by the labour of the land-toiler. So the labour power of a man in the city was more necessary to the Indian capitalist than that of a man in the village. Or in other words, the normal process of industrial revolution, impeded by a form of exploitation suitable for imerialism, began to assert itself with the rise of Indian industrial capital. British capital accomplished the destructive part of the industrial revolution in India, but prevented the constructive phase of it till, under its own regime, the native bourgeoisie rose to build the modern India on the ruins of the old, whose hollow skeleton had been preserved by the foreign ruler, in conjunction with the native conservatives.

Though the first power-driven factory owned by native capital was built in Bombay in the year 1851, it was not until the 80's of the last century that the real industrialisation of the country began. In the closing decades of the nineteenth century, a revolution in the movement of the population became quite marked. Several large cities had come into existence with their industrial centres, where a considerable number of workers were attracted from the villages. Since the industrial revolution in India was obstructed by a foreign agency, and the normal play of social forces was disturbed, the industrial centres of modern India did not grow in the same districts where, in the early days, had flourished the towns inhabited by a rich trading and prosperous artisan-class. Thus we find, that while traditionally Bengal used to be the centre of India's cotton textile industry in former days, the modern cotton industry developed in another part of the country. And in the place of the cotton-industry around Calcutta, the capital of Bengal, grew the modern factories for pressing, spinning and weaving jute. Modern industrial centres with a proletarian population began to develop since the last decades of the past century. But the native capitalists had to go through a protracted struggle with the foreign ruler before they could build modern industries to any considerable extent. Therefore, during the thirty years from 1880 to 1910, the growth of modern industrial centres in India was rather slow. The number of toilers living on wages accumulated in urban centres still remained very small. Nevertheless, considerable numbers of workers had been concentrated in the factory towns of Bombay and Bengal even in the closing years of the last century. Most of these workers were unskilled, fresh from the village to which they were still bound by family ties or the fascination of a miserable piece of land, heavily encumbered with debt. The city-worker of modern India did not come out of the ranks of expropriated artisans; he came mostly from the peasantry. After having lost his trade, the artisan was pushed back to the land, where he had come to stay two or three generations before the call of modern industry brought him again to the city. The normal course of industrial development was obstructed in India. Industry did not grow through the successive phases of handicraft, manufacture, small factory, mechano-facture, and then mass-production. So the Indian worker has not been trained in industry. He lacks the proletarian tradition. The presence of a vast number of pauperised population in the country makes the economic condition of the industrial worker of the city very uncertain. Not having had the traditional industrial training, the factory-worker of India is generally unskilled. All these factors taken together make the comparatively new industrial proletariat of India a loosely-knit mass of wage-slaves thrown suddenly into new environments, which are more pressing, more nauseating, more unbearable than their village homes, where they toiled and starved and which they have abandoned in quest of a more comfortable one but recently.

Since the beginning of the twentieth century, and specially during the last half dozen years, there has been a steady influx of workers from the village to the city. This movement of population is due to the growth of modern industries. The population of old industrial cities has swelled, and other urban districts have been industrialised. The working population of these industrial centres is mostly drawn from the ranks of the poor peasantry and agricultural proletariat. The growth of the new industrial cities having been rather sudden, the housing conditions of the workers is indescribably horrible. The cost of living is much higher in the towns than in the village. The needs, however modest, of a townsman are again more than those of a villager. Thus, after coming to the city in quest of a more comfortable life, the worker becomes disillusioned. Discontent follows disillusionment. In the village he did not feel the exploitation as keenly as he does in his new environment. The struggle for life is harder and more acute in the city. Here he misses the care-freeness of rural life; and the mutual sympathy that characterises the sufferers in the isolated villages is smothered in the bustles of a commercial city. But the activity of an urban environment infuses new energy in the worker, who but a short time ago was a patient toiler on the land, accepting his hard lot as ordained by providence. This traditional passivity receives a jolt in the city. The glaring inequalities of wealth and comfort, in contradistinction with the merciless intensity of exploitation of man by man disturbs his mental calm. The spirit of resignation, instilled in him by the teaching of religion during the ages, begins to be ruffled. He can no longer help doubting whether everything is for good, as he has been taught to believe.

Of course on the other hand, the first disillusionment in the city arouses in the worker the desire to go back to his village home. But it is not always so easy to do a thing as to want it. Often he lacks the wherewithal to pay his passage back to the far-off village. Then he actually does receive more cash money than he could ever get or hope to get in the village. The scandalously low wages of a factory worker are handsome in comparision with the dole recieved by an agricultural worker. And the poor peasant has never enjoyed the blessed sensation of slipping in his pocket a handful of coins, even if they may be of copper, without the apprehension that one or another of his innumerable creditors would be presently coming to take them away from him. In the town, he earns his wages, however small, and spends them as he likes. This is not a mean temptation to resist. To return to the village, allured by the fresh air, would be at the cost of the newly-earned freedom of naked wage-slavery, which is to a human being more exhilerating than the drudgery of village life. Indeed there are cases of returning to the old home. But these are rare, and only those few who happen to have their families still in the villages, go back. In cases of long-protracted strikes also, a number of the strikers go back to the villages, because it is impossible for them to live in the city without work. The strikes being spontaneous and the trade-unions being new, the workers are also utterly without any income during the strikes. The wages are so low that the worker begins to starve in the second week of unemployment. Therefore, after having starved as long as he can, the worker naturally feels inclined towards returning to the village where he can get a morsel from either the parents, or relations, or somebody else. But this tendency is on the decline as the result of the growth of unionism. Practical experience also tends to discourage the workers from returns ing to the village once they are in the city. Very few leave the village home on their own choosing; they are driven out by economic pressure. On his return to the village having been in the city for some time, the worker finds the place left by him occupied by somebody else. The town life has awakened new visions and new desires in him, which cannot be satisfied in the hackneyed village life. In the city, the last remnants of the caste bonds have been shaken off him, so on returning to the village he finds himself an out-caste. The recent exodus of the Assam Tea Plantation workers under the instigation of the Non-cooperation agitators ended in disaster. Thousands of workers returned to their village after years of absence, to find that there was no room for them there. The land they used to till had been occupied and leased to some other by the money-lender; the life in the plantations had completely freed them from those hollow caste-prejudices that still hold good in the villages; and if they were under-paid and ill-treated in the plantations, starvation and destitution greeted them on their return to the village.

The Secretary of the Railway, Mining, and Paper-Mill Worker's Union, who accompanied a batch of repatriated plantation workers to their villages makes the following statement:

"I found that the repatriation of the coolies had practically resulted in sending them to death. Most of the returning emigrants had no home, no lands. Many of them had been born in the tea gardens and did not even know the name of their villages. At least 60 % of the returning emigrants have no distinct caste, having inter-married with the Chamars (the lowest caste). The village people absolutely refused to have anything to do with them, and even denied entrance into the village to men who actually had houses still standing. The villagers themselves find it difficult to keep themselves from starvation, and therefore, feeding the returned coolies is an impossibility. In the villages there are no industries in which these men might be employed, not any kind of work can be found for the day labourers. It is futile to bring away the coolies from the gardens and send them to the villages, from which 50 to 60 men are leaving daily for the tea-gardens' owing to the famine conditions prevailing there. Strikes never succeed if the strikers leave, as their places are easily taken by others."

It is true on account of their youth and the comparative weakness of capitalist organisation, many factories in the new industrial centres of India work rather spasmodically. They do not offer steady employment to a given number of hands all round the year. Consequently, the workers in such factories are still in a state of semi-proletarianisation; because a part of the year they have to go back to the villages, the city failing to employ them. But development of capitalist organisation and the improvement of industrial production are rapidly changing the situation. The causes for the fluctuation in the urban working-class are being speedily removed. The modern towns of India are bound to grow at the cost of the villages. Primitive agriculture no longer suits the scheme of capitalist exploitation, neither of the imperialist nor of the native bourgeoisie. The Indian worker must produce more; and he cannot do so with the plough-share. Indian labour-power must be supplemented by machine-power. So the economic life of India, which more than a century and a half ago was pushed back to the village from the town of the trader and guildsman, is being shifted to the city of the capitalist and industrial proletariat. The urbanisation of Indian labour began 40 years ago. In the earlier days, the process went on rather slowly owing to the hostility of the imperialist capital; but during the last ten years all bonds have been broken, and many large industrial cities have come into existence accumulating large masses of proletariat. It is several years since the latter has ceased to be the docile Indian toilers of tradition. New material conditions have aroused new energy, new aspiration, new spirit in them. The will to resist has taken the place of resignation. In short, the worker of the industrial cities of modern India is a powerful social factor. He may not be fully conscious of his vital position as yet; he may be still unable to wield his power in the right way; he may still, occasionally, fall victim to the lingering religious and social prejudices, but he can no longer be ignored. Any social or political movement that fails to count on him runs a great danger, because he stands at the vanguard of the forces on which the economic life of the nation depends, and this vanguard will soon become conscions of the historie rôle it is destined to play.

CHAPTER V.

The Proletariat.

3. Present condition and Future.

The number of industrial wage-earners in 1911 was 17,515,230 making a total population of 35,323,041 with their families and dependents as against about 15,000,000 (33,000,000, with families) in 1899. While we take into consideration the fact that during the intervening period the rural craft industries dwindled, it becomes apparent that the number of workers employed in modern industries must have increased proportionately, since the total number of industrial wage earners showed a rise. This number did not include the workers employed in transport and domestic services. The number engaged in these two were 2,394,800 and 2,725,856 respectively, making a total population of 10,628,058 including families and dependents. About 15 % of the entire body of industrial wage-earners was employed in modern machine-industries. But a large portion of those engaged in handicrafts were also drawn to the towns, since their industries depended on the urban population or export trade. For example, the majority of the building workers lived in the towns; so also was the case with the carpenters and furniture workers, dress and toilet makers.

Thus while on one hand, the artisan class of the old towns was ruined economically and was absorbed in the ranks of the pauperised peasantry or land-workers after having been driven out of their urban homes, on the other hand, a new class of industrial wage earners employed in craft industry, was coming into existence in the modern cities. This new class of handicraft workers rested on a different social basis. They were not independent artisans owning their tools, but wage slaves; in their respective trade and profession they were not bound by the caste laws; and as an economic factor, they formed a part of the modern capitalist system. They were accumulated in cities owing to the growth of the latter. During the first decade of the present century the building industry in the towns had increased two-fold and the furniture industry had grown ten times. This was due to the migration of the rural population to the cities, thus creating need for more housing accomodation. With the exception of hand weaving and spinning, employing about 3,500,000 workers, all other craft industries of any importance, are in the towns.

The forcible penetration of foreign capital destroyed the equilibrium in the old system of national economy. It pushed the productive forces backwards; — by preventing the growth of machine industry it drove the semi-proletarianised craftsmen back to agriculture. But, as the inevitable consequence of capitalist exploitation, towns had to grow; and the new towns created their new industrial workers. At first these industrial workers were employed in small factories run more or less on handicraft basis; but small scale production could not prosper in a society reduced to the exploitation of industrial capital. Therefore, thanks to the rise of the modern bourgeoisie and its entrance into the industrial field, all the industrial wage-earners of the modern towns are being concentrated in large factories. This social re-adjustment has been greatly helped by the unexpected economic and industrial situation created by the war, which gave the Indian bourgeoisie the opportunity to increase the dimensions of the native capitalist industry. The rapidity with which the Indian bourgeoisie developed in the last ten years has been shown in the first chapter. In consequence of this sudden industrial development, the growth of large cities has been accentuated proportionately. For instance the pressure of population has been so enormous in Calcutta that the price of land went up 350 %, during the last 6 years; and house rent has increased by 200 %.

The classified reports of the census of 1920 are not yet available; but it is shown by other sources of information that the number of industrial workers employed in large capitalist concerns is more than 9,000,000 at the present time, as against a little over 3,000,000 before the war. It is estimated that 4.5 % of the total population is to-day employed in the three principal industries viz. transport, textile, and mining. That is, the number of workers in these industries is 14,400,000. The portion of these particular industries still left to handicraft is not considerable. Therefore, the total number of proletariat can be reasonably put further above the estimated figure of 9,000,000. In any case, compared with the vastness of the total population, the numerical strength of the proletariat cannot be called very great. But what should be remarked is not the actual number existing at the present moment, but the process of growth of the proletarian class. The primal industry of the country viz, agriculture, has been overburdened for a long time; the number of people depending on wages derived from this industry is too large to be borne by it under any condition; there are in the country tens of millions of people without any means of livelihood worth the name. Therefore it is but natural that a heavy migration from the village to the town will immediately follow the growth of modern large scale industry offering employment. This redistribution of the population will inevitably bring in with it new orientation in the political life of the nation.

Imperalism reduced the toilers of the country to the economic state of wage-slavery, but by denying the native capital the opportunity of exploiting the workers with the aid of modern means of production, the class differenciation of the society was kept rather confused. The rise of a national bourgeoisie, followed by the increasing exploitation of the worker by native capital, has broken the social stagnation. Proletarianisation of the Indian worker has began, and the Indian society cannot be spared the inevitable consequences. It will be shown presently that these consequences have begun to make themselves felt since several years ago.

The following list gives the principal industries with the approximate number of workers employed: Cotton and jute-textile (machine-driven) 1,300,000; Transport (including railways, tramways and river steam navigation) 1,200,000; Mining, 800,000; Plantations, 900,000; Engineering and metal works, 150,000; Rice, flour, oil, paper and saw mills, 150,000; Cotton ginning and jute bailing, 100,000;

Printing press, 150,000; Dockyard and shipbuilding, 200,000; Marine transport, 300,000; Building, 1,900,000; Tanneries and leather works, 50,000; Sugar, 120,000; Arms and ammunition factories, 100,000; Tobacco factories, 38,000; Petroleum Refineries, 40,000; Gas and Electric works, 50,000. Other industries employing a smaller number of workers, are rubber works, tinning and packing, pottery, cutlery, chemical, pencil, sheet-metal, sporting-goods etc., etc. Then, there are about a million furniture workers living in towns, engaged in capitalist factories. The number of workers employed in urban mechanical factories can, thus, be estimated at 7,000,000. To these should be added the masses of non-industrial workers accumulated in the large cities, whose number can also be counted in millions. The urban non-industrial workers include domestic servants, carriage drivers, street sweepers, other municipal employees, porters, carriers etc. etc. These unskilled workers are also employed *en masse* and live on the outskirts of the towns in conditions absolutely revolting. Then, we have already seen the economic condition of the petty intellectual wage-earner. In short, the large commercial cities are populated mostly by propertyless wage-slaves of different categories, but belonging to the same social class.

Since the modern machine industry of India has not been built gradually on the background of craft industries, the proletariat, until recently was a mass of unskilled labourers. Machine-industry, built in India with English capital, usually employed skilled workers imported from the home country. The absence of Indian workers grown up in machine-environments with a mechanical training, obliged the British capitalist to import skilled workers from England even if he had to pay comparatively high wages to these workers. Gradually the latter proved to be a rather useful member of the exploiting class. Working men, wage-slaves themselves, these imported skilled labourers ceased to feel themselves workers as soon as they landed in India, readily getting absorbed into the class of colonial over-lords. Thus the working class employed in Indian industries remained divided into two sections, far removed from each other. The first of which, that is the British labour aristocrats, rendered the capitalist great help in exploiting the more numerous second, that is the native unskilled workers. The latter continued to be so miserably under-paid that the employer could well afford to pay handsome salaries to the former in recompense for the valuable colonial services rendered by them. Being unskilled and extremely exploited, the Indian industrial workers were not always steady in their urban occupations. The permanent pressure of a huge unemployed mass always made the economic position of the unskilled industrial labourer very insecure. They never became vital to the industry, which could at any emergency throw them out in favour of new recruits from the unemployed reserve force. Thus it happened that till 15 years ago, when the first big strike of the railway workers took place, the wages of the Indian industrial workers stayed stationary. In the early years of the twentieth century, the average wages of the urban worker was half a pound a month. Since then, the rise in the wage scale has not been more than 100 % whereas the cost of living has gone up 300 % only in course of the last 4 years.

The economic condition of the Indian industrial worker is horrible. He is much worse off than the workers of any other civilized country. It is dangerous to draw parallels in history; but it could be said that the social readjustment felt in Europe, and especially in England, as a result of the Industrial Revolution, has at last come to India. The effect of this readjustment is a sudden concentration of workers in the new industrial centres. And this concentration of labour forces in rapidly growing factories has brought in its train untold sufferings. The living condition of the Indian factory worker is intolerable. The sudden concentration of population in the cities has made the housing problem very acute. In most of the large industrial towns no accomodation at all is available for the working people who, therefore, have to dwell in the surrounding villages, often 6 or 8 miles away from where they have to work. The working day is of 12 hours which has only lately been reduced to 11 and in some cases 10. Thus in order to present themselves at the factory at 6, when the work starts, the labourers have to start from their dwelling quarters as early as 4 in the morning. Then again in the evening, utterly exhausted by the long day's hard labour, with what can just as well be called an empty stomach, the worker has to walk the distance back home after leaving the factory at 6. Owing to the lack of cheap suburban transportation, it is necessary to walk this distance twice a day; and even had there been any, his scanty earning would not permit the worker to pay the fare.

As to the condition of the urban workingmen's quarters, when there are any, the following description is taken from the report of the Indian Industrial Commission (1916—18). We take the cases of the two most important and typical industrial cities, viz. Calcutta and Bombay. The living condition of the jute mill operatives in the suburbs of Calcutta is pictured as follows:

"We have little doubt that the long hours passed in the uncongenial, if not unhealthy, surroundings of a factory, from which the labourer returns at night to a dirty, crowded and insanitary hovel, where his only relaxation is found in the liquor shop and the bazaar, are most unattractive to a man accustomed to rural life, and it is only the congestion existing in his native district and the desire to earn higher wages that lead him to submit to such conditions."

The slums of Bombay are described by the Industrial Commission as follows:

"The worse type of chawls (tenaments) consists of a two, three, or four-storied building, with single-room units either placed back to back or separated by a narrow gully (alley) two or three feet wide, usually traversed by an open air drain. The rooms, especially those on the ground floor, are often pitch dark and possess little in the way of windows. The ground floor is usually damp, owing to an insufficient plinth; the courtyards between the buildings are most undesirably narrow and, therefore, receive insufficient sun and air. They are very dirty. Water arrangements are very insufficient and latrine accomodation bad. A most insanitary smell hangs round these buildings. The rents vary according to the value of the ground. The monthly rent per room is from 3 rupees to 7 rupees, and the rooms themselves are usually 10 feet square. The standard of comfort is so low that the overcrowding entailed by taking in boarders or lodgers is readily tolerated for the sake of contribution to the rent received from them."

The Commission testify to having seen families occupying the same room, and single lodgers living in the same rooms occupied by one or more families. In the city of Bombay and its immediate surroundings, three-fourths of a million people are living in one roomed dwellings, described above. Among the urban population of factory workers, the death-rate is 60 per 1000, and the infant mortality is 650 per every thousand births.

It is but very recently that the British government has changed its economic policy of obstructing the growth of modern industrialism in India. In order to handicap the working of the new cotton-factories and to render their products unable to compete with the imported goods, the Indian Factories Act to "protect the labouring class" was passed as early as 1881. It happened that the interests of the rising native bourgeoisie and the government were not indentical in India in those days. In the early 80's it was not a very rare instance when a worker worked 18 hours a day in the cotton mills. This inhuman practice was not much affected by the government measure; because the officials, who were to enforce the factory regulations, could be easily bought. And the tragedy of the whole situation was that, as in all government departments, these petty native officals helped the rich capitalist to abuse and infringe the laws to protect the poor labourer. The Factory Act of 1881 fixed the maximum working day at 15 hours; but even this did not satisfy the thirst of the employers. The original Act was again amended in 1891 making it more stringent; but with no avail. The brutal exploitation went on until the workers rebelled. In the later 90's a number of strikes took place in the cotton factories of Bombay and Ahmedabad as well as in the jute mills of Calcutta. The situation remained practically unchanged till 1906 when the boycott of foreign goods, declared by the Indian National Congress, gave the first great impetus to the indigenous machine-industry. This impetus was felt very largely in the cotton industry. Mills after mills were erected and the old ones extended. The number of urban workers was suddenly increased. In order to break down the boycott movement, the banks handling the import of Lancashire cotton fabrics, kept on under-selling this commodity during the years of 1906, '07, '08. The only available weapon, with which the Indian manufacturers could fight this economic battle, was the cheap and unorganised labour. They made such an inhumanly excessive use of this weapon that the situation became scandalous, and in 1908 the government, which thrives on the exploitation of the Indian masses, appointed a Commission of Enquiry to investigate the condition of factory labour and recommend means of improving it. In its reports published in 1911, the Commission says: "the hours of labour are excessive, being from 14 to 22 per day. Sanitary provision is gravely defective in most factories." One witness., of practical experience, stated that "any man would feel exhausted even if he merely sat in a chair in some of the work rooms for eight or ten hours, the atmosphere was so foul".

On the recommendation of the Commission of Enquiry, the Indian Factories Act was amended in 1911. The new legislation established a maximum 13 hour day for men, 11 hours for women and children, with a thirty minute break for a meal in the middle of the day. But in practice very little improvement was made in the life of the factory worker by the new legislation. The fact that the overwhelming majority of the Indian workers was unskilled and that, owing to the existence of a hungry mass of unemployed, it was long before they could begin to organise themselves, made them helpless victims of the employing class. The abuse of child labour was particularly brutal. In short, the harrowing scenes that followed the Industrial Revolution in England were repeated in India, in spite of her much-vaunted spiritual civilisation. And the extortion of labour was the most scandalous and disgraceful in the cotton-factories of Bombay, owned mostly by native capital.

Indian factory production was originally modelled on the English system which gives a privileged position to the skilled worker. With the rapid development of capitalism, the American method of standardised mass-production is, however, gaining preference of late. Up till a few years ago, the Indian factory workers were divided into the widely separated classes of skilled and unskilled. There were very few Indians in the first class, which was almost exclusively reserved for imported English mechanics and engineers. The monopoly was quite complete in the railways and other industries owned by the state or foreign capitalists. In the textile industries, the skilled weavers were mostly native. But all the responsible positions, and especially those belonging to the mechanical branch, were held by Europeans who, on account of the disproportionately high wages and treatment they received, could by no means be recognised as members of the proletarian class. But the Indian skilled workers did not enjoy such a privileged position, either in wages or in treatment. The only advantage they had over their unskilled colleagues was that their employment was not so unsteady as that of the latter, because it was not so easy to find skilled weavers, carpenters, molders, designers etc., to replace the ones under employment. The native craftsmen, in spite of their knowledge of the trade, could not readily handle the mechanical tools; and to employ European workers would increase the cost of production enormously. Thus, while in the earlier years of the twentieth century, the unskilled urban workers were still but a mass of fluctuating wage earners not altogether divorced from their village bonds, there had come into existence, nevertheless, a class of skilled workers domiciled permanently in the city and dependent exclusively on industrial wages.

In 1910 the numerical strength of this class of pure proletariat was about 1,000,000, that is nearly 50 % of the total number of urban factory labourers of that time. The European element in this skilled labouring class numbered 15,000 employed in factories and 80,000 employed on the railways, — traffic and workshops included. The number of European skilled factory workers has increased since then; last year in the cotton mills of the province of Bombay alone 23,000 of them were employed. But, on the other hand, the English monopoly over the field of skilled mechanical work in the transport and other industries owned by the government and British companies, has been broken. The number of Indians employed in these branches has increased considerably. This change was forced by war conditions.

The import of skilled workers from England had to be stopped, and Indian industries, extended and placed on a war basis for the production of military supplies, needed an additional number of skilled workers. Thus, native workers had to be admitted into the heavens of expert mechanical positions, so far reserved for the workers belonging to the ruling nationality. This process brought the Indian closer to the machine, and therefore, proportionately farther from the village life and traditions. Consequently, the number of industrial wage-earners domiciled in the towns, divorced from all connection with the village, increased.

Before the war, the textile industry, owned mostly by native capital, had to import foreign mechanical and engineering workers from abroad along with foreign machines. The obstructed growth of machine-industry had prevented the rise of a class of expert mechanics among the Indian proletariat. This obligation to employ highly-paid English mechanics constituted a heavy burden on the industry. But in spite of their desire to get rid of this burden, the native capitalists went on employing the imported experts in order to maintain the efficiency of the factories. The war conditions told on this practice also; and the mechanical jobs in the textile industries were opened to the native workers.

It is generally held that Indian labour in machine-industries falls short of the required standard of efficiency. Evidence is not lacking to prove that, in spite of the miserably low scale of wages, Indian labour can produce as cheaply as the Western workers. The comparatively inferior stage of organisation, in which the Indian capitalist industry found itself until recently and the unspeakably bad living conditions together with the artificially forced low standard of comfort of the Indian workers, are the causes of the small productivity of Indian labour in spite of the low wages. The Industrial Commission (1916—18) arrived at the following conclusion on the subject:

"It is true that the inferior physique and tropical conditions contribute to this state of affairs (low rati of production), but there is great reason to believe that the former is to some extent the result of preventible disease, whilst other causes, which are even more obviously remediable, are factors that unnecessarily increase the difficulties of our labour problem".

Major White M. D. of the Indian Medical Service, said: "a large part of the relative inefficiency of Indian labour is due to removable pathological causes". Indian employers, lacking a long experience in driving large herds of wage slaves, still believe in the antiquated theory and practice of paying the least possible wages. But the wrong economics of this practice is beginning to dawn upon them. The steady and uninterrupted growth of industry requires a settled class of urban workers; and the prevailing intolerable condition in which the factory labourer has to live in the towns, is not very conducive to make him forget the village, with which in he still maintains more or less connection. Of course it is no longer practically possible for the entire body of urban workers to go back to the village, thus leaving the modern industrial centres utterly deserted. But what actually happens is a constant fluctuation in the working population; — the movement back and forth between the village and the town. This in itself is very prejudicial to the productivity of the industry. So, of late there has arisen a movement, backed by the new economic policy of the government, to increase the housing capacity of the large industrial centres, in order that the working people can be accommodated near the factories. These housing factilities have been good for completing the proletarianisation of the city workers, because large numbers are settled in the towns once for all. But the condition in which they find themselves in their new environment is horrible. Driven from their holding on the soil, separated once for all from the village life and traditions, and rudely disillusioned in their pilgrimage to the shrine of urban industry in quest of higher wages, the Indian proletariat is bound to develop the psychology of its class, and it is doing so amazingly fast.

The relation which the Indian city worker maintained with the village until recently and still maintains to a certain extent, though to a diminishing degree, has its effects on the rural wage earners. The discontent aroused in him by the sight of glaring inequalities between the poor and the rich in the cities, is carried with him to the village and contributes to disturbing the resignation of the rural toiler. Coming to the cities, the worker finds out that he has been living a life not of a human being, but an animal; he sees how many things of necessity and comfort have been denied to him; his desire to live and enjoy is aroused; he becomes indignant at having been deprived of many things that are within the reach of the people living in the towns. He goes back to the village, but his new spirit does not die in him. On the country, it contaminates the inarticulate masses in the rural districts, and arouses in them the desire to go themselves to the cities. The result is an increased migration from the village to the town. Even those who come back from the cities, return thither with new comrades. Thus is growing a new social force motivated by the changed economic condition of a large section of the people. The economic basis of the country has been changed; the corresponding redistribution of the population is inevitable. The social equilibrium has been disturbed. A process of readjustment must follow. With all their traditionnal resignation and apathy, the wage-earners cannot any longer stay and starve in the villages. The small-scale, backward agriculture cannot provide them with employment. The attractions of city life are felt in the remotest corner of the country. The wages-slaves must flock thither. And the concentration of a numerous social class doomed to the same misery will inevitably give rise to a situation impregnated with revolutionary possibilities. The signs are already very manifest. The revolt of the wage-slave against the propertied rich is rocking the country. The nationalist pre-occupation can no longer calm it down. Side by side with the national struggle, which is assuming alarming proportions, the class-struggle is also developing. The modern bourgeoisie, which is leading the national struggle, could not have come into existence and power without bringing in its train the other side of the social picture, viz. the proletariat, which in its turn must initiate and lead the struggle for the emancipation of the exploited class. The class-struggle is raging in India simultanaeously with the struggle for national liberation.

Whether nationalist pre-occupations — the historic necessity for political independence of the Indian people, — will be sufficient for keeping the class-struggle in the background indefinately, is to be judged by the actual class differentiation in the present social organism and by the possibility of this differentiation growing wider. A comparative study of the economic condition of the different classes of the society is helpful for making this judgment. Since the entire Indian people is under the exploitation of a foreign imperialism, it is true that until about half a century ago, no social class had any considerably great wealth accumulated in its hands. On the contrary, in the early days of the British rule, the riches of the upper class were exploited and taken out of the country. For more than a century the propertied class was not allowed the freedom of investing their wealth in profitable means of exploitation. Generally speaking, this brought down the economic condition of the entire nation approximately to the same level. National exploitation was naturally followed by national pauperisation. But this abnormal economic equilibrium could not be maintained forever. In course of time it was disturbed, and class-exploitation within the structure of the exploited nation became a social phenomenon. The rise of the modern bourgeoisie in India has been traced in the first chapter; the pauperisation and destitution of the peasantry has been shown in the second; now we will see that in recent years the enrichment of the capitalist class has caused impoverishment of the proletariat.

Let us take one industry, viz. the textile, in which by far the largest amount of Indian capital is invested and which employs a considerable part of the city proletariat. In spite of the fact that this industry was not very small in that period, the companies owning cotton mills in the last decade of the past century could not pay more than 6 %, 7 % dividend; in 1907—1908, in spite of the prosperity resulting from the boycott movement of 1906, the rate of dividend did not rise any further than 15 %. But in recent years, the profit made in the same industry has been increasing enormously. According to the Bombay Stock Exchange List of 1919, the dividend paid by the cotton-mills exceeded 25 %. There were at least three mills paying 40 %, 2 paying 50 %, and 4 others paid 56 %, 70 %, 100 % and 120 %

respectively. Considering the fact that the capital invested as well as the total productivity of the textile industry have increased tremendously since 1919, it is to be deduced that the rate and amount of profit must have gone up in proportion. In 1918 the companies possessing jute mills paid to the shareholders an average of 20 %, or double the rate of the previous year. The profit from the jute mills has increased very much since then. (For the inereased rate of profit in Indian industries vide chap. I.)

A look at the other side of the picture makes the class cleavage of Indian society quite manifest. According to the evidence recorded by the Industrial Commission, the wages of the Bombay cotton mill operatives in 1918, ranged from 15 shillings and 10 pence to £ 3 2 s 7 d per month. The wages in the Calcutta jute mills were from 12 shillings to £ 2: and the average wages of the workers in the Bengal coal fields was 19 shillings per month. In the same year (1918), the cost of living had gone up 200 %. The price of food grains was 175 % wholesale and 400 % retail more than in the pre-war-period. But the wages had hardly been improved, the average rate of increase having been not more than 25 %. This unbearable economic burden exhausted the patience of the workers, and the result was the food-riots and the strike-movement which during the last three years affected every class of workers including those toiling on the land. By its three years' struggle for economic betterment, — a struggle much abused, dissipated and misled by the bourgeois nationalists, — the Indian proletariat has succeeded in securing an average 50 % increase in the wages, while the profit of the capitalist during the same period has grown much more, in proportion as well as in total amount.

The rise in the scale of average wages in the cotton industry is as follows:

Year		1895	1914	1918	1920
Wages per mouth	Rs.	14.5	18.5	21	24

The lowest scale of wages for unskilled labour was 7 rupees in 1915 and 8 in 1920 and the highest for the expert weaver was 36 and 40 respectively. The scale of wages in the same industry in another province, viz. Madras, was as follows:

Year		1895	1914	1918	1920
Wages	Rupees	9.5	17	21	25.5

The wages in the jute industry of Bengal showed the following scale of increase:

Year	1895	1914	1918	1920
Wages	11.8	16.5	17	23.5

The increase in the wages of the workers employed in the engineering industry has been as follows over the unit of 1880:

Year	Skilled	Unskilled
1914	11 %	7 %
1918	13 %	7.5 %
1920	15 %	9 %

The railway wages rose in the following scale. The rate of 1880 is taken for the unit:

Year	Skilled	Unskilled
1914	18 %	5.7 %
1918	20 %	7.5 %
1920	25.33 %	9 %

The average scale in several other principal industries taken together showed the following rate of increase:

Year		1895	1914	1918	1920
Wages	Rupees	9	18.3	19	25

From the above abstract figures it is evident that in all the industries, the percentage of increase in the wages has been more during the last period, that is, between 1918 to 1920. Remembering the fact that it was during this period of two years that the strike movement among the Indian proletariat became very strong and widespread, it is concluded that this meagre improvement in their economic condition was secured by the efforts of the workers themselves. Therefore it is natural that the Indian proletariat, however ignorant, however undeveloped they may be still, could not help learning from the experience of the last three years that they must fight to earn the right to live as human beings. They have also found out that in this struggle, they have to face the opposition of the native as well as the foreign employer, and that in case of emergency, the two don't hesitate to join forces in spite of the national struggle that makes them enemies otherwise.

The wages and living conditions of the working class vary so much from one part of the country to the other that one cannot get a clear idea about the situation from the average wage-scale in the principal industries. In fact, the actual income of nearly 80 % of the workers falls considerably below the average quoted above. For example, the daily earning of a miner in the coal fields of Bengal is seven annas, which is equivalent to 8 pence. With this he can hardly buy his food, not to take into account his family, housing and other primary necessities. The wages in the plantations are still worse, the average being as follows:

		1914	1919
Men	Rupees	6.2	6.35
Women		4.68	5,15
Children		2.9	3.15

The average wages of an unskilled urban labourer is 9 rupees per month. This buys him not more that 90 pounds of food-grains at the prevailing price. In order to have at least one full meal a day for himself and for his family, which averages two or three persons with very little earning capacity, he needs not less than 120 pounds of food-grains alone. Then there are other expenses which he must meet.

Such are the conditions under which the workers in the Indian cities live and labour. The cash payment they receive in the towns is indeed more than they used to get in the villages and more than the unskilled rural labourer still gets. Therefore, in spite of the wretchedness of the city life and the practically lower economic value of the wages earned there, urban employment offers a lure to the village toiler who wants to run away from the never-to-be-broken bonds of indebtedness and the hopeless drudgery of primitive rural life. Once in this city, his life is not by any means bettered; but the division of the society between the rich few and the poor many becomes manifest to him. In the village everybody seemed to be poor; everybody lived approximately the same kind of life; the sight of somebody benefitting by the labour of others is more vivid in the city than in the village. These factors act quickly on the psychology of the workers herded around the factories in horrible condition. Thus, notwithstanding their still existing ties with the village, their ignorance, lingering religious prejudices and the traditional spirit of resignation, — the most baneful product of the much-vaunted Indian culture, — the proletariat is forced to develop fighting qualities. The Indian worker has declared the class war, apparently unconscious of what he is engaged in. Under the regime of capitalist exploitation, Indian society stood divided into two classes since long ago. The cleavage has been growing wider and wider with the development of the native bourgeoisie. But the rise of modern industrial centres with their army of wage-slaves has brought the situation to a point where the cold facts have to be faced. They can no longer be softened by sentiment nor clouded by nationalist preoccupations.

That the unbearable economic conditions are making the patient Indian workers learn the necessity of fighting for their interest, and that this awakening of the labouring masses is no longer unnoticed by the upper classes of the society is shown by the discussion of the "Labour Problem" which is capturing the attention of the press as well as the platform. We quote below extracts from a typical article on the subject published in "The Hindu" of Madras, a nationalist journal of conservative school. The article was titled "The Labour Crisis — A Gloomy Outlook".

"The labour crisis in Madras is but the forerunner of what is in store for us in the future. I have observed with keen interest the first symptoms of the awakening intelligence throughout the country. In one word it is showing itself in the form of restlessness. The silent suffering and the stolid contentment of the poor and labouring classes have given way to a vehement desire to share the comforts of life wills the well-to do classes above them, the members of which are setting a bad example to the lower classes . . . The wheel of fortune in the villages has turned; the ancient simplicity of the village life has disappeared. The labouring classes have learned by silent suffering, helped by the instinct for self-preservation, to outwit their tyrants and masters by using the very same methods they have so long been practising to filch them out of their honest dues". The writer goes on describing at length the revolutionary changes that are taking place in the rural life; how the old caste divisions are breaking down and the society is getting divided into two classes viz. rich and poor; and how the latter are losing their traditional virtues and becoming turbulent. He remarks "They (workers) suffer, and cherish a strong dislike to the class which has compassed their ruin through quarrels and litigations, which are the village edition of the imperial "divide and rule policy".

So much for the pious alarm of the respectable bourgeoisie which is shocked at the impudence of the lowly. But the real strength and character of the awakening of the Indian working-class, urban as well as rural, are indicated by the strike movement of the last several years. The rebelliousness of the workers has added great potentiality to the struggle for national freedom. In the din of political fights, the economic struggle of the working class has been drowned; economic strikes have been invariably transformed into premature political ones; but to an observer with an understanding of the social forces, this complexity of affairs can not confuse the great outstanding motive behind it all. The working-class, and particulary the city proletariat, has begun to fight for its economic betterment, and signs are not lacking that before very long, the conscious desire for social emancipation will not remain beyond its mental outlock.

Ever since the class of city workers existed in India, the strike has not been an altogether unknown affair. But so long as the numerical strength of this class remained insignificant and the large majority of the workers were unskilled, strikes were very few and far between. Indian workers employed in modern industries were mostly unskilled until 10 or 12 years ago, and the permanent presence of a huge army of unemployed in the country constituted a standing menace to the steadiness of the factory workers' job. Under such circumstances, the only consequence of a strike would be the summary dismissal of the strikers, who could be replaced by new men at a moment's notice and at even lower wages.

Thus, although there occured strikes of the cotton-mill operatives of Bombay in the latter years of the 90's, of the railway-workers in 1906, of the coal miners around the same year, of the Calcutta jute-mill workers in 1907 etc., the economic struggle of the working-class did not take sufficiently organised and powerful form till 1917. In this year, the war conditions had on the one hand, given a tremendous impetus to the machine-industry in India, while on the other hard, they had pushed the cost of living several times higher. The number of workers accumulated and settled in the industrial centres had greatly increased; the proportion of skilled workmen among the Indian labourers had also increased. Owing to the sudden growth of industries, the towns were horribly congested and the housing condition was scandalous. The wages were so low that the workers could hardly buy anything with them. Such a situation could not help creating discontent, which was first expressed in the form of food-riots. Shops were looted by hungry work-people. The food-riots were quelled with the aid of armed forces.

Unable to drag along any longer in their unbearable existence, — unorganised, practically leaderless, — the workers of the textile-industry found the first weapon of the class-war. They instinctively learned to strike. The first strikes were declared in the latter part of 1917, and within the course of but a few months, not less than 120,000 workers took part in the same strike, tying up simultaneously a number of factories in several towns. The demand was for higher wages and shorter hours, which were granted to a certain extent. Since then strikes followed upon strikes, and the year 1918 found the entire country seething with labour unrest. Out of the strike movement were born labour organisations. Trade Unions were organised by the workers in various industries. The class-war became more naked. Even when forced to concede to the strike-demands, the capitalists refused to recognise the unions as legitimate bodies. The government endorsed the attitude of the employers, many of whom were Indians and not a few belonging to the nationalist movement. Recognition of the right of collective bargaining was included in the strike-demands. By the middle of 1918 "participation in the control of industry" was included in the demands of several strikes.

The story of the strike-wave that swept the country during the years from 1918 to 1920 is a history by itself. It needs special study; but lack of sufficient reliable material precludes our entering it at length. Suffice it to say that, side by side with the national struggle, the class struggle has also been developing. In the short space of four years, trade-unionism has made great progress in India. It shows that the Indian proletariat has been very quick in understanding the necessity of its class organism to fight for economic interests. In the earlier days of the movement, when almost every strike was followed by turbulent disturbances created by the workers, the nationalist leaders suddenly found in it a very good weapon to be used for the purposes of demonstration. Very soon all the strikers were led and organised by nationalist leaders, who in their enthusiasm, tried to read a political character in the economic struggle of the working-class. This led to the disasters of the Punjab, Bombay and other places in 1919. But the bloody baptism under nationalist leadership did not damp the spirit of the rebellious wage-slaves. What did happen was, that the failure of the bourgeois nationalist to understand the real significence of the labour unrest, prevented him from leading it into the right channel. Consequently, the leadership of organised labour began to pass into the control of conservative reformists and government agents. Nevertheless, mass-action still remains the backbone of the national struggle; and the masses are pushed on to the revolutionary ranks not so much by national enthusiasm, as by the instinct for self-preservation, which is the mother of the struggle for economic emanipation.

That the struggle of the proletariat is an affair distinct from the national movement and that what the Indian worker is really fighting for is freedom from his age-long economic bondage and social ostracism, can be seen from the innumerable strikes organised and led by the Unions. Today we find hundreds of thousands of workers all over the country, fighting with grim determination the battles of economic emancipation with the capitalist class.

irrespective of nationality. How far the sense of solidarity and will to fight have progreessed among the Indian proletariat can be judged from the following picture of the 50,000 textile workers of Madras who were locked-out for more than three months. The government extended full aid to the exployers in their efforts to break down the resistance of the workers, who were terrorized and proscuted in every conceivable way. A correspondent gives the following description of the spirit of the workers after 10 weeks of struggle and starvation:

"One sees in the faces of these workers, when they assemble in thousands in their union premises every evening, a deep and silent determination to carry on the struggle in spite of all the brutal devices that are now being practiced to cow them down to obedience and break the strike." Are you downhearted?" The answer "no" uttered by thousands of voices sends a thrill of joy among the vast assembly. But only a few can realise the real sufferings and privations of these brave people. Here is an example of endurance and suffering perhaps unparalleled in the strike phenomena of recent times, and which is destined to have far-reaching results all over the labour world. Still stubborn, still peaceful, still determined to endure and to suffer for their economic emancipation".

About a year ago, the labour unrest became so acute and wide-spread that the government found if necessary to recognise it as a problem separate from the general national movement. Commissions were appointed to investigate the causes of the unrest and devise remedies to counteract them. In its report, the Commission for Industrial Unrest in Bengal states that in nine months, from July 1920 to March 1921, no less than 137 strikes took place in the province of Bengal alone. The following figures quoted from the report of the Commission show that the strikes were very wide-spread and affected all branches of industries:

As regards the economic loss by these strikes, it is calculated that 244,180 employees were involved and that the aggregate duration in working days was 2,631,488.

"Five strikes or more occurred in the following industries:

	No. of strikes
Engineering and metal works	33
Jute mills	27
Transport and in the port of Calcutta . . .	19
Public utility services	12
Coal mines	7
Cotton mills	6
Railways	5
Printing presses	5

This Commission, composed of official employers, legislators and labour-leaders, made an exhaustive study of the causes of industrial unrest. In course of this study, the preoccupation that the labour troubles were due to political agitation was greatly dissipated.

"Industrial unrest is only a phase of the general unrest which has prevailed since the close of the war in every country in the world. The causes of the unrest are multifarious, political, social and economic. The economic causes are the most obvious and perhaps the most important. The increase in the cost of food-stuff, cloth and other necessities of life has been followed by a rise in the wages of all classes of labour, but the rise in wages has not at all times and in all industries, kept pace with the increase in prices. During the intervals, genuine hardship must have been caused to the labouring classes, giving rise to apprehension as to the future and a general feeling of unrest .... At all events, labour is developing a new consciousness of its solidarity and value."

Out of the 134 strikes recorded in the report of the Commission 110 were due to demands for higher wages or demands for wage increase together with other concessions. 13 were the continuation of the previous strikes after the original demands had been partially or completely satisfied. The strikes were renewed due to additional claims for overtime wages, strike pay, re-institution of dismissed strikers or other reasons connected directly with the immediate interest of the workers. One remarkable feature was that only on strike was declared for better facilities for prayers on the part of the Muhamedan employees. This analysis of the strikes demonstrate the fundamental character of the unrest that has contaminated the entire working population of India.

In recommending the introduction of Joint Works Committees (on the style of Whitley Councils) the Commission makes the following interesting and significant remarks. "It is a regrettable fact that, in spite of all that has been done during the last quarter of a century to improve the material condition of the work-people in the jute-mills and other large industrial concerns on the banks of the Hoogly, the relations between the employers and employed are much less intimate and cordial than they were twenty years ago".

It should be indicated that the owners of the industries referred to in the report are both foreign and native. The gravity of the industrial unrest can be gauged by the fact that the government found it necessary to appoint such a commission of enquiry and accept its recommendations. This shows that the employing class has been forced to recognise the proletariat as a factor to be contended with; and this position in the class-struggle has been reached only after four years' fight. The class-cleavage in India is very wide and the objective force of the proletariat tremendous!

It is not only in the province of Bengal that the industrial unrest has attracted the attention of the government. All the provincial as well as the central government are gravely concerned with this problem. Why? Because the growing consciousness of its class interest makes the working-class a powerful revolutionary factor, which will take part in the struggle for national freedom, not swayed by the wordy sentimentality of petty bourgeois libertarians, but in the pursuit of its ultimate economic and social liberation. To defect the most advanced section of the working-class from the national struggle by advocating the protection of its immediate material interests, appears to be within the present scheme of the government. The experienced British bourgeoisie, which stands behind the Indian government, does not fail to make a clear survey of the social forces underlying the revolutionary movement, and will avail itself of the inevitable results of the class-contradictions and antagonism in the national movement, if the awakening working-class is not led on to the revolutionary path according to its class interest. This is a task which appears to be beyond the wisdom and sagacity of the nationalist leaders, and naturally calls for a political party of the working-class.

The first stage of the proletarian struggle, which was marked by a mad wave of spantaneous strikes, followed invariably by riots and disturbances, seems to have terminated by the end of the last year. Since then, the proletarian movement has apparently entered the period of organisation and preparation for continuing the struggle with renewed vigor in the near future. Since the beginning of the present year the strike fever seems to have been on the decline. But now though the strikes are less frequent, they are better organised and are marked with the tendency of improving the immediate material conditions of the workers. In 1918 and 19, the first years of proletarian struggle under nationalist leadership, the strikes cost the workers heavily, but very little was achieved by way of improving their material conditions. The nationalists were more interested in turning out a popular demonstration than to develop the revolutionary consciousness of the masses by participating in their struggle of every-day life; of course this defect of tactics of the nationalists is due to their affiliation which puts a class-stamp upon their activities. The proletarian class must develop its own leadership and political career. Shortsighted nationalist tactics have temporarily driven the organised section of the proletariat into the control of those non-revolutionary elements who, however, are helping to solidify the worker's ranks. The influence of this non-revolutionary element has succeeded in curbing the strike-movement, and is trying to divert the proletarian energy into the channels of negotiation and conciliation with the employer. But this will simply embitter the antagonism, because the worker will come closer to the exploiter and will have more chances of seeing clearly the class-line that separates them.

Nothwithstanding the temporary slackening of the revolutionary fervor of the working-class movement, the situation in general has not changed very much. A note issued by the Labour Office states that in the province of Bombay, 6 strikes were declared in the month of April 1921, involving 103,850 persons and the loss of 184,450 working days. In May there 11 strikes and lockouts affecting 120,290 men and causing the loss of 227,115 working days; in June the number of strikes was 10 with 16,117 men taking part and the loss of working days was 79,804. The next month showed a further decrease.

The demands put forth by the strikers of late are better thought out than before, when the proletariat was led more by indignation, restiveness and agitation. Now the demands are calculated to further the interest of the class, immediately as well as ultimately. The fight for the recognition of the unions is still going on. In many districts, the working-day has been reduced to 10 hours. Demand for participation in the profits is not infrequent. In many industrial centres, especially in Bombay, the latest demand is for universal free primary education for the children of the workers. A movement has been started for the institution of a minimum wage-board and 8 hour day. In July, a resolution to that effect was moved in the Legislative Council, but met a united opposition from the British as well as native industrial interests and was lost. The Factory Act of 1911 has been amended in spite of the opposition from the Mill Owners' Association with slight concessions to the workers, including an 11 hour day for men, a 10 hour day for women and a 6 hour day for children. Almost in every province with a large industrial proletariat some sort of conciliation board has been appointed to settle the disputes between capital and labour. These are but signs which indicate which way the wind is blowing. The cityproletariat has become a social, economic and political factor in the national life.

It is the development of large-scale industry which is going to determine the future of India. The revolution has already begun and is marching with gigantic strides, disrupting the undermined structure of the village and building huge cities, whither the hapless wage-slaves are being driven by the force of circumstances. The vast masses of wage-slaves, which long since came into existence in the organism of Indian society reduced to capitalist exploitation, are in a process of concentration. The scattered forces are being mobilised into solid ranks. The consequence of this social readjustment cannot remain unfelt. In fact it is already manifesting itself very powerfully. It is the mass-awakening that has at last given real potentiality to the movement for national liberation; and it is the organised, class-conscious proletariat, aided by the pauperised peasantry, which will lead the national struggle to a successful end. An unconscious ignorant mob, excited by frothy sentiments, is no match for the mighty British imperialism. In spite of its rapid growth, the Indian bourgeoisie is still very weak and is bound to be unsteady in its purpose; but before the worker there is nothing but struggle. It is he having nothing to lose but his chains, on whom ultimately depends the national freedom; but national freedom does not mean anything to him unless it brings in its train his economic and social emanicipation. The national liberation of India is but a prelude to a greater thing — the social emancipation of the working class. National struggle and class-struggle are going on side by side; the noisiness of the former cannot conceal the existence of the latter.

CHAPTER VI.

Political Movement.

Before proceeding to deal with the national movement of modern India, it is necessary to review briefly the social and political events in the pre-British period. This study will help us to understand better the later developments, since these are but the inevitable consequences of the past. What is happening today has not been produced by the events exclusively of yesterday. Human history is connected with the dark ages of barbarism by the unbroken chain of evolution.

The English are not the first conquerers of India, which has been pratically under foreign domination since the thirteenth century. Before the English became the political masters of the country, it had been ruled by Mohammedan conquerers. Of course, the character of the medaeval empire of the Musalmans differed greatly from the modern capitalist imperialism. But the fact remains that the domination of a conquering race interfered with the free social development of the native people, precluding thereby the evolution of a national state.

The Musalmans began to invade India when the latter was in the first stage of feudalism. It was only among the Rajputs of the north that the feudal monarchy was fully developed, while the rest of the country still remained divided into a number of kingdoms, partly theocratic, partly patriarchal. Under such circumstances, national consciousness, embracing the entire population that inhabited the continent of India, was naturally an impossibility. The attempts made from time to time by one or another of these kingdoms to extend its boundaries at the cost of the neighbours, were not by any means actuated by the ideal of building up a great unified nation: dynastic ambition, pure and simple, was the motive behind such attempts. Nor could the heroic opposition put up by the Rajputs against the Moslem invaders be called national resistence, because the Rajput clans fought bravely to defend the feudal right of their chiefs, whose castles, womenfolk and patron-deity figured supreme among the holy objects to be defended at all costs. The Rajput chiefs led their legions to battle in order to defend the sanctity of "Rajasthan" (the abode of the kings) against the aggression of the barbarian invaders. No talk of defending India or the Indian nation was heard, unless interpolated subsequently by the zeal of patriotic writers unmindful of the process of social evolution.

Under the rule of Musalman emperors, the greater portion of the country was brought under one central state, but not as a nation, — because the court of Delhi was not the centre of a national state. The feudal imperialism of the emperors of Delhi was not based on the support of the loyal native nobility. It did not stand at the head of subordinate feudal nobles resting on serfdom as a social institution. The country was ruled, not by native feudal chiefs grown out of the people, but by nobles sent from the court of the foreign emperors. Feudal in origin, these nobles, nevertheless, could not count on the spontaneous support of the people they ruled over, because they had not grown out of the indigenous patriarchal society; power was not maintained by existing social forces within the country but by a mercenary army. The strength of Indian society lay in the decentralised village communities, which were far from being distintegrated by the advent of higher political institutions from outside. Therefore the Indian people were not unified under a centralized state power, the first requisite for the growth of a national political consciousness. The feudal hordes and mercenary armies of the invading Moslems were able to sweep the country because a united resistance could not be put up. The social development of the native population precluded it. Only Rajputana, where feudalism had attained a high degree of development, could never be completely subdued by the Musalman emperors, because in Rajputana, the strongly centralised feudal state was the outcome of a normal social growth, while Moslem feudalism was artifically foisted upon the country.

The result of the Mohamedan conquest was that the state-feudalism introduced by it, disturbed the free evolution of native feudal society. The theocratic and partriarchal Hindu kingdoms, which would otherwise have developed into feudal monarchies, were overthrown, to be replaced by imperial provinces ruled by the court nobles with the help of mercenary armies. Feudalism, which was in the process of evolution in the native social organism, was deprived of the possibility of political expression. The political state, imperial as well as provincial, was the apparatus of a dominant social class extraneous to the country. Its expression was mainly directed against the native feudal chiefs, an increase of whose power constituted a menace to the safety, — the very existence, of the Musalman authority. Thus the establishment of a more advanced form of political institution, instead of contributing towards, checked the social progress of the people. The forces that would have led the people eventually through the different stages of political and social evolution to a united national state or a number of states, were disturbed. But however suppressed, the growth of native feudalism could not altogether be thwarted. It kept on accumulating vigor, which was expressed in the form of innumerable revolts against the imperial authority. This rebellion of oppressed feudal chiefs against the supremacy of foreign state feudalism should not be mistaken for a national awakening.

Political nationhood is a comparatively recent phenomenon in the annals of human history. It is the result of a certain stage of economic development, affecting communities inhabiting a given geographical region. Diverse groups of peoples living in the same surroundings, are gradually welded into a national entity under the pressure of economic forces. So long as these forces are not sufficiently developed, the sense of nationhood remains unknown to a people. India is no exception to this law. The extensive peninsula called India, is a mere geographical expression; it is very distinctly marked out from the mainland of Asia by physical barriers. But to hold that this geographical accident has been in itself sufficient to create a sense of national unity among the diverse communities inhabiting India, would be to misread the history of human evolution. To weld the numerous races and tribes, divided by language and grades of culture, into one national unity was conditional upon the development of a material force which could make such fusion possible. As long as the productive forces remain so backward that the different groups of the people can live in self-contained isolated communities, the simple accident of their happening to be situated within the limits of a certain geographical area does not suffice to make a nation out of them. It is only economic development that induces these isolated communities to come into relation with each other to satisfy their mutual needs. These relations may be warlike or peaceful, according to the circumstances. In the period of barbarism, clans and tribes make war upon each other in quest of fertile ground; gradually the stronger one subdues and absorbs the weaker and grows into a theocratic feudal monarchy. Under the latter, the people are not united by national cnsciousness, but by common allegiance to the high priest or king or to both, as the case may be. The economic forces which eventually change this allegiance into rebellion are the source of political nationhood. Development of the mode of production brings into existence a new social class, the bourgeoisie, which struggles to control the production, distribution and exchange of commodities. In course of time, the political state power vested in the theocratic and feudal monarchy becomes a burden on social production, and the element controlling the latter originates the theory of nationhood, which is, that the sovereign power is not vested in an individual but in the entire community united into a nation. Under the influence of this growing social class, the bourgeoisie, which controls the productive life of the community, the national state, distinct from its feudal predecessors, is evolved. Economic relationships among the people united under such a state break down all racial, tribal, linguistic and cultural barriers; sectional isolation, prevailing hitherto, gives place to national cohesion.

Such economic development was not to be found in the resplendent Hindu kingdoms which flourished at the time of the Moslem invasions, not to mention those of earlier epochs. The Musalman conquerors naturally would not help the growth of the idea that their political power was the expression of the sovereign will of the people, subjugated by them. Since neither the Hindu kingdoms nor the Moslem empire were based upon the economic supremacy of the middle-class, those states could not produce a sense of national solidarity among the people superficially united under them. They could not unify the Indian peoples into a single national existence because the economic forces, which alone are capable of bringing about such a union, had not yet attained the adequate stage of development.

This absence of national consciousness in the early and medaeval stage of Indian development has been a great bone of contention between the two camps of historians, viz. the imperialist and nationalist. The former teaches that it was a peculiar defect of the Indian people that they never could unite upon a national basis; that this lack of national unity made the Indian people fall an easy prey to all foreign invaders; and that the unifying force of the British rule was indipensable for saving the Indian people from the political chaos and social anarchy in which they had been submerged for centuries. On the other hand, the patriotism of the nationalist historian revolts against this stamp of innate inferiority attached to his race, and he rushes to the other extreme in order to refute the imperialist interpretation of history, as if with a vengeance. He is untiring in pointing out how religious and cultural traditions knitted the peoples inhabiting the continent of India, into what he calls, a "homogeneous national unit". Scientifically judged, both of them, — the imperialist as well as the nationalist, — are bad readers of history. Their subjective attitude prevents them from looking at the history of human progress as it is. The imperialist distorts history to serve the purposes of insidious propaganda; while the nationalism of a subject people is naturally on the defensive. In his zeal to prove that the people of India are not inferior to other races, the nationalist historian goes so far as to assert that even among the peoples of primitive India, three or four thousand years ago, there existed a national consciousness. He forgets that, granted the existence of a certain religious and cultural solidarity, the presence of political nation hood is not necessarily established; it is with political nationhood that modern India is concerned, because political subjugation prevents the economic and social progress of a people. Political nationhood, and the struggle to attain a politically free national existence, in its turn, is conditional upon a certain grade of economic development in a particular people.

At the time of the British conquest, that is towards the middle of the eighteenth century, the economic and political evolution of India was such that her people could be called rather a number of nationalities inhabiting a continent, than a composite national unit. It is quite possible to imagine that but for the intervention of capitalist imperialism, which while obstructing the economic growth of her people, forced on them political unity, India would be today in a socio-political stage corresponding to that of modern Europe, — a continent composed of a number of free nationalities in different grades of economic and social development, but not one united nation. The march of historical events there, up till the eighteenth century did not appear to tend towards welding the diverse and often antagonistic communities into a unified national entity.

Nearly six hundred years of Musalman rule left the various Indian communities still in a more or less isolated position. The revolts against the central authority of the court of Delhi were local, being led by feudal kings, and had grown powerful in spite of the imperial suppression. They never took the form of struggle for national liberation. Different parts of the country tried, and at last succeeded in breaking away from the empire, in different times and under the lead of different chiefs, most of whom were interested in their own particular locality. The trading and intellectual middle-class, whose mission it is to lay the foundation of a modern national edifice, had not yet become a political factor. It was only towards the end of the Moghul Empire (at the beginning of the eighteenth century) that a middle-class was found to raise its head. Up till then, under the Musalmans as well as the Hindus, the state had been controlled either by the theocratic intelligencia of the Brahmans, or the military caste of the Kshattryas, or the Musalman feudal nobility having no organic relation with the native society.

Under such conditions, the idea of a national state embracing the entire country was inconceivable.

In the earlier decades of the eighteenth century the Musalman feudal imperialism broke down, after having ruled over the country approximately for five hundred years. By that time the middle-class had become an important factor in social-economics, but nevertheless, it was still hedged in by feudal fetters on one side and by the caste guilds of the village communities on the other. Although the village still retained its position as the productive unit, the exchange and distribution of commodities had given rise to large towns which had become centres of prosperous trade carried on by an opulent middle-class. Production itself could no longer be kept rigidly confined within the limits of the village community. It had greatly lost its former individualistic character. In the large towns were accumulated numerous classes of handicraftsmen producing more for exchange than for use. This transformation in the economic life of the country had not only created a prosperous middle-class engaged in trade, but enabled the rich traders to make their influence felt in the political field, in spite of the fact that the ruling feudal aristocracy, Hindu as well as Musalman, looked down upon them. The various independent states that sprang into being upon the ruins of the Moghul Empire, found themselves largely controlled financially by the trading class, although their political structure still remained feudal. This rising middle-class foreshadowed the development of a higher form of political state based no longer upon feudal or dynastic authority, but upon the theory of nationhood, — a political theory still to be evolved.

The collapse of the feudal empire of the Moghuls, however, was not caused directly and exclusively by the rise of the middle-class. The Moslem state-feudalism maintained by military force, was subverted by the growth of native feudal monarchies which were more virile because of their closer contact with the people, whose serfdom constituted the social basis of their power. In the days of the decay of the Moghul Empire, its armies had become mere bands of marauders, without any vital connection with the people. The leaders of these armies were more adventurers looking for personal aggrandisement than defenders of an existing economic and political order. Instead of defending the integrity of the Empire, the nobility of the effete court utilised their control of the army for the realisation of personal ambition, and a good many of them ended by establishing independent kingdoms headed by their respective dynasties. Its own internal disintegration, together with the rise of the Sikh, Rajput and Marhatta powers, caused the disruption of the Musalman Empire. These three might all be looked upon as the revindication of native feudalism, whose normal growth had been disturbed and delayed by the introduction of Moslem state-feudalism.

When the Moghul Empire declined in the first part of the eighteenth century, there existed in the country a trading and intellectual middle-class which objectively was the most progressive social factor. It was destined to capture the political state-power eventually, because its economic growth could not fully be realised under feudal political institutions. But it was not yet strong enough to enter the contest openly for political supremacy. A state which is to be the political expression of the middle-class must be based upon the theory of the sovereignty of the people, because the middle-class cannot overthrow and supplant the feudal power without the support of the people. So, on the eve of beginning its struggle for political power, the middle-class formulates the theory of nationhood based upon the so-called "natural right" of the people, to rule itself through delegated or elected representatives. But the Indian bourgeoisie in that period had not yet evolved a political ideology of its own. Its socio-economic position was such, that it was forced to remain the unseen power behind the throne on which the feudal monarchs still sat. There was therefore, no force to contest the absolute authority of the latter. Its political immaturity prevented the middle-class from initiating and heading a movement having for its object the establishment of a national state, based upon democratic principles. Consequently, the dissolution of the Moslem power was followed by a long period of chaos and anarchy from the midst of which arose the Marhatta feudal monarchy.

The rise of the Marhatta power marks the first stages of political nationalism in the history of India. The Marhatta kings, under the influence of their ministers, who belonged to the Brahman intelligencia, conceived the idea of establishing a Hindu federal empire on the ruins of the Moslem supremacy. This project of founding a national state was realised to a certain extent, not alone by the feudal chiefs, but under the rule of the Brahman ministers, who captured the political power of the state, peacefully replacing the royal dynasty. The federal empire of the Marhattas was consolidated, not under the leadership of the feudal dynasty which had originally started the revolt against the Moghul power, and which eventually contributed to its dissolution more than any other factor, but under the astute statemanship of the Brahman intelligencia in control of the state power, including the victorious military forces. Its political philosophy however, could hardly be separated from feudal traditions. Consequently, before the primitive Hindu nationalism of the Marhattas could crystallize itself as such, it degenerated into medaevel imperialism of the worst sort. The fact that the Marhatta Confederacy itself was, ere long, dismembered into several principalities fighting against each other, proves that the ideal of a national state had not been realised. It was not so much the awakening national consciousness as the military prowess of the Marhattas, which defeated the mercenary armies of the decrepit Moghul Empire.

The Marhatta Confederacy failed to consolidate the people into a national unit, because the economic foundation of the society on which such a political super-structure could be sustained for any length of time, had been shaken. The economic life of the country was no longer nourished exclusively by serf labour; the rise of the middle-class, given to prosperous trade and banking, signified a radical change in the productive forces. A state power that could, in that period, assume a national character, should have been built on the economic factor; should have been the political apparatus in the hand of the trading-class; should have brought peace and order out of chaos and anarchy in order to help the development of the new productive forces. Instead of using it for pillage and plunder, it should have wielded its military power as a police force. These are the characteristics of the bourgeois state; but the feudal character of the Marhatta power prevented it from adapting its nationalism to the contemporary economic factors and social tendencies. Thus, despite its patriotism, based on religious antagonism, the Marhatta power could not help but degenerate into rabid imperialism, which was instrumental in ruining the country, instead of contributing to the growth of nationhood. The Marhatta revolt against the Moslem authority failed to realise its original programme, viz, the building up of a unified Hindu nation, — because it was the political and military expression of native feudalism, which had been suppressed by Musalmen Imperialism. But feudalism, as a socio-economic institution had objectively reached the stage of decline; it could no longer be the state power. Therefore, in the latter part of the eighteenth century, the Indian people refused to respond to the reactionary cult of the religo-political nationalism preached by a feudal state. Instead of being a unifying force, the Marhatta power degenerated to such an extent that its very name became a terror all over the country.

By the time the representative of the English trading bourgeoisie began the first stages of struggle for political power in India, the Marhattas had reached the pinnacle od ascendency, and were already on the decline. The political chaos and social anarchy reigning since the beginning of the eighteenth century, had reached their climax. Civil war was the order of the day, and the economic life of the country was seriously injured. Feudalism, Hindu as well as Moslem, had landed in political bankrupcy, having failed to maintain an established government ruling over any considerable part of the country. It could not bring order out of chaos. A more advanced social factor had to appear on the field in order to build a political institution appropriate to the situation; — a social factor that could count upon the tacit support of the people at large by advancing social progress; — a social factor that could put an end to the ruinous civil wars and inaugurate an era of economic reconstruction and political peace. A progressive middle-class, controlling production and distribution by means of trades capital, was this power-to-be. This element did exist in the country at the moment, but its development had been rather stunted and immature owing to the troubled conditions obtaining just about the time that it assumed the proper social significance. The English bourgeoisie, which happened to appear on the scene in the person of the East India Company, as it were, took the hint from history and began to establish its domination over the country with the "aid of the Indian people themselves".

Marhatta nationalism, sanctified by religious traditions, failed to enlist the support even of the various Hindu communities; but a handful of foreign traders could become the paramount power of the country without meeting any serious popular resistence. The British East India Company happened to embody the social force which alone was able to secure what the Indian people badly needed. This was a form of government which could bring peace and order to the country. The people were craving for the cessation of the civil war ravaging the land. Every class, except the doomed feudal rulers and their henchmen given to plunder and pillage, cried for settled conditions, and would welcome any government which could assure it. Peasants, artisans, traders, intellectuals, all were sick of the civil war which had affected more or less seriously their respective material interests. The peasant could not peacefully till his land unless the danger of marauding hordes tramping over it was removed; artisans and traders suffered alike because the general insecurity of life and transportation had ruined commerce, and the heavy tolls levied by the irresponsible rulers were killing the economic life of the country; the intellectuals needed an established order of society in order to thrive. The foreign traders also required settled conditions. Thus it happened that the material interests of the would-be conqueror coincided with those of the about-to-be conquered. The representatives of the British bourgeoisie entered the field of political aggression with the standard of "peace and order", and soon became the paramount power of India with the aid and connivance of the Indian people themselves.

At the time of the British conquest, the Indian people were nothing but a mass of humanity, in the period of transition from a disintegrated feudalism to a higher stage of social evolution. The forces that could weld it into a national entity in the political sense, had not yet fully developed. The imperialist theory that the people of India were incapable of ruling themselves, and therefore, needed the protection and guidance of a more civilised nation, is preposterous. But what is historicaly true is that in the first part of the eighteenth century, India stood in need of a new social force which could lead her out of the chaos and anarchy resulting from the breakdown of the feudal states. In the bourgeoisie was to be found the saviour. The failure of the Marhatta confederation had demonstrated that a national state could not be built upon the basis of feudalism. A higher form of political institution was necessary, and this new institution should have been the bourgeois state resting on the theory of the sovereignty of the people — political nationhood. But the native middle-class failed to rise to the situation. It had not attained the necessary political maturity.

If a handful of English merchants could subdue such a vast population and one not in a barbarous stage of development, it was not, as the nationalists hold, simply because of the "devilish perfidy" of the invadors. There were deeper social reasons behind the tragic episode called the British Conquest of India. Such an outstanding historical event cannot be explained light-heartedly away with the flourish of such elequent phrases as "unsrupulous intrigues of perfidious Albion", marshalled by the conquered; nor as "an agreeable accident of history" piously pronounced by the apologists of British Imperialism. To an unprejudiced student, the British conquest of India does indeed appear more as an accident than as the result of consummate intrigues. But to call it an accident pure and simple, divorced from the gigantic scheme of human progress, might flatter imperial egotism, but it betrays sheer ignorance of social history. The British conquest of India is one of those accidents which are not very rare in human history, — accidents precipitated by the coincidence of events and forces developing with method, and in conformity with definite material laws. The English traders who came to the shores of India without any political pretensions, could eventually establish a great and mighty empire, because they happened to embody the social force which, in accordance with the imperious material laws determining all human progress, was next to assert itself over the political life of the country.

The British East India Company succeeded in establishing its political domination over India with the help of, and subsequently at the cost of, the native trading class which, together with the intelligencia, constituted the progressive and objectively most revolutionary factor of Indian society in the middle and latter parts of the eighteenth century. In order to consolidate its power, the Company's government had to enlist the support of a sufficiently strong social class, since otherwise the political domination of a handful of foreigners could not be expected to endure. The natural ally was of course, the native trading class, since it belonged to the same social category as the foreign invador. In fact, the native trader did enter into an alliance with the British Company even before the latter had entered the political struggle, and rendered it valuable services. It was a social struggle, in which national differentiation was overwhelmed by imperious economic necessities.

The glorious role of freeing the people from feudal fetters did not fall to the lot of the Indian middle-class libertarians. It was misappropriated by the British bourgeoisie, represented by the East India Company. The facility with which English aggressor could defeat one after another of the feudal monarchies with armies recruited from among the native peasantry, demonstrated that the social foundation of Indian feudalism was decayed. The forces for overthrowing feudalism had grown in the social organism. The tragedy was, that it was not the native bourgeoisie which marshalled and led these revolutionary forces on the path of social progress, but a foreign agency which appeared on the scene at the critical moment and exploited the revolutionary forces for its own benefit, thereby throttling Indian social progress and causing national stagnation.

The thread-bare feudal political structures collapsed like so many houses of cards before the attack of the foreign commercial bourgeoisie, because the latter objectively corresponded to and was actually backed by the native social forces which would have preformed the same exploit, perhaps somewhat later, had not the English intruded. Thus, by overthrowing feudalism from the political power, the English invadors did perform a revolutionary act; but it was not long before they transformed themselves into a counter-revolutionary force by obstructing the progress of those very native elements which had helped them come to power. The British bourgeoisie was interested in the establishment of a colonial state, which did not need the same economic foundation as a bourgeois national state. The exploitation of an imperial bourgeoisie governing a colonial country, does not follow the same line as that of a national bourgeoisie. The progress and prosperity of the latter require the fomenting of national consciousness and then of jingoism in the people, while the former obstructs the growth of national consciousness. To let the social forces develop, which brought the English traders to political power, would have meant the inevitable rise of the native bourgeoisie, a factor positively dangerous to the safety of the foreign domination. Therefore, the policy of the British Indian government was to crush the native trading class. Its power of resistence broken, feudalism was perpetuated in the persons of newly-created landed aristocracy and impotent native states, both of which factors became the mainstay of British rule. The reinstatement of the feudal show however, put the peasantry back into practical serfdom. All economic progress was made impossible by the coersion of the state. Thus, the British conquest of India, which could be called a coup de etat made by a foreign bourgeoisie with the help of a series of rather premature revolutionary forces, brought peace and order. But the peace soon proved to be the inactivity of the exhausted. The British power secured its own position in India by economic suppression and the social stagnation and political slumber that unavoidably followed it. First utilised and misled, then betrayed and ultimately wantonly destroyed by its more developed foreign prototype with a state power behind it, the Indian middle-class remained practically non-existent politically, for a considerable time after its fore-fathers had helped the English lay the foundation of their Indian Empire. The economic suppression of the propertied and intellectual middle-class, made a liberal bourgeois political movement impossible. The absence of a bourgeoisie precluded the evolution of those forces that make for the national consciousness of a people. Such was the background out of which has evolved the modern political movements of India. The political nationalism of modern India expresses the political ideology and aspiration of a youthful bourgeoisie, which has risen in spite of innumerable obstacles and which has never had the opportunity of utilising the state apparatus for disseminating and inculcating in the people the idea of nationhood. But at the same time, it enjoys the advantage of shielding its exploitations under the cry against foreign oppression. The nationalism of contemporary India lacks the tradition of a national unity, but it rests on the reaction against a common oppression. This negative basis however, renders the national liberation movement led by the bourgeoisie, inherently weak. Therefore, the political liberation of the oppressed people of India depends less on the nationalism of the bourgeoisie than on the struggle of the exploited masses for economic and social emancipation. It will be seen presently how the political movement in the India of today is being strengthened by the class-struggle that is overshadowing the nationalist sentiment, which has never gone beyond the limits of a certain section of the middle-class.

CHAPTER VII.

Political Movement-Conted.

The first hundred years of British rule was a period of social and political stagnation resulting from the ruthless destruction of the progressive tendencies in production. The political power passed on to the control of a foreign bourgeoisie which, instead of helping the development of higher productive methods, pushed the society back to the stage of agrarian economy. This told heavily on the native middle-class, which had already reached an advanced stage of trades capitalism and was standing on the eve of large-scale industrial production. Economic suppression of the native middle-class precluded the possibility of a political movement of a modern democratic character. There was no other element in the native population which could resist or be hostile to the foreign ruler. The program of "peace and order", which was gradually realised, secured the foreign conqueror active support from certain sections and the passive connivance of the masses of the population. The much longed for peace put the society, as it were, to a political sleep.

Peace established by a bourgeois state is usually followed by social progress and economic prosperity of a certain section of the people. But the peace, which the British conquest gave to India, turned to be the listlessness of the paralytic; the order was not that of a new society evolved out of the decayed old. — It was the artificial maintainance of the status quo which had been disturbed by the rise of new social forces. The fact of its being a colonial government turned the bourgeois state established by the English in India, into a reactionary force, because its safety and continued existence had to be secured by the destruction of all progressive forces in the native society. The practical elimination of the bourgeoisie from the political field made the growth of the spirit of nationhood an impossibility. The government was a bourgeois political institution, and as such was indeed an improvement on the older forms the country had evolved; but it was not a national state. Therefore its policy was not to foment national consciousness by means of public instruction, a capitalist press, ceremonies etc., but to keep the people in their primitive ignorance. In order to hold the society in a backward state, skeletons of the undermined feudal structure were maintained and pampered. These impotent feudal rulers, together with the newly-created landed aristocracy to which the rich trading class was cleverly diverted, constituted the social basis of the British rule for more than a hundred years. So in spite of being in itself a bourgeois state, the British Indian government allied itself with the conservative and reactionary element of the native population. This unholy alliance enabled it to betray and choke its former partner, the native trading and intellectual middle-class. The elimination of the latter caused a social reaction inevitably followed by political apathy.

Such a social atmosphere, which prevailed till after the middle of the nineteenth century, was not conducive to the evolution of any political movement of a national character. The revolt of 1857 was the first serious attempt to overthrow the British domination; but by no means could it be looked upon as a national movement. It was nothing more than the last spasm of the dying feudalism. In so far as it aimed at the overthrow of foreign domination, which had obstructed the social growth of the people, the revolt of 1857 was revolutionary; but socially it was a reactionary movement, because it wanted to replace British rule by revived feudal imperialism, either of the Moghuls or the Marhattas. This objectively reactionary character was the reason of its failure. It could not have been suppressed had it been a progressive national movement, led by the native bourgeoisie with advanced social ideas and political program. But such a movement was impossible in that epoch. The necessary social elements were absent. The following opinion of the imperialist historian Seeley is on the whole a correct interpretation of the situation:

"We could subdue the mutiny of 1857, formidable as it was, because it spread through only a part of the army, because the people did not actively sympathize with it, because it was possible to find Indian races who would fight on our side. The moment a mutiny is threatened, which shall be no more mutiny, but the expression of a universal feeling of nationality, at that moment all hope is at an end of preserving our empire. For we are not really conquerors of India, and we cannot rule her as conquerors."

The revolt of 1857 was predominantly a military mutiny brought about by the intrigues of the deposed and discontented feudal chiefs. The people at large had very little to do with it; the majority of them either remained passive or helped the British government. The only powerful Indian community with some sense of national solidarity, rendered valuable services to the British. It was the Sikhs, who had maintained an independent national state until but a few years before the mutiny, whose military aid contributed largely to the suppression of the rebellion. The English system of education introduced in the 30's, had brought into existence a small class of modern intellectuals who could be looked upon as the forerunners of the national movement of the subsequent epoch. The mutiny found all these intellectuals with modern and progressive thought, on the side of the British government. Only in some of the minor native states the people were somewhat drawn into the revolt because feudaism was still a living force in those parts. The failure of the mutiny proved that the intrigues of a backward social force, doomed to death by history, could not realize a national unity in opposition to a foreign domination which, nevertheless, objectively embodied an advanced political thought. The country was still undergoing a reaction against the long period of chaos and anarchy through which it had passed, and would thus stand by that political power which could insure peace and order, however dearly the latter might cost.

Orthodox nationalists of a later period looked upon and interpreted the rebellion of 1857 as a great struggle for independence. This tendency betrays the grave danger of reaction which is contained in the nationalism built on a religious basis. No Indian nationalist who stands for the social progress of his people and who struggles for political independence as a step towards that goal, would be treading the right path by clinging to the sentiments that lay behind the Revolt of 1857, which was not merely a military effort to overthrow the foreign domination. It was provoked by a fierce spirit of social reaction, being a revolt not against the British government in particular, but against the advanced social and political ideas it embodied, — the ideas which were hailed by the intellectual middle-class of India, because the latter was materially prepared for them, and would itself have evolved them, had they not been brought into the country through the agency of a foreign conqueror. In fact, the foreign "barbarians", against whom the ideological leaders of the mutiny sought to incite the Indian masses, were detrimental to the untrammelled evolution of progressive social and political thought in the native middle-class, inasmuch as they obstructed the latter's economic development.

A hundred years had passed since the British began to implant their political domination in the country. The earlier years of their rule were marked by wanton economic suppression, which was executed partly by plunder and spoliation, partly by destroying the native handicraft industry in competition with the machine production of England. The former method was used against the feudal rulers, while the latter served to reduce the trading class to social inaction and political impotency. The wisdom of the policy of basing British domination on the landed aristocracy, inaugurated under the direction of a semi-feudal Parliament at home, came to be questioned by not a few Englishmen in the government of India. These representatives of the English liberal bourgeoisie held that it was dangerous to rely on a reactionary social element. They suggested that the middle-class was the natural ally and that its intellectual growth should be helped by the government. This new tendency was expressed in the desire to introduce Western education into India. The object was to allow the progressive forces of the native society an intellectual expression, which, however, being devoid of any economic might, would not be able to be politically dangerous, but at the same time would constitute a bulwark against possible reactionary upheavals. A pure political manoevre on the part of the British rulers, this policy was interpreted by the apostles of reaction as a clever design to undermine their hold on the people; nevertheless, obviously contrary to the expectation of its promotors, it marked the birth of modern India. Inadvertantly, it let loose that dynamic social force which was destined to prove eventually mortal to the British, and in order to be able to fulfill its historic mission, had to prove itself an enemy of the native reactionary elements, which stood on the way of progress in the name of national culture and traditions. As a result of this policy of introducing Western education, a class of intellectuals with modern thoughts and progressive tendencies had come into existence already in the 30's of the nineteenth century. Still in its infancy, this progressive element showed signs of vigor in social and religious reformism, if not in the political field, which was naturally closed to it owing to the economic stagnation in which it was forcibly kept. But its very existence, which happened to be still under the fatally miscalculated patronage of the British government, was a challenge to the old order of things. The social significance of the Revolt of 1857 was the reaction it embodied against this revolutionary force, which had not appeared as such till then, but which was the harbinger of a new India, to be dominated neither by a foreign imperialism however liberal, nor by the native conservatism however glorified.

"All the vested interests connected with the old order of things in the religious as well as in the political domain, felt the ground swaying under their feet, and the peril with which they were confronted came not only from their alien rulers but from their own countrymen, often of their own caste and race, who had fallen into the snares and pitfalls of an alien civilization." These words of Valentine Chirol can be taken as a picture of the social background of the Mutiny, if only the last phrase is substituted by "who had awakened to the idea that the old social and political institutions were detrimental to the future progress of India". The failure of the Mutiny proved conclusively that the people of India were not united by the old social institutions and religious traditions,—that the future of India was to be secured not by the impossible revival of the old order of things, but by the birth of a new force arising upon the ruins of the old. The birth of this new was obtructed, but could not be prevented by the foreign ruler.

The safe continuation of the foreign domination however, still needed the sinister services of the reactionary forces in order to keep the masses of the population away from the influence of the progressive intellectuals. The social and religious superstitions were very useful in keeping the people in ignorance and resigned to their position. Therefore in the memorable Queen's Proclamation which followed the suppression of the Revolt, was emphasised the determination of the British Government "to abstain from all interference with religious beliefs or worship". This was obviously a concession to the forces of reaction, whose good graces should be enlisted as a counterpoise against the rising progressive intellectuals, who were always looked upon with suspicion on account of their objectively revolutionary character. The vanguard of the native society, they could not however be alienated, because their support was the most reliable foundation on which the foreign rule could rest itself. Therefore, in order to demonstrate that the British government was not inimical to the aspirations of the intellectuals, the following liberal and democratic clause was also incorporated in the same proclamation: "British subjects of whatever race or creed will be freely and impartially admitted to the offices in the services of the Crown, the duties of which they may be qualified by their education, ability and integrity duly to discharge. But in the same breath it is added "in framing and administering the law, due regard will be paid to the ancient rights, usages and customs of India" as if to reassure the conservative elements that their social rights and privileges would be protected by the government.

From such a background has arisen the forces which made for the political movements of modern India. The policy of the British government in the first half of the nineteenth century at the same time obstructed and contributed to the evolution of that social class, on which depended the formulation of the idea of nationhood of the Indian people. By protecting the factors which made for social reaction, even long after the feudal political power was broken, the government rendered the growth of national consciousness among the masses of people impossible; but on the other hand, in the person of the intellectuals educated in modern ideas, were allowed to be born the forerunners of Indian nationalism.

Ever since the earlier decades of the nineteenth century, by which time British domination was fairly consolidated, there had existed the tendency to enlist for the government the support of the native intelligencia, which, without an economically strong middle-class behind itself, could not constitute a political danger. This tendency naturally gave birth to the controversy over the introduction of the Western system of education. The opposition against it was strong, first from the English administrators, then from the conservative Indians. The former held that the introduction of modern education would sooner or later widen the political vision of the native middle-class. Putting forward this point of view, Sir John Malcolm sounded an alarm in the following words pronounced in 1813: "it will be something like suicide if we will increase the facilities for education in India". The class instinct and imperialist caution, which made him utter this warning, have since been very well justified. The Indians were against English education, because they saw in it a covert attack on their religious and social institutions. This apprehension was based on the fact that it was the Christian missionaries who first opened English schools.

The new policy of drawing the native intelligencia closer to the government triumphed when a Special Committee appointed by the Parliament after the Reform Bill of 1833, reported that "Indians were alive to the grievance of being excluded from a larger share in the executive government" and testified that "such exclusion is not warrented on the score of their own incapacity for business or the want of application or trust-worthiness". On the basis of this testimony it was laid down that "no native of the said Indian territories shall by reason only of his religion, place of birth, descent, colour, or any of them be disabled from holding any place, office or employment under the Company", which was the government of India in those days.

It was indeed a bold step on the part of the British bourgeoisie to have brought Western education within the reach of the Indian intelligencia. It broke the spell of reactionary nationalism, which subsequently took the violent expression of the Mutiny, but laid the foundation on which was built eventually the theory of the political nationhood of the Indian people. Macaulay, who is to be thanked more than anybody else for the introduction of Western education into India, appeared to have understood the gravity of the step he was advocating, and perhaps even the fatality involved in it. Because in course of the debate on the question in 1833 he put to the British Parliament these ominous questions: "Do you think we can give the Indians knowledge without awakening their ambition? Do you think we can awaken their ambition without giving some legitimate vent for it?" What induced the British imperialists to start on such a dangerous path in spite of having foreseen what lay ahead? It was indeed not the humanitarian mission of civilizing the backward peoples as the imperialist prophets preach. The object was to foment the growth of a native element which would consciously support the British government as the most beneficial political institution,—an element so educated as to understand that any other form of government based on native traditions, would be a step backward in the path of social progress. The wisdom of this policy was demonstrated by the part played by the modern intellengencia during the revolt of 1857. The immediate effect of the introduction of English education was the adherence of the most progressive native element to the rule of the foreign bourgeoisie. This adherence was complete, being moral and intellectual as well as political. With this achievement, British domination found itself planted on a more secure ground, that of the social class historically destined to be the political leader of the people. The young, progressive elements of Indian society of the early Victorian age proved to be a useful appendix to the foreign ruling-class. The economic suppression of the middle-class precluded the possibility of its being politically revolutionary, which it nevertheless was, as an objective social force. Therefore its activities were confined in the fields of social and religious reforms,—activities which invoked upon its members the wrath of the forces of reaction and conservatism.

The alacrity and enthusiasm with which English education was hailed by a section of the rich middle-class, shows that the latter was in a receptive mood. Modern political ideals and advanced social philosophies were studied earnestly by thousands of young men not only in the schools and colleges in India, but many of those who could afford went to the Universities in England, thus violating the old social prohibitions. Judged from the point of view of the native culture and traditions, the first generations of the modern-educated intelligencia could be called de-nationalised, because they were more English than Indian. Their religion was that of Spencer and Comte, their philosophy that of Bentham and the Mills. But they were the first rebels, boldly raising a voice challenging the old order of things, and heralding the birth of a new India which could not come into existence without shattering the still cherished religious and social ideals and institutions of old. In the earlier days they were politically impotent, but it was not long before these so-called de-nationalised intellectuals proved to be the fathers of the modern political nationalism of India.

With the suppression of the Revolt of 1857, feudalism was altogether eliminated from the political domain, notwithstanding the fact that for convenience, imperialist domination still perpetuated its hollow skeleton clothed in comic pomp and grandeur. The economic backbone of the native bourgeoisie had long ago been broken. The evolution of higher means of production having been obstructed for the benefit of colonial capitalism, the overwhelming majority of the population lived in villages, steeped in ignorance and submerged in social stagnation. Politics, forms of government, national subjugation or freedom remained matters outside their concern and beyond their conprehension. The only section of the people showing any sign of life was the modern intellectuals enducated in Western methods and thoughts. The numerical strength of this class was infinitesimal in comparison with the vast population economically suppressed, socially stagnant and politically inarticulate. Trained in the school of bourgeois liberalism and staunch believers in English constitutional traditions, these "de-nationalized" intellectuals were instrumental in bringing to India, for the first time in her long eventful history, political patriotism. The rise of a class educated in modern political thought marked the beginning of a movement which was to develop into a struggle for national liberation, to culminate eventually in the establishment of a centralized state embracing the various communities, united by common oppression, and represented by a native bourgeoisie strong economically, and ambitious for political supremacy.

The economic development of the middle-class having been impeded first by political instability and civil wars before the English government was established, and then by the capture of state power by a foreign capitalist imperialism, the modern ideology of bourgeois democracy could not evolve out of the native society. But when modern political thoughts became accessible by means of foreign education, Indian intellectuals responded to them enthusiastically. Being a bourgeois state, the Government of India was at first accepted by them as the best political institution. However, it was not long before they discovered the discrepancy between the theory and practice of British political philosophy, in so far as the Indian administration was concerned. Having been taught by English authorities that representative government was the noblest of the political institutions and that the world was indebted to the Anglo-Saxon race for this blessing, the Indian intellectuals found in the British government of India a total negation of the principle of popular representation. This discovery created discontent in them, their Anglicism notwithstanding. Thus was initiated the first stage of the struggle for representative government. This struggle of the radical intelligencia was not against an effete and antiquated political institution, but for the democratization of the existing government which, by virtue of its being controlled by the bourgeoisie, was the most advanced that the country had had till then. The ideology of this struggle had to be therefore, borrowed from the English bourgeoisie itself. Disciples of English schools of political philosophy and admirers of British constitutionalism, the pioneers of the Indian national movement could not question the legitimacy and authority of the government established and carried on in the name of that greatest constitutional democratic body, — the British Parliament. Their contention was that the Government of India should live up the doctrines of popular representation, the cornerstone of all bourgeois political structures.

The agitation for giving the British government of India a representative character was obviously based on the theory of nationhood inherent in the people. A central state had been established uniting the peoples of India in one political entity, which awakened in the liberal intellectual the vision of an Indian nation desiring to be represented in the administration of its public affairs. This new nationalism was not founded on the old traditions nor cultural unity of the Indian people. It was a political conception having for its object the establishment of a bourgeois national state. The idea of the political nationhood of the people led the intellectual democrats to think that they were their popular representatives, and as such had the right to be included in the government of the country. Their former docile admiration for the British government gradually changed into criticism,"loyal opposition". Such was the origin and evolution of the political movement in the 70's and early 80's.

The intellectuals trained in modern political thoughts laid down the theoretical foundation for the nationalism which was still to come, but the dynamic cause behind the movement was the economic revival of the native middle-class, after more than a hundred years of repression. The years following the revolt of 1857 were marked by a policy of reconciliation on the part of the British government. The modernized intellectuals and the progressive trading-class, which rendered valuable services in the critical days of the Mutiny, were patronized to some extent. The former, engaged in liberal professions and public administration, grew rich, while the latter was also becoming prosperous on account of the thriving internal trade, whose volume increased in proportion to the import of manufactured commodities and export of raw materials Considerable wealth was accumulated in the hands of both these elements, and consequently the desire for economic expansion was felt. The number of English-educated young men was rapidly growing. The liberal professions were becoming over-crowded. The government could not employ very many of these young men in higher posts without running the risk of losing control of the public administration. The native capitalist class could not be allowed to enter the industrial field without violating the imperialist monopoly.

Economic disablities created the necessity for political revolution. The time came when the most powerful elements of the Indian population felt their ambitions restricted by the foreign government. Intellectuals found the doors to the higher administrative positions closed to them; and the industrial expansion of the capitalist middle-class also met resistence from the government. The political movement was initiated by the former, armed with the doctrines of representative government learnt from English authorities, and was subsequently reinforced by the latter. Although the dynamic force of the movement against foreign rule is to be primarily looked for in the revival of the native capitalist-class, the formulation of the philosophy of Indian nationhood must be attributed to the liberal intellectuals, who are usually scorned by the orthodox nationalists as "de-nationalized patriots". Opposition to the British government could not be put up otherwise than in the name of the nation. A common school of education united the intellectuals on a common field of activities in order to realize the same aspirations. They began the struggle in the name of the people of India as a political unit which they claimed to represent, and whose national interest they pretended to defend. Thus, the forerunners of Indian nationalism, who were as much divorced from the national life and tradition, culturally and ideologically, as the English rulers themselves, assumed the role of popular representatives.

The fathers of Indian nationalism could be called rather constitutional democrats and reformers than nationalists. They believed more in English political ethics than in the social and cultural teachings of their forefathers. Their cult was not of nationalism, but of representative government. Unlike the progenitors of the European bourgeoisie, they were not evolving the doctrines of a new state based on new social relations. Socially they were revolutionaries, while politically they were but reformers, because the political revolution with the object of building a bourgeois state on the ruins of feudalism, had been accomplished in the form of the British conquest. Therefore their political struggle consisted in pointing out that the British Indian government did not comply with all the teachings of the prophets of the English school of constitutional liberalism. They constituted an opposition,—but a "loyal" opposition, to the policy of maintaining a strict British monopoly on the administration of the country. Their class instinct made them conform with the established government, so long as it was controlled by the bourgeoisie, nationality making no difference. They were not against the fundamentals of the bourgeois philosophy of state. They were convinced that any other form of state would not be compatible with their progressive social ideals, which were antagonistic to native traditions of feudal autocracy, absolute monarchy, religious reaction and patriarchal conservatism. They implicitly believed with their English preceptors, that the progress of the people, the civilization of the nation, would be realized under the protection of an enlightened government. But such a form of government could not be evolved from the contemporary Indian society, in which the educated, progressive and propertied middle-class still remained an almost negligible factor. Therefore they accepted the political institutions introduced by the British bourgeois imperialist as the best that the country had had till then. But according to the doctrines of bourgeois democracy, which were supposed to be the guiding principles of British rule, these institutions should be representative. An enlightened modern government should draw its authority from the people, in whose name it must rule. The government of India should be representative of the people; it must become a democratic institution by including the progressive intellectuals in its structure. Here in this demand, if it could be called a demand in those days, lay the germ of the idea of nationhood developed later on in accordance with the growth of the native middle-class.

Behind this demand for representative government, which looked like academic discussions indulged in by young intellectual visionaries, lurked the urges of economic interest which eventually supplied the motive-power of the national movement. So far, in return for the peace and order which it undoubtedly established, the British government in India had kept the natives excluded from the domain of political and military authority, in order to secure for the imperialist bourgeoisie a position of great privilege in the field of economic exploitation. Permitting the dissemination of modern education, which awakened the Indian intelligencia to a new political vision, had not in any way changed the policy of the British government, formulated as far back as 1833 in these words of the then Governor-General: "our very existence depends upon the exclusion of the native from military and political power". Ruthless economic exploitation, aided by the policy of obstructing industrial development through native capitalist enterprise had prevented the rise of a class which might contest this monopoly. In its earlier generations, the modern intelligencia did not constitute a political factor; on the contrary, it served the purposes of the imperialist bourgeoisie by denouncing the native social and religious institutions as well as political backwardness. This attitude of the most enlightened and progressive element of her people was used by the imperialists to prove that India could not govern herself and needed the protection of a civilized nation. But the growth of a middle-class, notwithstanding all obstacles, changed the attitude of the intelligencia, which retaining still its admiration for and faith in British constitutionalism, began to agitate for representative institutions. The representation sought for was evidently in the interests of the middle-class. The claim was that the government of the country should not overlook the aspirations of the propertied and intellectual middle-class, in order to be recognised as the best political institution for the country. The spiritual vanguard of the modern bourgeoisie, that is, the Western-educated intelligencia, was the first to register its claim, joined subsequently by its capitalist colleague. The intellectuals wanted to be admitted to the higher administrative positions as representatives of the governed, and later on this program of administrative reform was supplemented by the demand for fiscal autonomy, which voiced the aspiration of the nascent native capitalist-class.

The expression of the aspiration of a social class with identical economic interests but still in its infancy, was clothed in the language of the democratic scriptures of "National Will", "Sovereign Prerogative of the People" etc. The rise of the modern middle-class, capitalist as well as intellectual, marked the laying of the foundation of Indian nationalism in the political sense. In order to prove that, according to the principles of democracy, they were entitled to be parts of the government, the bourgeois intellectuals began to talk of the Indian people as a political unit whom they claimed to represent. Had not the forerunners of the Indian bourgeoisie been suffocated in the middle of the eighteenth century by historical accidents, they would have built, most prohably, several modern nations out of the mass of humanity living on the continent of India. A hundred and fifty years later began the renaissance of the Indian bourgeoisie, but under different circumstances. History had deprived it of the noble role of liberating the people from feudal serfdom, but its new mission was no less imposing and no more altruistic. It was to assume the leadership of the Indian people, united and led in the struggle for national-liberation, which would be achieved by replacing the foreign domination with the democratic dictatorship of the native bourgeoisie.

As soon as the young intelligentsia began to extend its activities to the political field, the British government found in it no longer a support, which it really had been, so long as it had occupied itself in attacks against native social and religious institutions. The British government was not slow in foreseeing the invitable. It could read a serious menace in the apparently tame and impotent agitation for representative institutions and an "open door" to the public services. The demand for popular representation, however mild at first, heralded the appearance of a class which would sooner or later dispute the political supremacy of the British, and would do so in the name of the people united into a nation, demanding autonomy and democratic government.

In the years preceding the organization of the Indian National Congress in 1885, the industrial aspirations of the native capitalist class had been expressed in the growing number of modern factories, which however, could not thrive on account of the competition of imperialist capital, as well as the determined hostility of the Indian government. It was imminent that the intellectuals with political education would constitute a revolutionary factor, by agitating for the interests and grievances of their own class, as well as those of the struggling capitalists. The causes for a potential political movement had been accumulating, and the very disciples of English liberalism were going to put themselves at the head of this movement. The National Congress was founded with the object of ventilating "popular grievances" and formulating "national aspirations",—in other words, to forward the grievances of the intellectuals who craved for higher positions, and the aspirations of the capitalist-class to enter the industrial field. But the real sponsors of the Congress were not Indian nationalists, conscious of the full significance of what they were initiating, but a few patriotic English liberals, who were disturbed by the ominous clouds gathering in the political sky. The unfilled aspirations of the young intellectuals, backed by the nascent capitalist-class, could be very well expected to turn into dissatisfaction, which might lead to developments more dangerous when too late to control the situation. A retired British official (A. O. Hume) of Gladstonian creed, who is called the Father of the Indian National Congress, called the attention of the government to the unrest of the „masses" of India caused by the increasing alienation of the educated natives from the administration of the country. In helping the young liberal intellectuals organize the National Congress, Hume expected to provide them with a glittering toy so that they could be kept out of harm's length. He seemed to have impressed on the then Viceroy, Lord Dufferin, the policy of conferring on the Congress the official benediction, with the object of making it assume the role of "Her Majesty's Opposition" at home. But one cannot conspire against history. Social forces cannot be deceived, not even by the cleverness of imperial liberalism. Subjectively disciples and admirers of British Constitutionalism, the Indian intellectuals objectively were the defenders of the interests of the rising native bourgeoisie, the standard-bearers of nationalism. Therefore it was not long before the Indian followers of John Bright turned traitors to their political preceptors and became rank protectionists.

The first session of the Indian National Congress was celebrated in Bombay (1885), which was then the main industrial centre of the country, under the presidency of W. C. Banerji, a prosperous lawyer. The tame character of the first Congress can be well judged from the fact that the English governor of the Province was requested to take the chair, and that it emphatically declared its loyalty to the Crown. The principal resolutions contained 1. the demand for the appointment of a Royal Commission on which the "people of India" should be represented, to enquire into the composition of public services and 2. the request for the expansion of the Legislative Council. So it is evident that it was only the grievances and claims of the intelligencia which the Congress consciously focussed. The economic interests of the bourgeoisie still remained an unseen force behind the scene.

But it was not long before the Congress took such a turn that its official and semi-official patrons had to lament their judgment. It was soon looked upon as a seditious body trying to create disaffection; because in spite of protestations of loyalty to British rule, it demanded the recognition of the "living forces of elective principles" which, it contended, could not be realised without "representative institutions". The Government of India made some efforts to retain the loyal support of the intelligencia. The Local Government Act of 1888 made some concession in the municipal administration and the Indian Councils Act passed by the British Parliament in 1892, declared that the Government of India should rely more on the experience and advice of responsible Indians. These were evidently attempts to convince the Congress that the British Government was not a negation of the principles of democracy. But the political consciousness of the Indian liberal intellectual had outgrown the stage of apprenticeship. The demand was "not for Consultative Councils, but for representative institutions".

Although it represented the interests and expressed the grievances of the most advanced section of the Indian people, politically the Congress retained its reformist tendency. Education, constitutional convictions and above all, instinctive class-affililiation prevented the Congress leaders from questioning the "benefits" of British rule. All they desired was that the government should become representative by including them in its organism. They could not possibly conceive of the idea of national independence, because their social position did not enable them to go to such an extent. Administrative reform to be achieved by constitutional means, therefore, remained their program. The political ideal of the Congress in its earlier years is best typified in the following quotation from the speech made at its second annual session in 1886 by Madan Mohan Malavya, today a radical nationalist demanding nothing less than complete self-government:

"It is not to the great British government that we should demonstrate the utility, the expediency, the necessity of representative institutions: it is surely uncessary to say one word in support of such a cause to the British nation — the descendants of these great and brave men who fought and died to obtain for themselves, and to preserve intact for their children, these very institutions, which, taught by their example, we now crave. What is an Englishman without representative institutions? Why, not an Englishmen at all, a mere sham, a base imitation, and I often wonder, when I look around our nominally English magnates, how they have the face to call themselves Englishmen, and yet deny us representative institutions, and struggle to maintain despotic ones. Representative institutions are as much a part of the true Briton as his language and literature".

This passionate admiration was, indeed, not for the British government as such, neither did it signify "de-nationalization", because the man who pronounced the words is still a partisan of Hindu culture and has been one all through his long public career; it was fomented by the spontaneous enthusiam for certain ideals held sacred by the liberal bourgeoisie of all countries. Democratic government is the political reflex of bourgeois society. Therefore it was but natural that the pioneers of the Indian bourgeoisie would hail enthusiastically the doctrines of democracy. In its earlier years, the ideal of the Congress was not a national government, but a democtratic government, by which was meant that the civil administration of the country should be entrusted to the liberal intellectuals,—the forebears of a new social order.

The political reformism of the Congress was unavoidable. Its leaders were the pioneers of a national renaissance. They dreamt of an India marching in the path of social progress and economic evolution under the guidance of a government infused with the spirit of bourgeois liberalism. To them, absence of British rule signified the active revival of the forces of reaction in every aspect of life, political, social and religious. Therefore radical nationalism, having for its object the subversion of the British domination, could not be the program of the Congress, not only because it was an impossibility, but such an idea could not be entertained by the liberal intellectuals. Radical or extremist nationalism in those days, could not but be based on reactionary forces, whose success would entail a political retrogression to a monarchical state and the reinforcement of social and religious conservatism which such a political setback would surely bring about. The forces which would make for the overthrow of the foreign bourgeoisie without at the time threatening a social reaction, were yet in the process of evolution. The political reformism of the Congress was augmented by these revolutionary forces accumulating behind the scene. Revolutionary nationalism,—nationalism which does not stand for social and political reaction,—could not be evolved before the liberal bourgeoisie had acquired sufficient strength. The national liberation of India, which would put her people on the road to moral and material progress, is not to be realised by political movements with orthodox reactionary ideology. This is the mission of the progressive bourgeoisie, and those spiritual pioneers of the rising progressive bourgeoisie, the liberal intellectuals assembled in the first sessions of the National Congress, heralded the birth of a new India. Historically they were revolutionaries. They rebelled against two mighty forces, viz, those of social conservatism and religious superstition still dominating the Indian society, and the absolute political monopoly exercised by the foreign bourgeoisie.

The revolutionary role of these men becomes more apparent when we turn to their social tendencies. A man of the type of Mahadeva Govinda Ranade, whose patriotism has always been unimpeachable and whose personality stands as a landmark of the political renaissance of India, worked with the firm conviction that the progress of the India people depended on a radical readjustment. The patriotism of Ranade and his co-workers was revolutionary, in as much as it recognized the banefulness of the old religious corruptions and social customs and boldly declared war on them. It would be a serious mistake to call those brave men servile imitators, an epithet often ascribed to them by the adherents of orthodox nationalism, which originated as a reaction against the social radicalism of the Congress. If the fathers of the Congress devoted more time and energy to the discussion of social questions than to the agitation for a popular franchise, it was because they were the embodiment of a revolutionary force which was eating into the vitals of the old order, doomed to destruction. By bravely condemning the old they voiced the judgment of history, and indicated that the forces of native reaction were more detrimental to popular progress than the political domination of a foreign bourgeoisie. Based on social foundations of a higher order, the British power was not to be shaken till the people of India would be stirred up by progressive ideals. New social relations bring about new political institutions. This law determined the psychology of the Indian intellectuals. A national state conducive to the growth of the bourgeoisie could not be expected to be built on the foundation of a social organism still greatly dominated by feudal traditions, patriarchal conservatism and religious superstition. These obstacles must be removed before India could be reborn to a new life. By declaring their desire to struggle on against time-honored customs and institutions, those men proved themselves to be the vanguard of a social revolution to be carried through, not by the reformistic measures advocated by them, but by the imminent rise of the native bourgeoisie as the leader of the new society.

In its earlier days the social significance of the Congress outweighed its political role. Its program of social reform was not actuated, as is generally believed, by the "de-nationalizing" Western education of its leaders. None but a rank jingoist discriminates against knowledge on racial or national grounds. In course of its continuous evolution, the human race passes through various stages, which are everywhere marked by corresponding social ideologies and institutions. The simple accident of being born in diverse countries does not make of the various human communities isolated units, with different paths marked out for each. To discriminate against certain branches and kinds of human knowledge as outlandish and therefore to be looked upon with suspicion and as injurious is not a sign of healthy nationalism. One must not be ashamed to learn from the other when necessary. The period in which the European peoples made great progress in political social, economic and cultural fields, saw India infested with civil wars and thus unable to keep pace with the modern world. Foreign conquest kept her in stagnation another hundred years. Consequently it was but natural that, in the scale of material civilization the people of India lagged behind. Not to recognize this historical fact and to sublimate this backwardness by clothing it in the glorious garb of a "spiritual" civilization is the effort of reactionary forces. The so-called "aggressive" nationalism, which refuses to learn anything from others and hugs the old traditions, is a questionable phenomenon, as its tends to prefer ignorance to knowledge.

The ideals of bourgeois society and the doctrines of a democratic state, which are the foundation of the material civilization of the modern world, happened first to be evolved by the European peoples. Left alone and uninterfered with by foreign conquest,

India would have evolved political and social ideals of a similar nature. Because these are not the outcome of a particular European civilization, but are realised by every human community at a particular stage of economic progress. Foreign domination had been harmful to the Indian people, chiefly because it prevented their development and deprived them of the full benefit of these modern thoughts and institutions. If the foreigner could continue to dominate over India, it was because there did not exist in her population an element which tended to break down the old, in order to build a new social and political structure. The fact that the Indian intellectuals responded to the European social and political thoughts did not by any means betray slavishness; on the contrary, it proved that they were objectively revolutionary. Because these thoughts were not European,—a monopoly of the so-called Western peoples,—they were progressive ideals, and any one who would respond to them must have reached a stage of material development which spontaneously gives origin to such tendencies. Therefore Western education, instead of being a de-nationalizing factor, caused a national renaissance.

From the very beginning the Congress did not raise the standard of political revolution, but it did lay down the foundation on which the political nationalism of India was built subsequently. The demand for representative government challenged the right of the British rule in India, and established the theory that in the people was vested the sovereign authority. This was indeed a new departure in the political history of India. It not only questioned the legitimacy of the benevolent dictatorship of the British, but also signified opposition to that school of nationalism which in the name of freedom, would revive backward political institutions under native rulers. The program of the Congress remained one of "nation-building" till Tilak swept it with his doctrine of "integral nationalism" in the closing years of the nineteenth century. Tilak's was a revolt more against the ideology and tactics of the Old Guard of the Congress than against Government. His theory was that the nationalism of India should be nourished with the native traditions, and that the nationhood of the Indian people was an accomplished fact in view of their religio-cultural unity. We will deal with this phase of nationalism later on.

The Congress assumed the title „national" as if the bourgeoisie whom it represented, was ordained providentially to be the custodian of the popular welfare. The small number of government officials, merchants, manufacturers, progressive landlords and intellectual liberals constituting it, believed themselves to be natural and legitimate representatives of the inarticulate masses. The grievances of the office-seeking intellectuals were put forth as those of the people. The ambitions of the native capitalist class were identified with the right of the nation. In the Congress were crystallized and through it were expressed the social ideals and political aspirations of an element of the people, which in spite of its numerical smallness, was intellectually competent and materially fitted to advocate the theory that India was a national unit and as such, should have the rights and dignities of one. To this element, nationhood was a political conception, and the National Right of a people was to be asserted in the domain of material progress. The struggle against foreign Government was, therefore, in so far as it stood on the way of those sections of the people which were consciously feeling the urge of material advancement. This discontented class began to fight for its own benefit, but in order to prove that the foreign government was in the wrong, it must talk of national interest and popular representation. Thus the modern nationalism of India was based on the economic interest of the native bourgeoisie, and the program of securing the needed protection for the latter's development as a potential factor in social-economics, was taken for that of nation-building.

The program of "social reform" which had been given precedence over political demands in the first sessions of the Congress, was gradually abandoned. This was not because the men assembled therein had lost their radicalism on social questions, but because it began to dawn upon them that the old customs and traditions could not be shaken until material conditions helpful to their preservation, were changed. Or in other words, they instinctively felt that until and unless the economic basis of Indian society was revolutionized, no radical change could be introduced in the social domain by criticism of the past and adoration of the golden future. For example, the caste-system, which was a legitimate object of assault, could not be abolished by legislation, nor by agitation. Higher means of production, based on new property relations had to be evolved before it could be uprooted. Even such a program as the "uplift of the depressed classes" could not be realised, because educational facilities were not available from the foreign government and the native bourgeoisie was not in a position to tackle the problem without the backing of the state. Indian society could be freed from the galling bondage of religious superstitions only by the dissemination of scientific knowledge; but the foreign government would be safely seated in power only so long as the people could be kept in ignorance. Therefore public education, one of the boons of the bourgeois state, was withheld determinedly, and the liberal reformers with all their sincere zeal, could not do anything worth while to dissipate the ignorance of the people. Its enthusiastic program of social reform having been thus rendered futile and not to be realised, under the contemporary economic and political conditions, the Congress became a purely political body, given to the struggle for administrative and fiscal reforms. Its demand was to "Indianize" the public services by giving more employment to the native intellectuals, and protection to the nascent indigenous industrial enterprises.

If the Indian adepts of English liberalism dared question the justice and beneficence of the doctrine of Free Trade, it was not that their faith in the bourgeois political philosophy had in any way been shaken, but because of the growth of an economic force which stood behind and determined their political ideology and activities. The modernized middle-class, led by the liberal intelligencia had entered the political arena. But its political struggle would remain impotent till sufficient economic power was acquired. Therefore the slogan of the national movement was the "development of home industries", which meant the strengthening of the native capitalist class. The political nationalism inaugurated by the Congress thus promised to become a bitter struggle between the two capitalist classes,—the native and the imperialist. The former sanctified its cause by christening it "national", while the latter claimed to be ruling India for the welfare of her people. The struggle between the two elements of the same social character however, could not break out into open hostility owing to the fact that one controlled the state power of a mighty capitalist empire, while the other was still in its infancy economically, and socially its leadership of an oppressed nation was but theoretical. It did not make any difference to the masses of the people, unquestionably oppressed by foreign capitalism, by whom they were exploited. National consciousness in the political sense, awakened in the bourgeoisie, was not to be found in the people. Under such circumstances, the struggle could not be anything but "legal" and "constitutional", as the Congress termed its agitation.

The aspirations of the intellectual and propertied middle-class were pressed with all the sanction of the precepts learned from English political seers. The tactics seemed to be to beat the British bourgeoisie with its own arguments. But already in the closing years of the century not much illusion was left. Newspapers voicing the sentiment of the Congress wrote in this strain: "as there can be no revival of the Indian industry without some displacement of British industry, we understand the difficulty of ruling India for the people of India". With the growth of this spirit of mistrust in the liberalism of the English bourgeoisie was brought to a close the first period of the modern political movement, which unquestionably laid the theoretical foundation of the struggle for national liberation, but did not exceed the bounds of constitutional agitation for democracy.

The period that followed was apparently more revolutionary, because its guiding principle was a challenge to the authority of a foreign power ruling another nation. Even the possibility of recognizing this authority, when democratized by including the available native element in it, was not admitted. But in socio-political significance this new phase was less revolutionary than the former, because its theory of "integral nationalism" when put to practice would push the country into a backward stage of development in spite of national independence. Youthful impatience and unseen forces of reactionary conservatism, brought about the apparently revolutionary violent outbursts which were the characteristics of this phase of the movement. And in these very causes lay its inherent weakness. But its unmixed influence was but of short duration, because in order to be potential, the interests of the rising industrial capital had to be made the motive force of the movement, which nevertheless, retained its orthodox and religious phraseology.

The new movement was not only a reaction against the political impotency of the Congress. Fundamentally it embodied the revolt of the spirit of orthodoxy and conservatism against the social radicalism of the prominent Congress leaders, particularly of Ranade in Bombay and Telang in Madras.. Himself a young intellectual, educated according to the so-called de-nationalizing Western methods, and a disciple of Ranade, the leader of the new movement was Bal Gangadhar Tilak, who started his career as an enthusiastic worker in the field of social and educational reform. In the 90's, tendencies of religious reform were being expressed as if to counteract the wave of radicalism headed by the modernized intelligencia. These tendencies took organized form in the "Arya Somaj" in the north and the "Ramkrishna Mission" in Bengal. The object was the rejuvenation of the teachings of Hinduism in order to make them compatible with the psychology created by modern education. But in fact, it was the resistence of the forces of conservatism and reaction trying to adapt themselves to the new environments. The glaring social corruptions and stifling religious superstitions could not be overlooked, even by the stoutest admirers of the spiritual civilization of the Aryans. The best that could be done and was done by those elements, which constituted the bulwark of the old, was to lay the blame on the degeneration brought about by time. The pristine purity of the original doctrines was vigorously upheld. And a national revival was advocated with the slogan of "back to the Vedas" which even in the present moment finds an apostle in Gandhi. The new movement headed by Tilak perhaps unconsciously transplanted into the political field this tendency of looking backward, in order to find inspiration for a forward march.

The advanced social views of its leaders had naturally kept the activities of the Congress confined within a narrow circle of rich intellectuals and liberal bourgeoisie. The great majority of the population was left entirely outside its influence. The material and intellectual condition of the masses had not changed in response to the political postulates and the social radicalism of the men assembled in the Congress, which therefore, failed to enlist any large following. The far-sightedness of its constructive program was not understood by the youthful elements, which had more reason to be dissatisfied with the British government. There was a great unemployment among the lower middle-class to which these youthful elements belonged. They were mostly students, many more of whom were annually graduating from the schools and universities than could be absorbed in the government services or the liberal professions open to them. The students in the colleges looked ahead in their life and found all roads to prosperity and distinction blocked. New education, new environments of the modern cities had aroused new ideas, new aspirations in them.

Economic desperation drove them to an extreme, one way or the other. The majority succumbed in the struggle, turning into semi-proletarianized petty intellectuals submerged in degenerating apathy, devoid of all social and political vision. A small number rebelled. But not having considerable incomes from government service, or profitable professions, or trade or industry or landed property or several of them combined, as was the case with the members of the Congress, the rebellious elements of the lower middle-class found no consolation in the idle deliberations and program of gradual reform of the Congress. They wanted to have an immediate change and a radical one at that. Constitutionalism did not appeal to them. They were driven to violence which however, proved futile to lead them anywhere.

The satisfied members of the lower middle-class jeered at the Congress, because the redress of their grievances was not included in its program, which advocated the interests only of those who were already in a relatively better position than themselves. It demanded more positions for those who were already well posted in comparism with the lower middle-class youths, whose university degrees hardly enabled them to keep starvation off their doorsteps. The demand for protection of the native industries was calculated to help the rich become richer. In short, the petite bourgeoisie found itself left out of the scheme of national advancement put forth by the rich intellectuals and capitalists assembled in the Congress, which however, had repeatedly held British exploitation responsible for the economic backwardness and bankruptcy of the Indian people. Having learned from the Congress leaders that foreign exploitation was the root of all the economic suffering of the people, the lower middle-class youths revolted against the tactics of their political preceptors. The rational economic theory of the Congress that India was poor because she was kept in an agrarian stage in an industrial age, was not appreciated by the impatient youths, who argued that nothing could be achieved unless political autonomy was realised and that it was not to be gained by prayer and petitions. As leader of this point of view, Tilak vigorously assailed what he called the "piece meal" policy of the Congress, and put forward his program of "integral nationalism" which meant to say that the nationhood of the Indian people was an historically accomplished fact, and that its right to self-government was not conditional upon any preliminary evolution, either social or economic. This challenge to the older leaders rallied the discontented and rebellious lower middle-class youths aroound Tilak.

But to have condemned the old policy as impotent was not enough. It still remained for Tilak and his followers to find the force with which their "integral nationalism" could be rendered more effective. If the old leaders had failed to make the Indian people appreciate the philosophies of Bentham and the Mills, neither could the "Duties of Man" as depicted by Mazzini nor the "Social Contract" of Jean Jaques Rousseau make any better impression, the patriotic efforts of Tilak notwithstanding. The people of India, excepting the small circle of the middle-class, were not materially fitted to respond to one or the other. The forces that could unite them in a fight for political independence had not yet fully developed. In the bourgeoisie was to be found the force, but the bourgeoisie could not be politically powerful until it should have reached a certain stage of economic advancement. By advocating the growth of the bourgeoisie, the Congress stood at the vanguard of the objectively revolutionary force. The theory of nationalism expressed in the person and preachings of Tilak, ignored the social law that political nationalism in modern times could not exist without an economic foundation. The task of creating a modern nation out of a people in a backward stage of social progress belongs to the middle-class, which under normal conditions, leads the struggle against feudal autocracy. In India this struggle happened to be against a foreign ruler which had largely destroyed feudalism as a factor of social-economics, but the exploitation of imperialist capital had prevented the people from outgrowing the social and economic order that prevails under patriarchy and feudalism. However, divested of idealistic verbiage, both the socio-political formulas, viz, Liberation from Serfdom and National Independence, make for the economic aggrandisement of the middle-class. In the first case, the evolution of higher means of production necessitates the mobilization of wage-earners freed from the feudal yoke, in order that they can sell their labor-power in the open market of capitalist competition; and the second signifies the installation of the native bourgeoisie in the political power so that it can carry on freely the exploitation of the manpower and the natural resources of the nation. Therefore the political nationhood of a people is conditional upon the rise of the bourgeoisie; and the economic evolution which makes the bourgeoisie a paramount factor in the society, destroys all old social institutions of a feudal and patriarchal character.

Indian Nationalism, indifferent to or scornful of the steps necessary for the development of the bourgeoisie, was therefore, not more revolutionary, but was actuated by forces of social and religious reaction against the progressive tendencies of the Congress, which focussed the ideology of the coming society. The reactionary forces contributing to the doctrines of "integral nationalism" stood revealed, when Tilak declared that Indian nationalism could not be purely secular, that it must be based on Hindu orthodoxy. In its earlier days, orthodox nationalism assailed the Congress more for its social radicalism and religious heresy than for its reformistic political program. A national independence, which would push Indian society back to Hindu orthodoxy, was indeed not a very revolutionary ideal. If material welfare should be sacrified for things spiritual, then why should the people be asked to fight for political independence which, after all, is a secular matter? Hindu religion had not been violated by the British conquerors; so it was not necessary to defend it. On the contrary, the British government had always been very anxious to insure the perpetuation of the religious superstitions and beliefs which kept the people in blissful ignorance, resigned to their lot however hard, as ordained by a super-human power. Advocates of Hindu orthodoxy consciously or unconsciously desired to keep the people in the darkness of ignorance and submission.

When we remember that Tilak parted ways with his preceptor on account of the controversy over the Age of Consent Bill of 1891, the social tendencies behind his political theories become palpable. His fierce and bold criticism of the Bill, brought him before the public eye as a stout defender of Hindu orthodoxy. The Age of Consent Bill proposed to increase the age limit to twelve instead of ten when a girls consent to her marriage would be legally valid. Being intended for reforming the custom of child marriage, which had given origin to unspeakable abuses, this measure enlisted the sympathy and support of the liberal intellectuals of the Congress. Tilak's argument was that the foreign government should not be allowed to interfere in the social institutions. He entered the political arena as the champion of orthodox nationalism as against the "de-nationalizing patriotism" of the Congress leaders, and sought to unite the people in a fight for the defence of national religion and culture. He put forward the theory of "integral nationalism" because the evolutionary nationalism of the Congress was calculated to disrupt the national life. He demanded that on the strength of her old glories and traditions, India should have self-government at once in order that her national heritage of religious orthodoxy, social conservatism and patient resignation to earthly suffering for the sake of spiritual uplift, might not be defiled by the rise of a progressive social force.

The movement of national renaissance inaugurated by the Congress, which in its earlier years was but the spiritual reflection of the social forces most revolutionary at that period, threatened to be more destructive to the reactionary elements than had been the British government. The constitutional democracy or evolutionary nationalism advocated by the liberal bourgeoisie led by the intellectuals, spelled doom to the old social heritage and religious orthodoxy. Orthodox nationalism was and still is more of a spontaneous reaction of the moribund old order against this progressive force, than a revolutionary struggle against foreign rule. In fact, the British government had always been rather friendly disposed towards the reactionary forces as expressed by religious orthodoxy and social conservatism, and those elements of the population which actively focussed these reactionary tendencies had always been the mainstay of the foreign domination. The British government, in spite of being a bourgeois institution, patronized the reactionary tendencies because, by keeping the people ignorance on the pretext of spiritual uplift, these proved themselves greatly helpful to the former. The memorable Queen's Proclamation of 1858 and other protestations made solemnly on various occasions, assured the native reactionary forces of a free hand in the field of social and religious exploitation. This being the case, it is to be deduced that orthodox nationalism, which sought for political power in order to preserve the ancient culture and save the purity of religion, was a revolt primarily against the native forces making for the disruption of these cherished treasures of the past. And these revolutionary forces were crystallizing in the Congress under radical leaders, whose program was not to revive the India of the Rishis (patriarchal sages) with its contented handicraft workers saturated with ignorance and dosed in the name of religion, but to build a new society on the ruins of the old. Orthodox nationalism, in the social sense, was the resistence of the forces of reaction against the ominous radicalism of the "de-nationalized" intellectuals who led the Congress. The same forces, whose military explosion was the Mutiny of 1857, could be discovered behind the political theories of the orthodox nationalism of half a century later.

National Social Conferences had been held annually ever since 1887, in spite of the opposition of the conservative elements which found their way into the Congress. The growth of orthodox nationalism strengthened the latter, whose point of view on the question of social reform was thus formulated in the Congress of 1895:

"The raison d'être for excluding social question from the deliberations of the Congress, is that if it were to take up such questions, it might lead to serious differences, ultimately culminating in a schism, and it is a matter of first importance to avoid a split".

The position of the radicals, on the other hand, was put forth by their leader Ranadé, who held that the political movement of a people could not be separated from its social problems. In 1900, Ranadé said "you cannot have a good social system when you find yourself low in the scale of political right, nor can you be fit to exercise political rights and privileges unless your social system is based upon reason and justice". Here is raised the sanctimonious voice of a petty bourgeois moralist. The intricate social problems of India, with their roots struck deep in the traditions of the hoary past, could not be solved by the reformism of a moralist. But the "reason and justice" of a bourgeois intellectual, whose sincerity, by the way, is not to be questioned, were not hollow words. They were based upon an imperious force which would bring about in time a new society based upon a new code of ethics. They meant to say "you can not make the people at large a conscious political unit so long as you are for keeping learning a monopoly of the Brahman oligarchy; you cannot unite the people in a struggle for political advancement so long as you tell them to sacrifice material things for a spiritual life: you cannot make the people fight for national independence or democratic government, which will put you in power, unless you tell them that the future will be better than the present; you cannot expect the people to move forward carrying you to power on their shoulders, unless you free them from the influences of feudal and patriarchal customs, which are hostile to the modern political concepts". These words meant all this and many more revolutionary doctrines preached by the bourgeoisie of all countries in a particular stage of social development. It is nevertheless true that society based on the „reason and justice" of the bourgeois libertarians, does not end, but intensifies the exploitation of the majority by the minority. Only then does it become naked, shorn of all the religious and spiritual hypocracies which kept the people in ignorance, resigned to their slavery. In bourgeois society, the sting of exploitation is felt by the masses directly and the reaction against it is eventually provoked. That is, the people consciously begin their march on the road to progress and emancipation. The justice and reason of a bourgeois libertarian are the spiritual expression of a rising social force, which breaks up the decayed and stifling old order and plunges society into a bitter struggle which exacts torrents of tears and rivers of blood. Patient suffering comes to an end, and the stagnation of the ignorant becomes a struggle of the awakened. This is a movement forward, and the radical nationalism of the Congress stood, though unconsciously, for this revolutionary forward movement. Consequently, it was a sworn enemy of the forces of reaction, still strong under the fostering care of the British government. Orthodox nationalism was the political outburst of these dying forces of reaction.

The problematical realization of the program of "aggressive nationalism" depended on the political potentiality of these forces of reaction and conservatism. The aggressive exponents of orthodox nationalism, including Tilak himself, invoked the teachings of the Hindu scriptures and philosophy to serve the purpose of a modern political movement. It was an impossible task fraught with grave danger. For example, the Anti-Cow-Killing Society, founded by Tilak obviously as an instrument of political agitation, soon degenerated, as was to be expected, into an organ of extreme religious orthodoxy. He delved into history to find inspiration for the present and thought to produce a magnetic charm in the personality of the Marhatta hero Sivaji. Festivals to celebrate Sivaji's birth-day were organized and stirring speeches were made in the name of religion, which was supposed to be defiled by the foreign rule. The orthodox spirit of "aggressive nationalism" crystallized in the formation of such organizations as the "Society for the removal of obstacles to Hindu religion".

The very name speaks for the nature and social tendency of such organizations.

Orthodox nationalism, however, remained impotent in the field of practical politics. It thrived in the secret revolutionary societies somposed of a small number of discontented middle-class youths. Orthodox nationalism, which rallies all the forces of reaction under its banner, may temporarily appeal to the imagination of the ignorant people, but never can be of any permanent strength. Because the national liberation of a people from capitalist domination, such as the British government is, can be achieved only by the development of progressive forces objectively revolutionary. Modern political nationalism is a progressive movement, therefore its motive force cannot be found in religious orthodoxy and social conservatism. This social law was vindicated when the orthodox element in the national movement, subsequently organized as the Extremist wing of the Congress, had to take the cue from the evolutionary radical leaders on the stage of pragmatic politics.

In spite of its orthodoxy and the desire for reviving the golden days of yore, the Extremist Party became a political force only when it came to the conclusion that the real fight had to take place on the economic field. Aggressive nationalists proved themselves more revolutionary than the old constitutionalist leaders when their aggressiveness was brought to bear upon the tactics, not of social reform, but of the best and most effective way to foment the growth of the native bourgeoisie. It criticised those who believed that the government would ever concede protection to Indian industries. Swadeshi (to encourage the use of indigenous articles) and Boycott of foreign goods were put forward as the best means of helping the development of national industries. The evolutionary radicals, who were called Moderates, accepted the program of Swadeshi and Boycott which, however, proved to be premature in practice.

This doubtful tactical triumph of the Extremists was gained when they recognized the necessity of giving predominance to material questions. By adopting the program of Swadeshi and Boycott they repudiated their own principles and abandoned their original orthodox ideal. Because these measures were resorted to with the object of helping the growth of native industries, that is, for strengthening the national bourgeoisie, which by its very nature, was an irreconcilable enemy of the old traditions and established social institutions based on orthodoxy. The prospective rise of a modern bourgeoisie heralded such a revolution in the economic foundation of Indian society, that the national heritage of spiritual culture and religious beliefs, the defence and glorification of which was the motive force of orthodox nationalism, would become untenable. The reborn Indian nation would outgrow them, and its fight would be for progress still further ahead.

The political ascendency of the Extremist Party forced the National Congress to adopt the program of Swadeshi in its twenty-first session held at Benares (1906), and of boycotting British goods the next year. The triumph was the more remarkable because the Congress gave up its former policy of agitating the government and accepted the Extremist point of view under the presidency of two of its most outstanding veterans, who had been staunch believers in constitutionalism and evolutionary progress both in the economic and political fields. Gopal Krishna Gokhale, the great political opponent of Tilak, launched the program of Swadeshi, which had already been adopted in Calcutta under the leadership of Bepin Chandra Pal, as an answer to the Partition of the Province of Bengal. So long as orthodox nationalism had desired to prove itself more revolutionary by its religious fervour and social conservatism, the Marhatta country in the Province of Bombay remained its stronghold, and Tilak its greatest expounder. But its political strength, expressed in the form of the Extremist Party, was first felt in the Province of Bengal under the leadership of Bepin Chandra Pal and Arabinda Ghose, both of whom were men of modern education and keen intellect.

It had been long since the British government looked for some pretext in order to nullify the Permanent Settlement of Bengal, which had created and perpetuated a rich landholding class. The necessity for having such a privileged class, to the detriment of the public exchequer, had ceased to exist. The government of Lord Curzon divided the Province of Bengal into two parts in 1905. The object was twofold. First, to nullify the Permanent Settlement and second, to foment the ill -feeling between the Hindus and Mohamedans. The first object would to achieved by ordering a new settlement of land in both the new provinces, which were so constituted territorially as to include areas Regulated and

Non-regulated under the Permanent Settlement. The second object was to be realized by creating an overwhelming Hindu majority in one and Moslem majority in the other province. Such a distribution of the population would enable the government to play the one community against the other, on the pretext of protecting the minority.

Religious nationalism of the orthodox as well as reformed school had begun to come into evidence in the province of Bengal since the first years of the twentieth century. Although its political philosopher and leader were found subsequently in the persons of Arabinda Ghose and Bepin Chabdra Pal respectively, its fundamental ideology was conceived by a young intellectual of petit bourgeois origin. He was Narendra Nath Dutta, subsequently known by the religious nomenclature of Swami Vivekanada. While still a student in the University of Calcutta, Dutta felt the rebellious spirit affecting the lower middle class intellectuals. It was in the early nineties. He was moved by the sufferings of the common people. De-classed socially, possessing a keen intellect, he made a spectacular plunge into the philosophical depths of Hindu scripture and discovered in his cult of Vedantism (religious Monism of the Hindus) a sort of socialistic, humanitarian religion. He decried scathingly orthodoxy in religion as well as in social customs. He was the picturesque, and tremendously vigorous embodiment of the old trying to readjust itself to the new. Like Bal Gangadhar Tilak, Dutta was also a prophet of Hindu nationalism. He also was a firm believer in the cultural superiority of the Indian people, and held that on this cultural basis should be built the future Indian nation. But he was not a partisan of orthodoxy in religion: to social conservatism, he was a veritable iconoclast. He had the couragous foresight, or perhaps instinct, which convinced him that if religion was to be saved, it must be given a modern garb; if the priest was still to hold his sway over the millions of Hindu believers, he must modify his old crude ways; if the intellectual aristocracy of the fortunate few was to retain its social predominance, spiritual knowledge must be democratized. The reaction of native culture against the intrusion of Western education ran wild, so to say, in the person of Vivekananda and the cult of Universal Religion he formulated in the name of his preceptor, Ramkrishna Paramahansa. He preached that Hinduism, not Indian nationalism, should be aggressive. His nationalism was a spiritual imperialism. He called on Young India to believe in the spiritual mission of India. The following quotation from his voluminous writings and speeches can be taken as the fundaments of his philosophy, on which was subsequently built the orthodox nationalism of the de-classed young intellectuals, organized into secret societies advocating violence and terrorism for the overthrow of British rule. Vivekananda said:

"Materialism and all its miseries cannot be conquered by materialism. Armies, when they attempt to conquer armies, only multiply and make brutes of humanity. ..... Spirituality must conquer the West. Now is the time to work for India's spiritual ideals penetrating deep into the West. We must go out. We must conquer the world through our spirituality and philosophy. We must do it or die. The condition of Indian national life, of unashamed and vigorous national life, is the conquest of the world by Indian thought."

This romantic vision of conquering the world by spiritual superiority electrified the young intellectuals, whose desperate economic position made them restive. Victims of the existing order, they were rebelling against it and would destroy it, if possible. The British domination stood in the way as the root of all evils. Thus, an intelligently rebellious element, which otherwise would have been the vanguard of the exploited class in a social struggle, had to give in to national pre-occupations, and contribute itself to a movement for the immediate overthrow of foreign rule, not for progress forward, but in order to go back to an imaginary golden age — the fountain-head of India's spiritual heritage. This youthful band of rebels' fanatically believing in the spiritual mission of their Motherland, embodied in themselves the clash of two forces; that of Reaction inducing them to put their nationalism on a religious basis, — to hoist the banner of so-called „aggressive nationalism" which proposed to put up a determined resistence to the menaces of materialism in order to preserve the assumed superiority of their spiritual heritage; and that of Revolution, driving them to political nihilism, together with tendencies towards religious or utopian socialism without, however, any appreciation of the laws of social progress. In their religiousness and wild spiritual imperialism, they embodied the reactionary social forces. Their no less sincere and ardent desire, on the other hand, to educate the people, to improve the latter's conditions, to revive the golden age unsullied by the vices of the existing system, were generated by the objectively revolutionary forces heralding a coming social struggle. Despite the apparent predominance of their religious tendencies in the ideological domain, it was the latter spirit of revolt, generated as it was by a powerful material cause, which really determined their activites and made them a power behind the Extremist Party. But the de-classed character of the members of these secret revolutionary societies becomes clear when we see them pay but little attention to the program of the Congress, which, whether under the leadership of the Moderates or the Extremists, advocated the interests of the bourgeoisie. Their de-classed character enabled them to avoid falling helpless victims to the reactionary tendencies running through them. Revolutionary forces expressed through them got the upper hand.

The revolutionary idealism of the secret societies was sumptuously fed with suitable interpretations of the Hindu scriptures. Aggressive nationalism must be self-sufficient. It must exclude the necessity of outside inspiration for its development. Therefore, the ideology of a modern political movement had to be drawn from the fountain of national philosophy. Complete national independence, which was its ideal, was to be more of a spiritual uplift than political progress. The philosopher of aggressive nationalism, Arabinda Ghose, — he who adapted the teachings of Vivekananda to political purposes,— said, „achievement of Swaraj (self-government) will develop Indian spirituality". On another occasion he declared; „British rule and Western civilization for which it stands, threaten the very life of Hinduism". Thus the ideal of aggressive nationalism could not be realized, unless foreign domination was overthrown. And for the destruction of foreign domination, all sorts of foreign means were welcome. For example, the spiritual idealists resorted to bombs and dynamite and pistols: and this practice was justified by rulings from the scriptures.

The partition of Bengal brought a new element into the anti-British movement. It was the landholding class, which had so far been the most loyal support of the government. But the partition threatened to injure the privileged position of the landed aristocracy, whose traditional loyalty was thus tampered with. The agitation against the Partition brought the aggressive nationalists led by

Bepin Chandra Pal, into political prominence. Bombs and dynamite were supplemented by the program of fomenting national industries by means of Swadeshi and Boycott. It was argued by those who came to be known as the Extremist Party that nothing could be secured by petitioning which, they held, had been the tactical principle of the Congress so far. Demands must be made, and means should be devised to back the demands. Thus the Extremist Party, in spite of its ideals of spiritual nationality, materialised itself on a political platform, which was ratified by the Twenty-second Congress held in Calcutta (1907) under the presidency of the veteran constitutional democrat, Dadabhoy Naoroji, who not only approved the fighting program of Swadeshi and Boycott, but declared that the ideal of the Indian National Congress was Swaraj, that is, Self-government.

The cause of this change in the policy of the Congress is not to be looked for in the apparent vigorousness of the orthodoxy which characterized the youthful revolutionaries standing behind the Extremist Party. It was not the spiritual nationalism of the orthodox that proved itself more revolutionary, and consequently more powerful, than the „de-nationalized" patriotism of the Congress. On the contrary, it was the material forces of revolution which proved triumphant over the reaction clothed in orthodoxy. Three material factors contributed to the victory of the Extremist Party: 1. the still slow but steady development of native industrial capital, 2. the discontent created by growing unemployment among the lower middle-class youths, and 3. the disaffection of the landed aristocracy, whose privileged position was threatened by the Partition of Bengal. If the Congress abandoned its former tactics of seeking government protection for the development of native industries, it was not that its old leaders had turned orthodox nationalists. They still believed that the national regeneration of India was conditional upon the rise of a modern bourgeoisie. The program of Swadeshi and boycott was intended for the advancement of national industries. In 1905 the Congress adopted this program because it perceived the rise of those forces which heralded the advent of a new industrial India.

The adoption of the program of Swadeshi and Boycott did not signify the defeat of the progressive liberals; on the contrary, it vindicated their social tendency, which was objectively revolutionary. It was the orthodox nationalism which was vanquished, because by subscribing to the program of industrial development, it practically surrendered its fundamental principles. It tacitly admitted that it was not the old spiritual heritage, but a modern bourgeoisie with a materialistic philosophy, that was going to save India as a nation. In moving the resolution on the poverty of the Indian people in the Benares Congress of 1905, Tilak himself admitted that the growth of modern industries would alone solve the problem. Thus, the greatest prophet of orthodox nationalism was forced to pay homage to that force against whose social tendencies, as expressed in the earlier Congresses, he revolted, and which would make the cherished ideal of spiritual civilization an impossibility.

The theory of „integral nationalism" formulated by Tilak was subsequently accorded a philosophico-spiritual sublimity by Pal and Ghose; but it had to cut loose from its rigid orthodox moorings, which invoked only the forces of reaction of an apparently violent nature, but of little durable strength. The surrender of its intrinsic principles in favor of more revolutionary social forces, signified the inherent impotency of the reactionary tendencies that ran through its ideological structure. It revealed the impossibility of building the future after the image of the past, however admirable, however ideal the latter might be. It gave an ominous warning that it was the sordid material interest of the bourgeoisie, a comparatively small class of the society, and not the „spiritual uplift" of the people, that was the motive force behind the movement for national independence. The „integral nationalism" of the Extremist Party became a political force when it entered the struggle for material benefit, and that too of a small class of exploiters. Although its abstract philosophical ideology still remained couched in modernized orthodoxy with a tint of mysticism, the cardinal points in its political program dealt with things temporal. It could hardly be distinguished from modern nationalism, in that it also advocated the development of a new economic basis of society, which the growth of capitalist industrial production would inevitably entail.

The rise of the bourgeoisie and the dissipation of the old social order, were factors indispensable for the success of Indian nationalism. Everything should be sacrificed on the altar of the coming national diety, the bourgeoisie. This was to take place, in spite of all the talk about the spirituality of Indian nationhood.

Besides the struggle with the foreign enemy, there was another struggle of greater significance inside the national movement. This was a social strife, -a struggle between the old and the new, between the forces of reaction and those of progress. As was ordained by the imperious verdict of history, the latter proved triumpant. The nationalism of the lower middle-class, whose economic condition must make it more revolutionary than the rich liberal intellectuals, went on gradually extricating itself from the quagmire of orthodoxy. In the field of pragmatic politics, it took the lead from the progressive elders, and soon went ahead of them. It could do so, not on account of its orthodox and spiritual philosophy, but in spite of it, because the latter failed to prevent the material laws from asserting themselves. The lower middle-class was economically bankrupt; there was no hope for it but in a radical change of the existing order of society. The rich intellectuals and the propertied bourgeoisie could not help being cautious, despite their social progressiveness, since they needed the protection of an established government. But the proletarianized lower middle-class, which was the social origin of „integral nationalism“ had nothing to stake, and therefore could afford to be more reckless and more extreme in its political views.

In 1907 the program of the Extremist Party, as formulated by Bepin Chandra Pal, stood as follows:

1. Promotion of education as widely as possible,
2. Raising of national volunteers,
3. Development of national industries,
4. Establishment of a political organization with the object of assuming the functions of national government when the time will come.

With this program, conspicuous by the absence of its original orthodoxy of creed as formulated by Tilak, "integral nationalism" dominated the Congress of 1906 which declared Swaraj to be its political ideal. Defence of Dharma (religion) and the Cow (held sacred by the Hindus) were replaced by Swadeshi (encouragement of home industries) and Boycott. Thus it was proved that orthodoxy was not the weapon with which such a mighty modern enemy as British Imperialism could be fought. A hundred and fifty years of determined, systematic suppression could not kill the germs which were to develop into the modern bourgeoisie, which eventually was to be born in the course of evolution. In order to fall in with the scheme of this process of social evolution, orthodox nationalism had to bow down before imperious material laws, in spite of its ideal of spirituality. It could not have become a factor in the modern political movement had it persisted in clinging to its original practice.

The Boycott however, failed to achieve any serious result. Swadeshi propaganda found the common people rather luke-warm. Economic fallacies involved in these steps were responsible for the failure. Nevertheless, machine industries owned by native capital received a considerable impetus, and the political leaders learned a lesson. They discovered that the popular support behind the Congress was not strong enough to warrant an uncompromising struggle with the government. The latter, on its part, met the liberal bourgeoisie half-way with petty concessions, and came down on the Extremists with the heavy hand of repression. Lord Morley's policy of "rallying the Moderates" was a recognition of the dynamic forces of revolution contained in the progressive element of Indian society. The object, however, was not to give full sanction to the aspirations of the bourgeoisie, but rather to deceive it by worthless administrative reform. The Moderates accepted the Morley-Minto Reforms of 1909, not as valuable concessions in themselves, but as the beginning of a new era.

The following years saw a steady growth of native industrialism, in spite of the fact that the government still persisted in its policy of obstruction. But the economic basis of imperialism itself had changed. Capital was being exported to the colonies, in an ever increasing amount. The industrialization of India had begun, and the native bourgeoisie could no longer be excluded altogether.

The questionable success of aggressive tactics once more convinced the Moderates of the prudence of evolutionary methods. They looked dubiously upon the sentimental enthusiasm stirred up by the orthodox nationalists, whose reactionary social tendencies appealed to the people, kept in ignorance by the carefully manipulated policy of the British government. But the forces of reaction also had lost their potentiality, in consequence of the loss of an economic basis. They were largely maintained by the artificial stimulation given by the British government. Therefore, the faint popular response to orthodox nationalism was merely sentimental and temporary. If the masses of the people remained apathetic to the national movement sanctified with religion, it was not the foreign rule that was to be blamed for it. The popular apathy was the result of the social institutions and religious teachings of the past. In order to be successful, modern nationalism, instead of glorifying those instituions and teachings making for the present apathy, should base itself upon the forces and tendencies that tend to disrupt and dissipate them, and that promise to infuse new vigor in the social organism as a result of new property relations.

The attempt of the Moderates to rescue the Congress from what they considered the reckless tactics of the Extremists, resulted in the split of 1907. The following years saw the Moderates in the background, leaving the political arena not so much to the Extremists as to the extra-Congress revolutionary organizations, which dominated the situation less by political agitation than by terrorist activities. Persecution of its principal leaders including Tilak, who was sentenced to six years hard labor in 1908, broke down the Extremist Party. A year and a half in jail (1908—09): brought the philosopher and ascetic in Arabinda Ghose into predominance, and he practically retired from politics. Pal appeared to be bewildered by the extremely contradictary tendencies of his own ideas. Bourgeois radicalism coupled with religious reformism rendered his political vision rather foggy. He migrated to London (1908) to propagandize the British democracy, thus undertaking an act for which he and his partly fellows had heaped insults on the Moderates. The astounding change in his political convictions became evident when on leaving London in 1912 he declared:

"Should Providence offer me choice of absolute independence for India with one hand, and the alternative of self-government within the Empire with the other, I would unhesitatingly accept the latter".

This statement betrayed the modification, if not abandonment, of his former theory of "aggressive nationalism" which would not permit any foreign element to enter into the making of the Indian nation. It was admitted that the spiritual civilization of India would not satisfy the needs of a modern nation, and that the benefits of the "soulless" Western civilization were necessary. Progressive liberalism was getting the upper hand of the religious mysticism in Pal's nationalistic philosophy. Revolutionary tendencies overwhelmed the forces of reaction focussed through him. His pathetic desire for the imperial connection, in itself, was but a sign of subjective weakness; but this desire originated in a hidden mistrust of all those ideals cherished by orthodox nationalism.

The practical extermination of the Extremist Party did not stamp out orthodox nationalism, which found a stronghold in the secret revolutionary societies, whose program was the overthrow of British domination by means of terrorist campaigns, to culminate in an uprising at a suitable opportunity. The members of these secret organizations, which outlived years of severest persecution by the government, were more romantic ascetics of jesuitic character than revolutionaries with a political vision. Through them were expressed the forces of reaction and revolution. They were the product of a society in a great crisis, which was marked by a fanatic resistence of the old to the inevitable appearance of the new. Both these conflicting forces with their origin in the material background of social disintegration on the one hand and readjustment on the other, acted and reacted on the psychology of these young men organized in secret revolutionary societies, and produced in them political nihilism, social confusion and mystic religious orthodoxy. To them national independence meant spiritual imperialism. Clarification of the political tendencies of these fanatical ascetics could not take place until the class cleavage in the society became more glaring amd more cruel. And since class cleavage was to follow the development of the bourgeoisie, the field of activity of these ardent revolutionaries remained confined to futile conspiracies, until the society underwent the necessary tranformation. In every respect proletarianized by the capitalist society, these lower middle-class intellectuals were objectively social anarchists. National pre-occupations clouded their vision of social antagonism, and made them fall temporary and unconscious victims of the forces of reaction. Their natural tendencies towards religious socialism were taken by storm by the romantic ideal of a great spiritual mission awaiting the Indian nation.

The years preceding the great world war saw the recuperation of the bourgeois political tendencies in the revived Congress, which had played a rather insignificant role in the years following the disaster of 1907. In 1910 the Congress was reorganized by the right-wing moderates. An English liberal, Sir William Wedderburn, was called to preside, as if to vivify the thanks for the Morley-Minto

Reforms. Then followed a period of calm, to be disturbed by a violent storm in the first years of the war, when the secret revolutionary societies made a determined, but abortive attempt at a national uprising. Subsequently, the Congress became the fighting political apparatus of the bourgeosie united upon a common platform, until the Montague-Chelmsford Reforms of 1919 brought a split. But the most outstanding feature of this period was the appearance of a new factor on the political field. This was the working-class.

CHAPTER VIII.

Present Situation-Review and Perspective.

Strong cross-currents have always been the feature of the political movement of modern India. In the last three years, this feature has becomes more and more remarkable in proportion as the nationalist movement acquired strength and assumed dimensions positively alarming to the British authorities. It is since 1918 that the movement for national liberation began to spread beyond the narrow circle of the middle-class and affect the masses of the people. The growing disaffection of the people at large has added potentiality to the nationalist movement. But the very awakening of the masses, which has enabled the political movement of the bourgeoisie to outgrow the stage of agitation and propaganda and enter into an active fight, has at the same time brought into evidence another cross-current which threatens to turn the tide in the near future. It marks the initiation of a triangular fight, in which class anatagonism and the national struggle will be intensified side by side. The development of the bourgeoisie stiffens the national struggle as well as intensifies the class-cleavage by creating a proletarian class. This process of class-readjustment has been going on in India within the last few years and the political movement must be affected by it.

Indian nationalism, whether of the progressive character and of evolutionary tactics, as advocated by the Moderates now in League with the Impe rialist Government, or based on the integralist theory of the Extremists, orthodox in social tendancies, is fundamentally a bourgeois movement. Excepting the religious orthodox, — whose violent outbursts not so much against the British Government as against the "Western Civilization" it stands for, do not make them any less the exponents of the forces of reaction, — all shades of opinion in the national movement tend consciously or unconsciously, to the enhancement of the material interests of the intellectual and propertied middle-class. Even the reactionary nationalism of the orthodox religionists, in its purely political activities, finds itself obliged to back the bourgeoisie. This was proved when the greatest stalwart of religious nationalism, Tilak, formulated the theory of attaining Swaraj by fostering the growth of indigenous industries. As the present moment, Gandhi also tries to save the spiritual civilization of India through the aggrandizement of the merchants and manufacturers.

The representative institutions demanded by the evolutionary Moderates, when fully inaugurated, will open the gates of the paradise lost more than a hundred and fifty years ago, to the intellectual and capitalist bourgeoisie. Free access to the higher administrative posts will be allowed to the former, while fiscal autonomy will mean the protection of Indian industries by means of tariff barriers against all foreign competitors, including England herself. Only in that case, Boycott of foreign goods, considered by the Extremists to be a powerful weapon in the political struggle, can be used with effect. The following extract from the address of the Chairman of the Reception Committee of the Calcutta Congress 1890, contains the fundamental doctrines and object of bourgeois liberal nationalism.

"It is perfectly correct that the ignorant classes whom we seek to represent are still unable to take an active interest in the many social and administrative problems which are now engaging the attention of the educated class; but history teaches us that in all the countries and in all ages, it is the thinking who lead the unthinking, and we are bound to think for ourselves and for those who are still too ignorant to exercise that important function".

Himself a rich lawyer, as well as belonging to the landed aristocracy, the speaker of these words voiced what his class, still in a backward stage of development, understood by a national government based on principles of popular representation. It is the rule of the national bourgeoisie which the Congress sought for; the Moderates as well as the Extremists, the progressive liberals as well as the orthodox religionists, all agree on this political conviction in their nationalism.

The Extremists, who have always based their nationalism on the superiority of India's spiritual civilization, in the field of pure politics prove themselves equally ardent defenders of the material interests of the national bourgeoisie. On supporting the Resolution of Self-Government in the Lucknow Congress of 1916, Tilak, the great advocate of the „common people" said; "I would not care if they (rights of self-government) are granted to the lower and lowest classes of the Hindu population, provided that the British Government considers them more fit than the educated classes of India for exercising those rights". These words contain a challenge to the possible thought that the lower classes are and can be better fitted than the educated classes to exercise the rights and privileges accruing from political autonomy. In answer to a question put to him "whether the Indian masses would be any less exploited by the native bourgeoisie wielding political state power", Lajpat Rai once told that he would prefer to be kicked by his brother than by a foreigner. And above all, the program of fostering native industries betrays the bourgeois character even of the orthodox nationalism of the Extremists.

The movement for national liberation is a struggle of the native middle-class against the economic and political monopoly of the imperialist bourgeoisie. But the former cannot succeed in the struggle, nor even threaten its opponent to make substantial concessions, without the support of the masses of the people. Because the Indian middle-class is still weak numerically, economically and socially, hence the necessity of nationalism in the name of which the people can be led to fight; the victory gained in this fight however, will not change very much the condition of those whose blood it will cost. The Constitutional Democratic theories of the Moderates are beyond the comprehension of the common people, and therefore cannot be the motive force of Indian nationalism. Their economic program, which proposes to foster modern industries with native capital by every means, is bound nevertheless, to revolutionize the position of the toiling masses, and will eventually bring them within the reach of political agitation. But the development of a native capitalist class will at the same time, inevitably intensify the class-antagonism between the bourgeoisie and the working-masses. When the latter will begin the struggle earnestly, it is expected to be more of a social nature than a political movement for national liberation. Since 1918, the Indian movement has entered this stage. It may still have the appearance of a national struggle involving masses of the population, but fundamentally it is a social strife, the revolt of the exploited against the exploiting class, irrespective of nationality.

The Extremists, now called the Non-cooperators, have had better success than the Moderates in drawing the masses under the influence of Nationalism. But a closer study shows that it is not the demagoguic methods nor the religious character attached to the nationalist compaign to which this apparent success is to be attributed. There are deeper economic reasons behind it. It is not by a better understanding of the social problem that the Extremists have succeeded where the Moderates failed. In fact, the reactionary tendancy of orthodox extremism makes it blind to these social problems on whose radical solution depends the success of the Indian movement. The discontent and growing unrest among the masses, brought about by economic exploitation intensified during the war, was seized by the Congress under the leadership of the Extremists, and turned into a popular demonstration demanding national liberation. But in spite of their religious ideosyncracies and orthodox inclinations, the social affiliation of the Extremists is identical with that of the Moderates. In the spontaneous mass-upheaval, they discovered the force which could be utilized for the triumph of the native bourgeoisie. But they could not develop the potentiality of the mass movement by leading it in accordance with its economic urges and social tendencies. Their tactics were to strengthen the nationalist movement by the questionable method of exploiting the ignorance of the masses. And the best way of exploiting the ignorance of the masses was to make a religion of nationalism. This tactics led to the appearance of Mohandas Karamchand Gandhi on the political horizon, and the temporary eclipse of all other politico-social tendencies in the shade of Gandhism, which has reached a crisis after having swept the country for two years.

In Gandhism culminates all the social tendencies that have always differentiated the two principles of Indian nationalism. In fact, Gandhism is the acutest and most desperate manifestation of the forces of reaction, trying to hold their own against the objectively revolutionary tendencies contained in the liberal bourgeois nationalism. The impending wane of Gandhism signifies the collapse of the reactionary forces and their total elimination from the political movement.

Ever since its inception, the political movement of modern India has contained two tendencies of diverse character. Progressive politically and revolutionary in social questions, the one has always been evolutionary and compromising in tactics. In spite of its apparently intransigeant attitude towards the foreign domination, the other is reactionary socially. Notwithstanding its subjectively reformistic character, the first is and has always been objectively revolutionary because its social basis is the bourgeoisie, and it is conscious of the fact. But this tendency has failed and will always fail to play any outwardly revolutionary role because the conditions for a purely bourgeois revolution do not exist in India. The Indian national movement is not a struggle of the commercial and industrial middle-class against decrepit feudalism. The Indian bourgeoisie is not engaged in a class-struggle. The basis of the national movement is the rivalry of a weak and suppressed bourgeoisie against its immensely stronger imperialist prototype controlling the state power. To its great misfortune, the Indian middle-class was long ago deprived of its historic role of freeing the productive classes from the fetters of feudal bondage. The present fight of the Indian bourgeoisie cannot be, therefore, unrelenting. Its growth and prosperity are not necessarily conditional upon the total destruction of its present enemy. Owing to this relative weakness of its social foundation, nationalism of the progressive tendency headed by the class conscious bourgeoisie, is bound to be compromising. It is inherently more inimical to the possible revival of social and political reaction than to the British rule which, in spite of itself, promises protection to the advent of capitalist civilization in Indian. A mass revolt temporarily swayed by the influence of orthodox nationalism, or actuated by the vigorous spirit of class-struggle, will be looked upon with equal apprehension by the progressive national democrats, conscious of their economic interests and social affiliation. Because, if the first is the case, it will signify a social and political reaction seriously detrimental to the still weak progressive movement, whereas a revolt of the working-class is always very disquieting to the bourgeoisie. Both eventualities are more menacing to the interests of the liberal bourgeoisie than the British government. Therefore, the constitutional democrats, in spite of their revolutionary significance as an objective force, are not only not in a position to stir up and head a mass movement, but are very likely to be driven to the protecting arms of their imperialist peer in the event of such a movement, which is mortally menacing to the bourgeois institutions, so precious, so profitable, so congenial to the peaceful development of the middle-class.

Orthodox nationalism, on the other hand, is closer to the understanding of the people, and for this reason succeeds in provoking enthusiam from time to time; but the reactionary tendencies inherent in it preclude the possibility of its ever becoming a dynamic revolutionary force, which alone is able to shake the foundation of foreign rule and start the people on the road to further progress. The backwardness of the people makes them respond more to religious nationalism than to constitutional democracy. The inevitable incapacity of the progressive bourgeoisie to assume the leadership of the national movement on a mass basis, left the ground at the command of orthodox nationalism which sought to incite the people against the foreign domination in the name of religion and culture. But they also failed, because the masses remained equally passive to the national movement based upon religion. At last the stings of economic exploitation exhausted their patience and religious calm, which owed their baneful origin and durability, to the very spiritual national culture they are called upon to defend. It was the narcotic effect of the much-vaunted "spiritual civilization" which kept the Indian masses apathetic to any movement for material progress. They have been taught to sacrifice the hallucinations of the phenomenal world in expectation of a blissful existence hereafter. The present awakening is a reaction against the age-long resignation, created by religious teachings and the tenets of spiritual culture. Therefore it cannot be used for a national movement tending towards the revival of the spiritual civilization of India. Here lies the contradiction in the orthodox nationalism as expressed of late in the cult of Ghandhism. It endeavors to utilize the mass energy for the perpetuation or revival of that heritage of national culture which has been made untenable by the awakening of this energy. The orthodox Extremists in control of the Congress. freed from all Moderate influence, assumed the leadership of a popular mass movement national in appearance which contains, nevertheless, a challenge to all the fundamental doctrines of orthodox nationalism. Therefore, the intention of the present Congress, which has acquired the status of a political party, to unite the people of all classes in a struggle for national liberation to be carried on under the banner of Gandhism, is bound to be defeated. The signs of the impending defeat are already perceptible.

Gandhism will fall victim to its own contradictions. By

Gandhism is meant the school of nationalism which has been reigning supreme in the Indian movement during the last three years. It can be put in another way: The Indian national movement, actuated by the spirit of Gandhism cannot succeed, because in that case it would defeat its own end. In spite of the pious desire of its leaders, post-British India cannot and will not become pre-British India. The Indian people will not be able to overthrow foreign domination until and unless all that is cherished by orthodox nationalists have become things of the past, of venerable memory. Sanctimonious antagonism to the "satanic Western civilization", a tendency which in spite of its pathetic impotency, smacks of reaction, cannot be the life of a movement whose success will be marked by the crowning of the native bourgeoisie, who will prove to be as disruptive as the British ruler in so far as the social and religious ideals of orthodox nationalism are concerned. The victory of Indian nationalism will be the victory of the progressive middle-class, which may build a monument to the memory of the Mahatma for the valuable services he rendered them involuntarily, but which will never share his pious indignation against Western civilization, which is after all only a certain stage of social development through which every human community has to pass. This victory will be won, not through "suffering and soul-force", but with blood and tears and will be maintained by blood and iron. But it must come. The introduction of "Western civilization" so heartily hated by Gandhi is the reward of the fierce fight for national independence to which he seeks to lead the people. He is working for something which is mortally antagonistic to the reactionary forces operating through him, and whose standard bearer he unconsciously is.

Before proceeding to review the happenings in the Indian movement since the beginning of the world war from the point of view stated above, it will be worthwhile to analyze Gandhism, because in it has found ample expression all the ebbing vitality contained in orthodox nationalism. The imminent collapse of Gandhism will close a romantic and exciting chapter of the Indian national movement. It will demonstrate that a socially revolutionary movement cannot be influenced by reactionary forces. It will disclose the incompatibility between the national struggle having for its object the aggrandisement of the bourgeoisie and the revolt of the working masses against class exploitation, — a revolt which nevertheless has contributed strength to the Congress in the last years of its activities.

Although somewhat unique in its idiosyncracies and fanaticism, the Gandhi cult is not an innovation. Divested of the rebellious spirit and the shrewd politican in him, Tilak would resemble Gandhi in so far as religious beliefs and spiritual prejudices are concerned. But for his versatility in modern thoughts and characteristic looseness of conviction, Bepin Chandra Pal would perchance, join the Mahatma in the passionate denunciation of everything that adds to the material comfort of man. Had he been more of a monomaniac than a profound thinker with metaphysical pre-occupations, Arabinda Ghose would subscribe to Gandhi's philosophy, which pretends to command a rushing tide; "thus far shalt thou go and no farther". In the contemporary epoch outside India, Tolstoy has been the apostle of what Gandhi professes. In fact the latter is an avowed disciple of the former. Gandhism is nothing but petty-bourgeois humanitarianism hopelessly bewildered in the clashes of the staggering forces of human progress. The crocodile tears of this humanitarianism are shed ostensibly for the undeniable sufferings of the majority in capitalist society, but they are really caused by grief over the end of the old order, already destroyed or about to be so. It pines for that ancient golden age when the majority were kept in blissful ignorance in order that a few could roll in idle luxury, undisturbed by the revolt of the discontented; the spiritual culture of which was based on the barbarism of the people at large; the simplicity of which was the sign of its backwardness. This longing glance backwards is due, in some cases, to the consummate intrigues of the forces of reaction, and in others, to involuntary subordination to the influence of the same agency. Its tendency towards a sort of religious or utopian socialism proves that Gandhism, as well as its source Tolstoyism, belongs to the latter category. Or in other words, the services rendered by it to reaction, are involuntary.

It was in 1908 while still in South Africa that Gandhi formulated his philosophy of "Non-resistence" and "Soul-force" in a small book called "Indian Home Rule". It appears that since then he had not learnt anything nor had he forgotten anything till January 1921, when in the preface to the third edition of his book he confessed:

"It (the book) teaches the gospel of love in the place of that of hate. It replaces violence with self-sacrifice. It pits soul-force against brute force. I withdrew (in this edition) nothing... ..... But I would warn the reader against thinking that I am to-day aiming at the Swaraj described therein. I know that India is not ripe for it. ..... I am individually working for the self-rule pictured therein. But today my corporate activity is undoubtedly devoted to the attainment of parliamentary Swaraj in accordance which the wishes of the people of India. I am not aiming at destroying railways or hospitals, though I would certainly welcome their natural destruction. Neither railways nor hospitals are a test of a high and pure civilization. .... It requires a higher simplicity and renunciation than the people are today prepared for".

These passages make one suspect a wavering in the belief of the author. But the preceding as well as following paragraphs obviate such possible suspicions. Before declaring that the ideals of his philosophy are practically untenable in these days, Gandhi fortifies himself by the following confession of faith: "My conviction is deeper to-day than ever. I feel that if India would discard modern civilization, she can only gain by doing so". And he reassures himself by declaring: "If India adopted the doctrine of love as an active part of her religion and introduced it in her politics, Swaraj would descend upon India from heaven". Gandhi's quarrel is not with the British government, but with "Western civilization" which is satanic according to his estimation. An Indian government, which would stand for bringing or fostering the same civilization, would be no more acceptable to him. Is there anything more incongruous than this —, that a man with such a philosophy should be at the head of a movement which strives for the establishment of a capitalist society? And is there any doubt whatsoever that Gandhism must discredit itself before long if the movement for national liberation is to go ahead?

Gandhi's criticism of modern civilization, that is, capitalist society, is correct. But the remedy he prescribes is not only wrong. but impossible. One need not be a sentimental humanitarian, nor a religious fanatic in order to denounce the present order of society in the countries where capitalism rules. But the knowledge of material and social sciences makes one see through the Christian piety of Gandhism, not only Indian, but International (there are Gandhis in every country) and discover the sinister forces of reaction busy in its depths. Its true social character no longer remains unknown on finding such tenets in its philosophy:

"The more we indulge our passions, the more unbridled they become. Our ancestors, therefore, set a limit to our indulgences. They saw that happiness was largely a mental condition. A man is not necessarily happy because he is rich, or unhappy because he is poor. The rich are often seen to be unhappy, the poor to be happy. Millions will always remain poor. Observing all this, our ancestors dissuaded us from luxuries and pleasures."

This sanctimonious philosophy of poverty is not unfamiliar. It has been preached by many prophets who have not only been proved false by history, but the questionableness of their humanitarianism has also been revealed. Such philosophy serves but one object, — to gurantee the safety of the vested interests, whose character may differ in different epochs but which essentially is always the same, being based on the right of exploitation of man by man.

Capitalist civilization is rotten; but it cannot be avoided. Neither is it permanent. It must pass away in due course of evolution, giving place to a higher order of society, as the ones preceeding it were replaced by it. But it will not collapse because sentimental humanitarians find it full of cruelty and injustice. It will break down under the pressure of its own contradictions. Whether we want it or not, it must be lived through somehow. It must be lived through in order that the fetters of moral and material ignorance that kept the human race bound hitherto can be broken, and mankind in all countries may have the facilities to strive for a higher stage of civilization. National freedom will not enable the people of India to go back, but to surge ahead.

In itself capitalist society has many defects; but it is undoubtedly an improvement on the patriarchal or feudal civilization for which Gandhi and his kind pine. Indian society is inevitably heading towards capitalist civilization, in spite of the premonitions of Gandhi, among many other prophets of similar creed. The desire to see it hark back is as futile as to expect a river to rush back to its source. Caught in the morass of such hopeless contradictions, Gandhism cannot supply the ideology of Indian nationalism. The revolutionary character of the latter is contrary to it. Nevertheless, it is undeniable that Gandhism, better said, the personality of Gandhi, exercised a considerable influence on the Indian movement in the last three years. Or in other words, just about the time that the National Congress was finding the first response among the ranks of the working masses, it came under the domination of a spirit which is essentially reactionary and non-revolutionary in a very frank way. How did it happen? How could a revolutionary movement accept a leadership with antagonistic tendencies? This question leads us to a review of the movement.

The attempts made by the secret revolutionary societies to organize an armed uprising in the first year of the world war were easily thwarted. These organizations could be crushed, or prevented from constituting any serious danger, because they relied more upon conspiracies than upon revolutionary social forces. There was some discontent among the Indian soldiers, which was suffocated if not removed, by severe military measures. The masses of the people remained passive, while the educated lower-middle-class gloated over German victories and expected a possible defeat of the British, which prospect was conducive to the success of Indian nationalism. But the political parties, without any remarkable exception, protested loyalty to the British government and offered unconditional assistence in the prosecution of the war. Even Tilak, who had just come out of jail after six years, was not an exception. The Congress, under the leadership of the Moderates representing the rich intellectuals and capitalist class, outdid everybody in these protestations of loyalty. But behind this mask of loyalty was to be noticed either an anxious expectation or a spiteful glee on all faces. A whisper ran through the length and breadth of the country that the British power was crumbling. Even in the far-off villages this whisper raised an echo. There was a period of suspense and tension.

In 1915 the military strength of the British Indian government was depleted to the minimum. All the available troops were sent out, and the new recruits, British as well as native, were qualitatively and quantitatively incapable of resisting a possible national upheaval. If there had been a revolutionary national consciousness in the Indian people anywhere outside the small middle-class, that was the most opportune moment to strike a blow which would have been mortal in all probablity. The loyalty professed so vigorously was false; there was much discontent and disaffection, but it had not yet contaminated the masses. The potentiality of this discontent was reduced to almost nothing when the capitalist class, the backbone of nationalism, unexpectedly found opportunities for industrial development. The monopoly of imperialist capital was made untenable by war conditions; the competition of manufactured goods imported from European countries, including England herself, was removed. Indian industries suddenly entered upon an era of spectacular growth. This economic revolution deprived the political movement of its most powerful social foundation. The intellectual and capitalist middle-class found it profitable to stand by the government. Obstacles to its industrial aspiration removed, the bourgeoisie had no more quarrel with the foreign ruler, at least for the time being. On the contrary, the new era of industrial development needed the protection of an established government. Therefore the loyalty of the bourgeoisie became real, and the leadership of the Congress sank into such sycophancy that to preside over its session of 1915 was selected a man who combined in his person the landed aristocracy, rich liberal professions and officialdom. He was S. P. Sinha (later on Sir, then Lord, then His Britannic Majesty's Privy-Councillor etc. etc.) on whose head had been showered more blessings of governmental concessions than on any other Indian. He proved himself worthy of the innumerable distinctions received hitherto, and merited more that were to be bestowed subsequently, by uttering in his presidential address such sentiments as; „in that critical time it was the duty of India to prove to the great British nation her gratitude for peace and the blessings of civilization secured to her under its aegis for the last hundred and fifty years and more." These words should not be taken as expressing the sentiments of a slavish individual. They were the voice of the class that he represented.

This remarkable abdication of the Congress betrays the innate weakness of the nationalist forces. That element, which is the most revolutionary from the objective point of view, is liable nevertheless, to make compromises in every critical moment, by virtue of the fact that its revolutionary energy is not pitted against an enemy which would be unrelentingly hostile to it on the ground of class-struggle. Had the Indian bourgeoisie been fighting against a feudal absolution, no such compromise would be possible; because the two could never be accomodated as is the case in the relation of the former with capitalist imperialism, which will always readjust its method of exploitation in the way of making concessions to its native partner before risking the eventual conflict. This equivocal position of the socially revolutionary factor in the ranks of the nationalist movement, makes for the possibility of the latter's falling under the influence of the orthodox school. The reactionary forces behind orthodox nationalism make it subjectively more hostile to British rule. The antagonism between the reactionary tendencies of orthodox nationalism and the modern civilization which the British domination embodies, is much more deep-seated and uncompromising than the rivalry between the Indian and British bourgeoisies.

The interests and aspirations of the economically bankrupt lower middle-class not being identical with those of the rich intellectuals and capitalist bourgeoisie, the arrangements that give temporary satisfaction to the latter, do not remove the grievances of the former, thus leaving it in a discontented frame of mind which gets worse. When by virtue of their compromising tactics, the Moderates forfeit the leadership of the movement, the lower middle-class steps in. The latter's economic position makes it more intransigeant, more extremist in its political demands. But the petty-bourgeois social bearing of the Extremists makes them susceptible to the influence of the forces of reaction masquerading in the garb of such cults as spiritual civilization, humanitarianism and the like. On account of its reactionary tendencies, orthodox nationalism, embraced by the discontented petty bourgeoisie, is more uncompromising in its fight against foreign rule, which is the personification of a social order mortally inimical to its ideals. But doomed to death by the imperious verdict of history, it cannot infuse any vitality in the national movement in spite of its more revolutionary appearance. Nevertheless, its bitter hostility to modern civilization enables it to be more uncompromising to British rule, and therefore to take up the fight and carry it on further than the point at which the Moderates desert it. This was the social reason which explains how the Indian national movement in its most revolutionary period, could be actuated by such a reactionary philosophy as Gandhism.

The second year of the war found the rich intellectual and

bourgeois leaders of the national movement reconciled to the British rule and actively supporting it, at a time when it could possibly have been overthrown or at least substantial concessions wrung from its reluctant hand, by threats of withholding assistence to conduct the war. But such measures were altogether unthinkable for the Moderate Party, whose economic interest would be jeopardised more by the unsettled conditions that were most likely to follow a premature overthrow of the British government than by its continuation, specially when the latter was forced by unexpected circumstances to modify, if not abandon, its former economic policy. The position of the Moderates at that critical moment was very well formulated in the following words of B. L. Mittra, one of their leaders:

"The Moderates consider co-operation with the English necessary for national development, political, industrial, economic, and otherwise. The Extremists would straight away assume full responsibility of government; the Moderates think that would lead to chaos, and would proceed by stages. It is the difference between cataclysm and evolution. The Extremists' ideal is destruction of the existing order of things in the hope that something better will take its place, for nothing can be worse than what is; the Moderates' ideal is for formation of a new order of things on definite progressive lines".

But the very possibility of economic and industrial development which satisfied temporarily the aspirations of the rich bourgeoisie, promised the emergence of another social factor which would be more revolutionary than both the political parties hitherto sharing the leadership of the national movement. The rapid development of large scale machine industries and the emergency extension of the already existing ones, led to the concentration of the masses of working people in cities with utterly insufficient accomodation for the sudden influx of additional inhabitants. The sudden increase in the number of consumers was very readily taken advantage of by the speculating traders. Consequently prices went up so much, that they exceeded the limits of the miserable wages in the newly-grown capitalist industries. All the effects of a social readjustment resulting from a sudden industrial revolution were felt. Potential causes of a mass revolt were to be expected from such a situation. Increased export caused an acute scarcity of food grains. The burden of forced contribution to the war loans, so liberally subscribed to by the loyal landed aristocracy, who transferred then immediately on to the shoulders of the poor cultivators, prepared the ground for an agrarian revolt. Then, the petty-bourgeoisie and the lower middle-class were still smarting under their unredressed grievances; their hopeless economic condition could not be expected to improve in any way by the prospect of a great industrial development or administrative reforms. The surrender of the progressive Moderates left all these revolutionary forces either partially manifest, or still brewing under the surface, without political leadership. The field was clear for orthodox nationalism. Reaction sought to unite all these unconscious forces of revolution in a movement ostensibly anti-British, but really, and according to the confession of the orthodox leaders, to combat the advent of a new order which was denounced as "satanic" or "sordid materialism". All those revolutionary forces directly or indirectly tended towards the destruction of Imperialism, as the rankest manifestation of class-domination; reactionary nationalism also desired the overthrow of British rule; but with a different purpose. A common foe made for the alliance of these two most incompatible, nay antagonistic tendencies. And the ignorance of the masses, aided by the lack of social or political conviction of the petty-bourgeoisie, handed the leadership of the movement over to the orthodox Extremists.

The advent of native orthodoxy in the person of Gandhi was preceded by a reaction voluntarily or involuntarily serving the cause of Imperialism. Annie Besant was its apostle. She was seemingly an avowed spiritualist dreading all contamination of things material, but in reality a masked defender of the interests of the imperialist bourgeoisie to which she belonged, in spite of her Irish birth. She had always been a champion of the British Empire, which she chose to call the foundation of a real League of Nations. Her ideal of the League of Nations was evidently the incorporation of the whole world in the British Empire. The same instinct, which thirty years ago had induced the liberal imperialist Hume to promote the idea of founding the National Congress, led Mrs. Besant to arise from her theosophical esoterics, in which she had immersed herself ever since she came to India, and pollute her holiness which such sordid materialism as politics. Her instinctive zeal for the welfare (not spiritual) of the imperialist bourgeoisie disquieted her at the sight of the ominous clouds gathering on the political horizon. Long residence in the country and intimate relation with the lower middle-class intellectuals, enabled her to gauge the situation cleverly. She set out with the mission of stemming the rising tide of revolution.

Unnoticed by the bourgeois political parties, a new combination of social forces was in the process of consummation. The imminent spontaneous upheaval of the working masses, both in the cities as well as in the countryside, would open up a new vision to the de-classed young intellectuals dissipating their revolutionary energy in futile conspiracies. The revolt of the oppressed masses and the ruthless manner in which such a revolt would surely be suppressed by the government with the aid and connivance of the national bourgeoisie, would clarify their social tendencies, thus rescuing them from the vicious circle of orthodox nationalism, and push them forward into the healthy and envigorating atmosphere of an inevitable class-struggle against the native as well as the foreign exploiting class. Once launched on such a consciously revolutionary road, the Indian national movement would soon acquire real strength. It would throb with the vitality of mass-action. Neither British oppression, nor the compromising tactics of the bourgeoisie, nor the questionable orthodoxy of the reactionary religionists would be able to check or distort the victorious march of such a movement.

This was a gloomy prospect for imperial domination as well as that of which the native bourgeoisie was dreaming in the name of national independence. How could such a fatal eventuality be averted? An outburst of orthodox nationalism tickling the spiritual imperialism of the young revolutionaries, supplemented by a show of extremism in political demands, might be expected to save the situation. Mrs. Besant captured the imagination and admiration of the revolutionarily-inclined young intellectuals by preaching with her wonted eloquence the familiar gospel of the spiritual superiority of Indian over Western culture, and condemning the British government as the worst manifestation of Western materialism from which, she exclaimed, the innocent children of sacred India must be saved. Thus a wrong channel was opened for the great revolutionary wave that was raising its majestic crest on the offing of the society. Essentially a socio-economic struggle, the impending movement must assume a political manifestation with considerable latitude for nationalist pre-occupations. The astuteness of Mrs. Besant caught on to the familiar, but harmless, political slogan of "Home Rule" which swung the Extremists on her side, because it promised to lead the movement abandoned by the Moderates. In consequence. those who might have sought the destruction of British domination with the aid of revolutionary mass-action, committed themselves to the ambigous programe of Self-government within the British Empire. Mrs. Besant rendered a valuable service to the imperial cause so dear to her, although the bureaucratic government did not seem to appreciate her merits and made a pseudo martyr of her.

The prospect of a mass-upheaval completely drove the progressive bourgeoisie into the protecting arms of its imperialist peer, but inspired the orthodox Extremists, who stepped into the control of the movement. Under their leadership it assumed a politically aggressive character, but its social significance was confused for the time being. Mrs. Besant could not prevent the inevitable; she only prepared the ground for Gandhi, whose advent pushed her into well-merited disgrace. Both preached the doctrine of orthodox nationalism, but the difference lay in the respective objects in view. The former desired to save the Indians from modern materialism in order to insure the continuance of British domination, while the latter's hostility to Western civilization was fomented by the apprehension that it would strike at the root of the religious, intellectual and patriarchal vested interests which, in the name of spiritual culture, held the Indian masses in moral as well as material bondage.

In 1916 the National Congress entered upon a new chapter of its history. From that year it ceased to be the loosely organized deliberative body that it had been so far, and assumed the character of a cohesive political party-, a fighting organ. The political program of the Extremists was completely adopted, though the Moderates still participated in the Congress, and one of the most mediocre from their midst was chosen to preside over the session of 1916 held in Lucknow. The embarassing position of the imperial power, together with the first indications of a popular awakening, encouraged the Congress. It decided to demand an adequate price for the support which the Indian bourgeoisie was willing to render the British government. The latter had already shown an inclination to make concessions by placing with the native factories large orders for war materials, by encouraging war production in industrial plants owned by native capital, and lastly by appointing a commission to investigate the possibilities of modern industries in India and devise ways and means of fostering them by native capital. Something more significant happened to show that the British government was serious in its new policy of compromise. Just before his extended term of office was over in the middle of 1916, the then viceroy Lord Hardinge was known to be engaged in drafting a scheme of reforms which would cater liberally to the ambitions of the bourgeoisie, as represented by the Moderates. Then, the talk of a radical reconstruction in imperial relations after the war reached the ears of the Indian bourgeoisie. The British Premier Asquith's promise that in consideration of her war services India would be looked at from "a new angle of vision" was interpreted as the offer of dominion status with a government responsible to the Indian people. All these factors contributed to the crystallization of such a feeling that the Lucknow Congress (1916) swayed clear to the left. It was dominated by the Extremists' outlook in spite of its Moderate president.

It was not only the Congress dominated by Extremist politicians that reflected the vigor felt by the bourgeoisie. It was manifested in another and quite unexpected way. Before the Congress met, the elected members of the Legislative Council, which owed its existence to the Morley Reforms of 1909, presented a memorandum to the government demanding an immediate readjustment in the state administration. The repeal of the Arms Act and the organization of an Indian volunteer corps were very energetically pressed. The necessity of mending the autocratic character of the British Indian government and of transferring some of its power to the elected representatives of the people was emphatically urged. The memorandum expressed the point of view of that section of the bourgeoisie already in alliance with the government, which raised its voice to say that if the government desired to be assured of its valuable services, it must show an inclination to pay a reasonable price. Still looking up to the British government as an indispensable protection, the bourgeoisie was encouraged to assume such an aggressive attitude not only through its growing economic importance, but mainly because of the awakening mass-energy, which could be utilized for backing up the demands made. Constitutional agitation was replaced by the hagglings of a bargainer. The mass awakening was not yet a conscious movement. But the politically minded middle-class felt the impulse of strength proceeding from the knowledge that the people would follow its lead. The bourgeoisie's claim to national leadership was at last materializing.

What had been formulated as the ultimate goal of the Congress in 1906 was categorically demanded in 1916. In return for the Indian people's support of the war, immediate self-government (dominion status) and complete fiscal autonomy were asked for. Both the wings of the Congress, the Moderates as well as the Extremists, subscribed to this demand. It fell to the lot of Surendra Nath Banerji, the Moderate veteran and one of the founders of the Congress, to move the resolution of self-government. The president in course of his speech formulated the demand as follows:

"India must cease to be a dependency and be raised to the status of a self-governing state, as an equal partner with equal rights and responsibilities, as an independent unit of the empire".

He declared that a "bloodless revolution" was already in progress, and a resolution was passed requesting that "the King Emperor should issue a proclamation announcing that it is the aim and intention of the British policy to confer self-government on India at an early date".

Another epoch-making feature of the Lucknow Congress was the unconditional endorsement of its program and demands by the All-India Moslem League simultaneously in session in the same city. This rapprochment of the two great rival, if not antagonistic communities, culminated in the so-called Congress-League Scheme formulated and issued as the program of the Indian National Movement in August 1917. Self-government within the British Empire, with complete fiscal autonomy was the slogan, and the Congress in which its sister Moslem organization was incorporated, entered the period of an active political fight.

At this point it is necessary to make a retrospective study in order that the full significance of this rapprochement may be well understood. Except for one or two solitary figures, the founders of the National Congress were all non-Moslems. Orthodox nationalism was based upon aggressive Hinduism. The Extremist Party was born and developed as a Hindu party. It was actuated by Hindu religion; its ideology was derived from Hindu philosophy. The ruling power of the land till but a relatively short time ago, the Mussalmans, at least the upper class with the blood of the conquering race, did not consider themselves the same as the Hindu population. With their fierce fanaticism, they could not be expected to feel themselves an integral part of the Indian people, welded together by religious consciousness and cultural traditions. Then, on account of a higher grade of social development, the Hindu intellectuals responded more readily to those progressive political and social thoughts which made for the birth of modern nationalism and the eventual foundation of the Congress. When the Western educated Hindu intellectuals began the agitation for representative government, the Mussalmans would not have anything to do with them. The latter looked upon the former with suspicion. The Hindus were in the majority in the bulk of the population as well as in the intellectual and propertied middle-class.*) A government based upon the principles of national repre sentation threatened to be a Hindu supremacy. Naturally the Mussalmans were not very enthusiastic over a movement fraught with such possibilities. In fact, the landed aristocracy and the comparatively few intellectuals among them were decidedly hostile to such a movement. This attitude of theirs gave the foreign ruler the opportunity of using the large Islamic community as an opposition to the nationalism of the Congress. And the imperialist government did use this weapon very cleverly and not without effect. But the blame for this lack of unity among the Hindus and Moslems is not to be laid entirely at the doors of the government, whose "divide and rule" policy could not have succeeded had there not been conflicting interests between the two communities. As soon as both communities came to have identical material interests, their union in a political movement could not longer be prevented by the cleverest artifices of the government, nor by the traditional religious antagonism.

The masses of both the communities were equally indifferent to questions political. They lived for centuries side by side in the same villages, engaged in the same occupation of toiling for the maintainance of an extravagantly luxurious ruling class.

*) According to the census of 1921, there are 70,000,000 Mohamedants out of a total population of 319,000,000.

Religious antagonisms, which undoubtedly did exist, could not however interfere with the unavoidable phenomenon that the society was divided into two classes, the exploited lower class and the exploiting upper class. People professing antagonistic religions were to be found in the ranks of both classes. For convenience of exploitation, religious antagonism was kept alive among the people by the upper class of both the communities. Fanaticism fed upon ignorance made such strategy possible. But the relation between the rich propertied classes of the two communities could not be harmonious, either under the Mohamedan rule, nor afterwards. It was marked by bitter rivalry. The trading middle-class flourishing in the latter days of the Moslem empire was predominantly Hindu, while the ruling Islamic community remained in the backward social stage of feudalism. The British conquest found the Moslem population generally divided into feudal landlords and peasantry. In accordance with the policy of British imperialism in its earlier days, the feudal rulers as well as the landed aristocracy were crushed politically and militarily to a state of impotency, — to be preserved, petted and pampered later on. This being the case, the social basis for a liberal intelligentsia was absent in the Moslem community at the time of the British conquest, and it was long before such a social factor could come into being during the British period.

When the Hindu liberal intellectuals organized the National Congress, the few modern educated Mohamedans that existed in the country belonged exclusively to the landed aristocracy of feudal descent. By class affiliation, these were not prone to progressive ideas, either political or social. Sir Syed Ahmed Khan, an aristocratic intellectual, did the pioneer work in starting (1880) the Aligarh College, with the intention of bringing modern education within the reach of Moslem youths without tampering with the religious prejudices and susceptibilities of his reactionary community. Unlike the Hindu middle-class, the Moslems were still in a stage of social development which was not conducive to the introduction of secular education. The separation of education from religion was looked upon with great apprehension and was universally opposed. Despite his progressive tendencies, Syed Ahmed Khan had to bow down before the forces of reaction still rampant in the Moslem community and compromise on an adjustment of modern secular education with theological teaching in the Aligarh College. He sought to get as many young men as possible educated in modern ways compatible with the tenets of Islam, which, reflecting the tendencies of his community, he held to be indispensable for and more conducive to the welfare of Moslem society than Western civilization. Nevertheless, he looked upon British rule as a providential contact, — and implicit loyalty to it was the theme of all his educational and public activities. Under his zealous patronage, Aligarh came to be the Eton of Moslem India. The intellectual centre of the rich aristocracy, its concession to modern education amply counterbalanced by a good dose of theological training, Aligarh naturally failed to produce youthful elements holding social and political ideas similar to the Hindu intellectuals who conceived of a political nationalism as expressed in the organization of the National Congress. While the earlier generation of the Hindu modern intelligencia became "denationalized", or in other words, were capable of imbibing fully progressive social and political thoughts, the products of Aligarh were staunch Mussalmans above all, and implicit in their loyalty to the British government. This loyalty however, did not speak for any special characteristic of the Moslem community. It was a natural and inevitable outcome of the social position the Moslems occupied in those days. Besides it was provoked by instinctive rivalry and suspicion against a movement whose success, even partial, would mean a Hindu supremacy in Indian politics. And in those days, to the Moslem upper class of feudal origin, Hindu domination was by no means a better prospect than British rule, which was always willing to show them favoritism. The absence of a class-cohesion was responsible for the political divergence between the Hindus and Moslems. Those of the former, who inaugurated the agitation for representative government and social reforms, were intellectual bourgeoisie, whereas the Aligarh alumni, on whom were showered the good graces of the British government, belonged to the landed aristocracy with social and political tendencies predomiantly feudal. Elements so diverse socially could not unite in a national movement. The foreign ruler was not slow in finding this social divergence and communal rivalry, and made full use of them.

The Moslem intellectuals remained loyal to British rule because feudal class affiliation rendered them unresponsive to the progressive political thoughts embraced and propagated by their

Hindu contemporaries. Theirs was not loyalty to British rule as such, but loyalty to a particular social order they were zealous to preserve. If they were hostile to the Congress, it was not for its alleged "seditious" character, but because it represented a tendency inimical to the social, political and religious institutions and traditions cherished as ideal by them. Their support and sympathy for British rule were not purchased, as is generally believed, by petty favoritism, but originated in the belief that British rule would provide a protection for the social order and religious institutions they desired to preserve, and which, they apprehended, would be endangered if the Hindu liberals were to be given their way. This apprehension was corroborated by the growth of orthodox nationalism, which was bigotedly Hindu in character and therefore could not be expected to be looked upon with equanimityby the Moslems. It was not governmental favoritism, but class affiliation that first kept the Moslem intellectuals away from the Congress, and subsequently arrayed against it the forces of their community. The Moslems could not take part in the national movement until there should arise in their midst a modern bourgeoisie divorced from all feudal connection, whose economic vision would not be limited to land-owning, but extended to commercial and industrial horizons.

Till the earlier years of the twentieth century, politically the Moslem intellectuals were less concerned with Indian affairs than with Pan-Islamism, which embodied the dream of a federation of the Mussalman states; a sort of a romantic imperialism sanctified by religious authority. In this politico-religious movement, no force making for the growth of nationalism among the Indian Moslems was to be found. In fact, it was an impediment to the development of national consciousness. The Moslem intellectuals of modern India awoke, not to nationalism, but to the dream of an extra-national existence whose realization, however, had been made impossible by various other factors outside India and beyond their control and comprehension. When the politically independent or semi-independent Moslem states like Persia and Turkey felt the call of nationalism as expressed in the revolutions of 1907 and 1908, the impracticability and illusiveness of Pan-Islamism became apparent. The religious solidarity of the Moslem world also proved to be little more than a pleasant myth, due to the silence and passivity with which the declaration of Jehad by the Khalifa during the Tripolitan and Balkan wars was received by the faithful. On the other hand, the attitude of England during the Balkan war led the Indian Moslems to suspect the sincerity of the British patronage they had hitherto believed in.

This double disillusionment made the Moslem intellectuals of India turn towards home politics. They could no longer remain satisfied with the fond dream of Pan-Islamism, which failed to stand the test of experiment in a political as well as a religious sense; nor could they longer entrust the interests of their community entirely to the questionable patronage of the British. Pan-Islamism had been smiled upon by the British government so long as it remained a fashionable cult, harmless politically. It was a diversion for the young intellectuals who otherwise might run into mischief, in imitation of their Hindu contemporaries. But in the years following the Turkish revolution Pan-Islamism, under the spiritual leadership of the Comittee of Union and Progress (Young Turk Party) took on the character of incipient imperialism. Therefore the condescending smile with which the British Indian government had regarded the Pan-Islamism of Sultan Abdul Hamid, turned into a frown when it was converted into the Pan-Turanism of the Young Turks. The spread of Pan-Islamism of the new denomination threatened to be an anti-British movement, and could not be tolerated among the Indian Moslems. This led to a disruption of the relation hitherto subsisting between the Moslem middle-class of India and the British government. But mere anti-British sentiment could not make the Moslems consider themselves as part of the Indian nation, predominated by Hindu ideology and traditions.

It was a factor of an entirely different nature which contributed to the tendency towards political nationalism in the Moslem community. This was the mercantile and industrial class, which developed quite independent of the religious unity of the Moslem world. Its interest in Pan-Islamism, where it existed, was purely that for a fashionable cult, without any vital attachment. It was the political situation of India and the economie policy of the British government which had a vital bearing upon its own development. The anti-British feelings created by events outside India, and spreading among the new generation of Moslem intellectuals, did not affect the Moslem capitalist class, which looked upon British patronage as a necessary factor for its development. By the first years of the twentieth century had come into existence a small number of young intellectuals, the ideological pioneers of the Moslem bourgeoisie, who stood for nationalism in which religious and sectarian disputes should be submerged. But the first political expression of the Moslem community was rather anti-nationalistic than national. It was the organization of the All-India Moslem League, in which took part members of the loyal intellectual landed aristocracy and some of the mercantile and industrial class. In fact, the League was organized under the benign auspices of the British government, which wanted to make of it a Moslem opposition to Hindu nationalism. Under the leadership of the religious aristocrat Aga Khan and the official reactionary Ameer Ali, the League proved to be a willing instrument for the insidious designs of the British government. It emphatically protested "loyalty" as against the "seditious" attitude of the Hindu Congress, whose claim to national representation was challenged by the very organization of the League which pretended to voice the sentiment of the sixty-seven million Mohamedans.

Apart from being a bulwark against Hindu nationalism, the League served another purpose of the imperialist government. It raised an opposition against the spread of Pan-Islamism in India. Already in the latter 90's Syed Ahmed Khan as leader of the liberal Moslems of India, had repudiated the title of the Turkish Sultan to the Khalifat. For this act he had on his side the traditional authority of the Moslem emperors of Delhi, who never recognized the Turkish Sultan as their Lord Temporal and Spiritual. The founder and first leader of the League, Aga Khan himself claimed direct descent from the Prophet in his capacity as the spiritual head of the Khoza dissenters.

But the pronounced political significance of the Moslem League, under its founders and old leaders, was the opposition to the National Congress, the realization of whose program of representative government would be tantamount to Hindu rule. The League came into existence on the very eve of the Extremist triumph over the Congress. Orthodox nationalism with its pronounced religious ideology could not but arouse apprehension among the Mussalmans. Therefore the need of British protection was doubly felt by the latter. The Partition of Bengal, while a great butt of attack on the government from the nationalists of all shades of opinion, received the approval of the newly born Moslem League; because one of the objects of the partition was to create a large province with an overwhelming Moslem majority in the population. It was in this new province that the Hindu nationalism of the Extremists was very rampant, and the government did succeed in setting the religious fanaticism of the ignorant Moslem majority against it with disastrous results. The atrocities committed on the Hindu minority by the infuriated Moslem mob egged on by the police, seriously harmed the possibility of a national unity embracing the people at large. In spite of all these lamentable consequences of the Partition, the Moslem League went so far as to warn the government, when it was considering its repeal, not to make hasty concessions which would make for a Hindu supremacy. It was in deference to the point of view put forth by the League that the Indian Councils Act of 1909, which was followed two years later by the repeal of the Partition, was based on the principle of community representation, thus guaranteeing the Moslem minority a privileged position as a remuneration for its loyalty.

But events outside India weakened the faith of the Moslem intellectuals in the good will of the British government, notwithstanding the loyalism of the League and the reciprocal favoritism of the government. Not a few of the young Moslem intellectuals joined the nationalist movement, and began to participate in the Congress. A middle-class had come into existence in the Moslem community. It grew out of the poorer strata of the landed aristocracy and the commercial community. The modern educated youths of this class were violently anti-British on account of the ripples of Pan-Turanism reaching India. Therefore they swelled the ranks of the Extremists in spite of their religious diversity. The news of the Turkish revolution stirred up the imagination of these young enthusiasts, who sought connection with the Committee of Union and Progress, whose leaders were hailed as the saviours of the Moslem world. The loyalist policy of the Moslem League was assailed by these young intellectuals who could be called revolutionary, considering their anti-British sentiment. But they were far from nationalism as yet. They were willing to join hands with the Hindu Extremists in order to destroy British imperialism, not for the national liberation of the Indian people, but because they considered the British to be the mortal enemies of Islam. It was the spirit of Pan-Islamism which had an acute outburst in consequence of the triumph of the Young Turks, who aspired to launch on an imperialist venture in the name of Islam, with the questionable friendship of the Pan-Germans. This wave of Pan-Turanism in India, did not go beyond the walls of the modern Madrassas whose number was very small, but a few members of the thin lower middle-class were also agitated by it. The rich upper class remained unshaken in its loyalty, while the Moslem masses were electrified by it as much as the Hindus were by orthodox nationalism.

Nevertheless, the overthrow of reactionary loyalists like Aga Khan and Ameer Ali from the leadership of the League brought the political movement of the Moslems closer to the Congress. The new leaders of the League were mostly young middle-class intellectuals, and therefore susceptible to nationalism. Even before capturing the leadership, they had criticised the Leagues' advocacy of community representation as detrimental to national solidarity. The gradual subordination of religious orthodoxy to the political radicalism of the Extremists, on the other hand, removed another cause which might have kept, and to some extent did keep, the Mussalman intellectuals away from the Congress. The growth of a capitalist bourgeoisie socially distinguished from the aristocratic scions of the reactionary feudal landlords, made the conception of nationalism possible among the Indian Moslems. This nationalism was distinct from a politico-religious movement on behalf of an imaginary world-federation of Islamic states; it was the nationalism of an integral part of the Indian people. Reactionary Moslem landlords could be the object of governmental favoritism as against progressive Hindu intellectuals; but the interests of Mussalman capitalists were as hostile as those of the Hindus to imperialist exploitation. This being the essence of the situation, the years preceding the great world-war were marked by a steady closing of the ranks of the bourgeoisie, Hindu as well as Moslem, in the movement of political nationalism. In 1916, it was under the presidency of a rich merchant that the Moslem League made common cause with the Congress, which thus became the political organ of the national bourgeoisie, undivided by religious or sectional interests.

* * *

The firm attitude of the Congress, especially the Congress-League Scheme, commanded the attention of the government, which promptly showed indications of introducing such reforms as would placate the native capitalist class, till then the driving force behind the increasing vigour of the Congress. The first practical measure by way of these promised concessions was the increased rate of Customs duty imposed on the manufactured cotton imported into India. This touched a vital spot by conceding a partial protection, so persistently sought for, to the principal and most prosperous Indian industry. It appeared to have had the desired effect. The Indian bourgeoisie did not hesitate to pay the price demanded for this concession. A War Fund of £ 100,000,000 to be sent as a gift to England, was readily contributed. This partial protection was hailed by the Indian bourgeoisie as an earnest of further concessions that were to come, as the herald of the radical revision of the entire fiscal relation of the different parts of the Empire after the war, as promised by the government.

The schism between the two wings of the nationalist camp could no longer be averted, when the following declaration was simultaneously made by Montagu in the House of Commons and by the Viceroy, Lord Chelmsford, in Simla:

The policy of the British government henceforth was declared to be not only the "increasing association of Indians in every branch of administration, but also the greatest development of self-governing institutions with a view to the progressive realization of responsible government in India as an integral part of the British Empire".

This declaration complied with almost all the demands of the Moderates. For all those who happened to be free from distrust of the imperialistic policy, it was indeed a liberal promise. The Moderate Party, that is, the rich intellectuals and big capitalists, hailed this declaration as the advent of a new era. They obviously did not believe that the imperialist government would, without a struggle, concede to India that amount of Self-government which would practically make her lost to the empire. But they considered it a mistake to press any further at that point. According to their estimation, enough had been secured, and it was advisable to consolidate the new acquisition and prepare for a further advance in due course of time. Gandhi himself, still out of politics and engaged in humanitarian activities, in the beginning of 1915 defined Swaraj as partnership in the British Empire, and prescribed that the way to the realization of Swaraj was by services rendered for the successful prosecution of the war. At the outbreak of the war he had offered his services in an Indian Volunteer Ambulance

Corps, like the one he had organized and led to the great appreciation of the high command during the Boer War.

The British government, however, felt that the situation in India was much more serious than in 1908-9, in spite of the apparent loyalty of the bourgeoisie during the war and its grateful acceptance of the new reforms. Potential social factors, which did not exist before, had come into operation, and were beginning to make their influence felt on the nationalist movement. Imperial shrewdness did not fail to foresee that the wave of popular revolt following the cataclysm of the world war could not leave India entirely unaffected. A mass upheaval would add dynamic strength to the nationalist movement. Therefore it was found necessary to convince a powerful social class that it had a stake in the existing government. The Moderates could not be rallied by the government with so little as was found sufficient by the liberal Morley in 1909. The rich bourgeoisie must be made to understand that their further development would no longer be obstructed by the British, in order that, for the continued maintainance of law and order as against the threatening popular disturbances, their unconditional support could be counted upon. With a safe road to progressive development open before it, the rich bourgeoisie would certainly throw its weight against a movement mainly destructive in character. The instinct to preserve vested interests, economic as well as political, would make the rich liberal and propertied bourgeoisie together with the landed aristocracy, opposed to all popular upheavals, threatening the subversion of the established order in favour of something uncertain, which could be either too reactionary or too radical. Neither eventuality was welcome.

These considerations determined the policy of the British government in the latter part of the war and also in the post bellum years. The declaration made by the Secretary of State for India and the Viceroy in August, 1917 contained the following statement: "that substantial steps should be taken in this direction (of introducing self-governing institutions) as soon as possible, and that it is of highest importance that there should be free and informal exchange of opinion between those in authority at home and India". The latter purpose took Montagu to India towards the end of the year. But dominated by the political extremism of the orthodox nationalists, the Congress in December 1917, reaffirmed the resolutions of the previous year and declared that nothing less than

Home Rule would be acceptable. Here triumphed the spirit of Mrs. Besant who presided over the Congress of 1917. By introducing the slogan of Home Rule she saved India for the Empire; left alone, the Extremists, who controlled the Congress completely, might have repudiated the imperial connection, because the awakening mass energy had fired their imagination. The reactionary nationalism preached by Mrs. Besant and subsequently taken up by Gandhi, was not compatible with that form of political state which would be the corollary to Home Rule. But Mrs. Besant's reactionary designs concerned the political and not social aspect of the Indian movement. The reactionary tendencies contained in the orthodox nationalism of the followers of Tilak and the Gandhi-ites are social; therefore they would not brook any compromise with a political institution which would render them untenable. They would demand complete separation from the British Empire with the desire to save India from the unholy contamination of the sordid materialism of Western civilization, if they dared.

The publication of the Montagu-Chelmsford Reform Scheme forced a clear split in the ranks of the nationalists. The majority of the Moderates, though not fully satisfied by the reforms promised, accepted them as a big step forward, while the Extremists declared them to be utterly inadequate and rejected them summarily. The Moderates read a promising future in such passages in the Report on which the suggested reforms were based: "We must remember too that the educated Indian has come to the front by hard work; he has seized the education which we offered him because he first saw its advantages; and it is he who has advocated and worked for political progress. All this stands to his credit. For thirty years he has developed in his Congress, and latterly in the Moslem League, free popular convocations which express his ideals. We owe him sympathy because he has conceived and pursued the idea of managing his own affairs, an aim which no Englishman can fail to respect". These patronizing words tickled the vanity of the rich intellectuals, to whom they meant a recognition of their own importance by the British government. They also concluded from these phrases that their political point of view had been accepted by the government; the logical consequence of which acceptance was a matter of elation to them. They looked forward to the advancement of the interest of their class under the protection and sanction of the British government.

The bourgeoisie was further reassured of the prospect of its aggrandizement by the following statement contained in the Report: "We cannot stay their (of the intelligencia) progress entirely until education has been extended to the masses. . . . We have not succeeded in making education practical. It is only now, when the war has revealed the importance of industry, that we have deliberately set about encouraging Indians to undertake the creation of wealth by industrial enterprise, and thereby have offered the educated classes any tangible inducement to overcome their traditional inclination to look down upon practical forms of energy". The aspirations of the capitalists and liberal intellectuals on their way to be realized even if but partially, the Moderates gave up their opposition to the government. They condemned the uncompromising attitude of the Extremists as imprudent and detrimental to the constructive progress of the Indian nation. The Congress of 1918 was totally deserted by the Moderates. Gandhi himself, who as a member of the government Commission appointed for making inquiries in connection with the agrarian troubles in Champaran, had glimpsed the volcano of discontent seething under the hitherto unruffled surface of the society, expressed a favourable opinion about the Reforms.

But the government was smelling trouble in the air. The first indications of an imminent mass upheaval were to be noticed in the general restiveness all over the country. It was neither from the compromising rich bourgeoisie, nor from the objectively impotent but apparently aggressive orthodox nationalism of the lower middle-class intellectuals involuntarily under the influence of the forces of reaction, that the gravest danger was to be expected. Placating the Moderates did not put an end to the possibility of troubles from other quarters. Prolonged economic exploitation intensified during the war, had exhausted the traditional patience of the people, large masses of whom had been herded into the new industrial centres, where they found themselves in conditions worse than before. In the beginning of the war, several thousand workers came back from the United States of America where they had emigrated. These emigrants had experienced a higher standard of living in America; they had seen that the ordinary comforts available for the workingmen in other countries were luxuries in comparison with the miserable condition of the Indian toiler, urban as well as rural. Besides, while in America they had received political ideas of a revolutionary trend. They all came back with the intention of overthrowing the British domination. In this they had failed, since the conspiracies of the secret revolutionary organizations were frustrated in the earlier part of the war. But these returned emigrants did more revolutionary service than to take part in an abortive insurrection. Originally they all belonged to the poor peasantry of the north, especially the Punjab. The attempt to organize insurrections being frustated, these returned emigrants all went straight into their villages with their new vision and experiences acquired in foreign countries. It was not long before their spirit was caught by the people they came in contact with. There was another factor which rendered similar services in awakening the mass energy. More than a million Indian soldiers were sent out to different fronts where they fought side by side with Europeans. In the towns and village of Europe they found even the poorest people living in a condition better than theirs at home. These soldiers were also coming back changed men. The imminent demobilization would scatter these discontented and disturbing elements broadcast all over the country.

These were the potential sources of the impending danger. Discontent was no longer confined within the small middle class; it had penetrated the villages, it had rudely shaken the resignation of the masses of Indian people. This situation had not been created by the agitation of the bourgeois democrats, nor by the aggressive nationalism of the religious orthodox. It was brought about by the development of objective forces. Therefore it could not be handled succesfully merely by placating the Moderates and persecuting the Extremists. At last there was the menace of a huge popular upheaval, caused essentially by economic exploitation not alone of imperial capital, but by native agencies as well. The imminent popular upheaval was a social outburst-, the rise of a socially revolutionary force uncompromising, unrelenting, implacable, which would mark the commencement of the inevitable class-war.

Success in "rallying the Moderates" did not insure the situation in face of this theatening mass-revolt, which would add immense strength to the Extremists. In fact the latter could take such a firm stand on their political demands only because encouraged, though unconsciously, by the strength that would accrue to the nationalist movement as a result of a mass upheaval. The religious ideology of the orthodox Extremists was capable of influencing the zeal of the ignorant masses in the first phases of their struggle. The result would be an immense strengthening of the national movement, under the leadership of the Extremist Party. Mass-revolt provoked by a still confused class antagonism, could be easily diverted into the channel of anti-British sentiment. The National Congress threatened to become a really powerful body, in spite of the defection of its founders.

Consequently, the government launched upon a dual policy; it tried to combat the Indian movement with a double-edged sword. It adopted the policy of conciliation and concession on the one hand, and brutal repression on the other. The Montagu-Chelmsford Reforms typified the former, while the latter was ominously heralded by the introduction of the Rowlatt Bill in the Legislature. The apprehension of a great popular outburst, which induced the government to pass emergency legislation putting the country practically under Martial law, was manifest in the following words uttered by the Viceroy in defending the Rowlatt Bill in the Legislative Council. He sounded the alarm saying: „the reaction against all authority that has manifested itself in many parts of the civilized world are unlikely to leave India entirely untouched and the powers of evil are still abroad". The powers which the Viceroy had in mind were evidently dis covered outside the camp of the Extremists, whose following was still confined to a small section of the lower middle-class. The alarm was sounded in the beginning of 1919. The echoes of the Russian Revolution had been for sometime reverberating upon the horizon of India; the news of the great upheaval of the European working-class as expressed in the German, Hungarian and Bavarian revolutions was not althogether unknown; serious troubles were brewing among the toiling masses of Japan. There was indeed ample reason for the British government to be anxious about its position and to take precautions. The Rowlatt Bill was enacted in the face of unanimous opposition from all shades of nationalist opinion. Even the elected Indian members of the Legislative Council voted en bloc against it.

The agitation against the Rowlatt Bill brought Gandhi prominently into the political field. So far he had kept himself practically aloof from any note worthy political activities. Gandhi had seen active demonstration of massaction in South Africa, where he had led the struggle of the Indian emigrants. His recent works in connection with the agrarian revolts in Champaran had also given him a good idea of mass psychology. All his accumulated experience was brought to bear upon the mass energy on the eve of an outburst in India. While the political leaders, Moderates and Extremists alike, were agitating against the projected coercive measures, there appeared on the scene the magnetic personality of Mohandas Karamchand Gandhi, an ardent apostle of religious nationalism and a bitter opponent of what he called the "Satanic Western Civilization" which was being feverishly introduced into India in the form of large capitalist industries. By inaugurating the campaign of Satyagraha (passive resistence to evil), an active vent was given to the Opposition, which could thus transcend the limits of mere indignation meetings and passing resolutions of protest. Devoid of any other weapons to fight the British government, the Indian people were provided in the campaign of passive resistence with a way of making their energy felt by the opponent. Gandhi postulated that the Indian people would "refuse to obey these laws and such other laws", but would at the same time "faithfully follow the truth and refrain from violence to life, person and property". With this vow a committee was organized, which replied to the enactment of the Rowlatt Bill by calling a Hartal (national strike). Everybody should cease work; all shops should be closed; all business should be suspended.

For the first time in its history, the Indian national movement entered into the period of active struggle, and in doing so it had to call upon the masses of the people. A national strike cannot be carried on with any effect by the lower middle-class, which too is very small in India. The time for mass-action was ripe. Economic forces, together with other objective causes had created an atmosphere in which a spontaneous reponse could be expected to a call for a national strike. Had this step been taken several years earlier, there would have been hardly any response. Gandhi did not think of backing up the Congress-League demands of 1916 by a Hartal, not even by a big demonstration. Great ideas originate and are determined by the prevailing material conditions. In 1919 the state of affairs was such that the idea of a national strike could be conceived. A considerable portion of the population was in an inflammable state of mind. There had been various strikes in the industrial centres. The call for a Hartal was enthusiastically responded to by the working-class. It was a great mass upheaval, an essentially socio-economic, and not a mere national demonstration, that led up to the Punjab massacres culminating in Amritsar. The powder magazine was there; Gandhi set fire to it.

This mighty mass revolt scared the Moderates into the shelter of their spiritual home, under the throne of the Imperial bourgeoisie. They were not slow in issuing a manifesto condemning the Hartal which, apparently a demonstration against the government, was essentially a great social upheaval—the prelude to the coming class-struggle. Gandhi himself appeared to have surmised instinctively the dangerous character to be eventually assumed by the mighty forces he was instrumental in invoking. Therefore from the very beginning he firmly took his stand on the ground that "truth" should be followed by "refraining from violence to property". This strong instinct of preserving property rights above all betrays the class affiliation of Gandhi, in spite of his pious outbursts against the sordid materialism of modern civilization. His hostility to capitalist society is manifestly not revolutionary, but reactionary. He believes in the sanctity of private property, but seeks to prevent its inevitable evolution to capitalism. In the years following the Industrial Revolution, Great Britain was swept by a wave of anti-machine philosophy; but it was a revolutionary movement, because the attack against private property was its feature. A radical cure of that civilization so heartily hated by Gandhi, can be effected, not by returning to a backward stage of society based upon private property, but by eliminating property-rights root and branch. And before being altogether eliminated, private property must go through succesive stages of evolution, the highest being capitalism. Gandhi took his stand on dangerous ground. He embodies simultaneously Revolution and Reaction; he must perish in the fierce clash.

Before spreading to the Punjab, the strike was most successful in the industrial districts of the province of Bombay. Several hundred thousand workers in the textile factories mostly owned and managed by native capitalists, not a few of whom were Congressmen, were in a state of open revolt, which could be put down only by the free use of machine guns and bombing planes. It was clearly demonstrated that the military machine of the state would always protect the propertied bourgeoisie against any riotous action of the ignorant mob. Gandhi himself confessed that he had underestimated the "forces of evil" he helped let loose upon the respectable bourgeois order of society. Therefore, while in those stirring days of 1919, there were about fifty thousand textile workers on strike in Ahmedabad, and the railway workers were holding up the traffic in order to prevent the rushing of troops to suppress the Punjab revolts by wholesale massacre and terrorism, Gandhi could be found "co-operating" with the "Satanic Government" in restoring order in his home town (Ahmedabad).

The unerring instinct for safeguarding class-interest reigns supreme, even in the prophet of spiritual civilization. The valuable properties of the Guzrati capitalists—notorious for sucking the blood of the Indian people by means of usury—were endangered by the "infuriated mob". Was it possible for any respectable bourgeois believing in the sanctity of private property, to stand aloof? Not only did Gandhi rush to the rescue, but under his presidency the Satyagraha Committee ruled a temporary suspension of "civil disobedience" and ordered every patriot to follow the noble example of their leader in helping the government restore order.

The response of the Moslem population to the Khilafat propaganda also showed that the country was undergoing a great social transformation. The bulk of the Indian Mohamedans had never been well informed of, much less interested in Pan-Islamism, which remained a fashionable cult among the reactionary intellectuals. The fact that the declaration of Jehad during the Tripoli and Balkan Wars, as well as the entrance of Turkey into the great European conflict had, left the Moslem masses of India practically unmoved, betrayed the weakeness of the assumed religious solidarity on which Pan-Islamism was based. It proved that what could be possible several hundred years ago, had become untenable in the twentieth century. It was not the dismemberment of the Turkish empire that agitated the Indian Moslems in 1919, when they revolted en masse with the rest of the Indian oppressed class. Their revolt was also brought about by material causes, religion having very little to do with it essentially. Hunger, intensified exploitation, and above all the underminig of old property relations by the growth of native capitalism—all these factors contributed to the rebellious mood of the Indian masses, Moslems as well as Hindus. The agitation against the Rowlatt Bill and subsequently the Khilafat propaganda were succesful in stirring up a tremendous popular movement, because the ground had been prepared by these fundamental socio-economic causes.

The fiasco of the Hijrat (Khilafat emigration) revealed the superficiality of religious sentiment, held to be so strong among the Indian Moslems. It showed that movements which fail to take deeper causes into consideration and which are based on supposed forces, whose original vitality has been lost in the process of social evolution, are doomed to failure. The best that can be achieved by such movements is futile demonstrations, which but dissipate popular energy and provide some bitter and costly experiences.

By an ukase issued by the high priesthood, the faithful were enjoined to leave the Kafir-ridden India and migrate to the Mohamedan countries or to swell the forces of Ghazi Mustapha Kemal Pasha. This religious edict was very dubiously responded to. Hardly thirty thousand out of the seventy million Moslems of India took part in the holy Hijrat, and more than 90 per cent of these emigrants did not go further than a few dozen miles beyond the Indo-Afghan frontier. The treatment received from the government of the first Moslem country encountered convinced them of their error and of the advisability of returning home. A close investigation showed that in spite of the religious ardour which undoubtedly existed on the surface, it was some material motive or other which actuated almost every one of those emigrants. It was not so much the Fatwa of the Maulana Abul Kalam Azad as the declaration of the Afghan Ameer to the effect that every Indian Moslem coming to his territories would be given free land as well as some working capital, that induced most of the emigrants to leave home. Of course, there were some young visionaries among them, and a number of daring adventurers bent on making fame and fortune upon some unknown battle-field.

No, it was not the indignation over the violation of the Khilafat, nor the capture of the Holy places by the infidel that agitated the Moslem masses of India. They felt the impulse of the same social upheaval as shook their Hindu compatriots from their age-long resignation and apathy. The great wave of mass energy, which threw Gandhi and his colleagues in the national movement on to the towering crest of leadership, was raised neither by the awakening national consciousness of the Hindus, nor by the religious fervor of the Moslems. It was the revolt of the exploited masses, still unconscious of their purpose. It was provoked neither by the personality, however magnetic, of a prophet preaching a bankrupt gospel, not by the injunction of theological authorities, nor by the equivocal opposition of the bourgeois nationalist. The dynamic causes had been accumulating for a long time; the fire of discontent and unrest had been smoldering under the surface for years. At last the flames of open revolt broke out under such auspices that its essential social significance could be confused with wild political demonstrations. It is not the awakening national consciousness, but the socio-economic struggle of the exploited masses that has lent apparent potentiality to the political movement of the bourgeoisie. But the revolt of the exploited masses connot be for any length of time a dependable force behind the nationalism of the bourgeoisie. It was possible in the past, in countries in which different socio-political institutions obtained; in which the liberal democratic movement of the national bourgeoisie was based upon class antagonism. But the world has changed since then, and the relation between the classes of Indian society today do not correspond to those of central Europe in the forties and fifties of the nineteenth century, nor to those of the British American Colonies towards the end of the eighteenth century, nor to those of the Italian states in the sixties. Bitter war between the classes is being waged all over the world. This world situation cannot but be reflected in the Indian movement. The awakening of mass energy, which has strengthened the movement for national liberation and which alone is capable of making this movement a success, at the same time weakens the position of the bourgeois nationalist movement.

The present situation in India is not unique in history. It is a stage of social development marked by a sudden and rapid introduction of modern means of production, resulting in a dislocation of the status quo, economic as well as territorial, of the population. Great Britain passed through a similar epoch in the years following the Reform Bill of 1832 and leading up to the Chartist Movement. But the same development cannot be expected to take place in India, although similar social and political tendencies are to be noticed in the movement. The propertied middle-class, which eventually dominated the situation in England as a result of the Reform Bill and the failure of the Chartist Movement, does not occupy an identical socio-political position in India today. The struggle of the Indian bourgeoisie is not against a government controlled by rich landed aristocracy with strong feudal traditions; it is against the highest form of capitalism in an extremely critical moment of its existence. Consequently, there is a great possibility of compromise in this struggle.

Then, Democracy, the slogan of the English middle-class in the days of the Reform Bill and Chartism, has lost all its illusive charms. After the bitter experience of almost a century, it stands to-day naked in its true character, which is the dictatorship of the bourgeoisie heading towards a plutocratic Imperialism. The struggle of the English bourgeoisie took place when capitalist society was in the process of building. The Nationalism of India tends towards the aggrandisement of the native bourgeoisie at a time when capitalism has gone bankrupt—when it is collapsing under its own contradictions all over the world. In the thirties and forties of the nineteenth century, the bourgeoisie was a revolutionary factor in England as well as on the Continent. It was struggling to build a new civilization on the ruins of the old. To their great misfortune, this much cannot be said of the bourgeois nationalists of India. They have appeared too late on the scene. It is not their fault. They did not choose to be late. They were kept back by Imperialism. They are late, all the same; and, therefore, cannot be expected to play the same role as their kind played in other countries in more opportune times. In relation to the past and present Indian society taken as a whole, they are undoubtedly revolutionary. But they are trying to build what is crumbling the world over. They happen to be at the head of a revolutionary movement at a period when their class has ceased to be a revolutionary social force.

The Indian bourgeoisie today stands between two fires: one just beginning to break into flames still clouded with thick smoke, the other large and awe inspiring, but its imposing glare is not that of living flames—it is of burning embers, to be soon covered with ashes. On one side is the great social upheaval fomented by the rising tide of mass energy which it endeavors to manipulate according to its own benefit and convenience; on the other side stands the Imperial Power intent upon maintaining its political and economic hegemony, but at the same time showing inclinations to compromise. The unbridled advance of the first, which alone can deliver a death blow to Imperial domination, spells a serious menace to the designs of the nationalist bourgeoisie; while to enter into partnership with Imperial capital is not a bad prospect. But the Indian bourgeoisie, by itself, is too weak to make the Imperialist Government pay heed to its demands. Therefore it must depend upon mass action for imposing its will. This is playing with fire, digging one's own grave. It has been demonstrated on various occasions during the last three years, that the mass movement cannot always be kept within the limits set according to the convenience of the bourgeoisie. Signs are already to be seen that the workers and peasants, who are steadily emerging from the first confusion of a great social upheaval, do not find the Congress and Khilafat programs include their interests. The inevitable consequence of these tendencies is the eventual divorce of the mass movement from bourgeois leadership. In that case, bourgeois nationalism will end in a compromise with Imperial supremacy. and the liberation of India will be left to the political movement of the workers and peasants, consciously organized and fighting on the grounds of class-struggle.
